Notorious H.I.V.

Notorious H.I.V.

The Media Spectacle of Nushawn Williams

Thomas Shevory

University of Minnesota Press
Minneapolis • London

Published by the University of Minnesota Press
111 Third Avenue South, Suite 290
Minneapolis, MN 55401-2520
http://www.upress.umn.edu

Library of Congress Cataloging-in-Publication Data

Shevory, Thomas C.
    Notorious H.I.V. : the media spectacle of Nushawn Williams / Thomas Shevory.
        p.   cm.
    Includes bibliographical references and index.
    ISBN 0-8166-4339-3 (alk. paper) — ISBN 0-8166-4340-7 (pb : alk. paper)
        1. Prisoners—Diseases—United States—Case studies. 2. AIDS (Disease)—United States—Case studies. 3. AIDS (Disease) in mass media—United States—Case studies. 4. Williams, Nushawn. I. Title.
    HV8838 .S54 2004
    364.1'42—dc22

                                                                2003019657

Printed in the United States of America on acid-free paper

The University of Minnesota is an equal-opportunity educator and employer.

12 11 10 09 08 07 06 05 04   10 9 8 7 6 5 4 3 2 1

Contents

Preface

N o worthwhile work of social analysis is the result of only one person's efforts. Writing is a political activity, and those whose contributions make it possible must be publicly recognized.

This book would literally not have been possible without the efforts of my mother, Joan Shevory. During her many years as a reference librarian at Jamestown Community College, she honed formidable research skills, which she was, fortunately for me, happily willing to put into the service of this project. She culled articles from the *Jamestown Post-Journal, Buffalo News,* and *New York Times*; gave me books and other materials to which I would not otherwise have had access; and kept me updated on events in Jamestown as they unfolded. She offered numerous suggestions about individuals I might interview, sometimes made connections for me in the community, and gave me innumerable insights into Jamestown's history, politics, and social life.

George and Irene Lawn, across-the-street neighbors and long involved in Jamestown's civic affairs, generously spent time discussing the history of racial discrimination and civil rights in the community.

Other community members who contributed in various ways were former mayor Richard Kimball, Dr. Robert Berke, James Subjack, Mayor Sam Teresi, Russ Tilaro, Matt Milovich, Elaine Forbes, Donna Vanstrom, Joan Patrie, Greg Brinks, Police Chief William MacLaughlin, the members of the Downtown Dialogue on Race Unity, Dr. Neil Rzepkowski, Sheila McCarthy, Philip Shevory, and Mike Koplik. Many of these people may disagree with some of the conclusions I have reached, but I listened carefully and very seriously took account of each person's views.

Without Nushawn Williams's willingness to talk openly about his various activities, often illegal, in Jamestown and other places, this work would have lacked the insider perspective that I hope adds to its richness. I also thank Ruth Williams and Lou Shipano.

Zillah Eisenstein, as is her practice, read every page of the manuscript and made detailed and insightful criticisms, while also being a constant source of encouragement. Every academic writer should be so lucky as to have such a colleague.

Sections of the manuscript were presented at the American Political Science Association's Foundations Symposium on Myth, Rhetoric, and Symbolism. In particular, I would like to thank John Nelson, who organizes this annual event and who has been extremely generous with his criticism of my work over many years. Other participants in the symposium whose criticisms I found helpful were Bob Boynton, Al Damico, Ron Terchek, Roger Green, and Glenn Perusek.

Manuscript readers Cindy Patton and Jeffrey Ian Ross made numerous useful suggestions, all of which I took quite seriously and many of which I incorporated into the final manuscript. Carrie Mullen's active interest in the project at the University of Minnesota Press helped to sustain me through the process of responding to reviewers and making final revisions. Ithaca College provided summer grant support for my writing.

As always, Tamara is a source of support, inspiration, and love.

Introduction

L et me be clear right from the start: I do not condone the deliberate and knowing endangerment of one person by another from HIV infection. In fact, if an individual were to infect another deliberately, and that could be demonstrated beyond a reasonable doubt, I would fully support criminal sanctions to punish such a person. Having said that, however, I want to alert the reader to the many complexities that I uncovered in re-searching the Nushawn Williams case. The deepest complexities lie within the character of Nushawn Williams. As my research progressed, I decided that I wanted to meet the "monster" named Nushawn; what I discovered was a human being. It is not uncommon for outsiders to find humanity within the confines of prison walls. The documentary film *The Farm: Angola, U.S.A.,* directed by Liz Garbus, Wilbert Rideau, and Jonathan Stack, and books such as Ted Conover's *Newjack: Guarding Sing Sing* and Jennifer Wynn's *Inside Rikers* are recent and articulate manifestations of a tradition that can be traced to Jean Genet and Fyodor Dostoevsky. The present work, in some respects at least, borrows from that tradition. Rec-ognizing a person's humanity is not the same as condoning that person's irresponsible or criminal actions, and through this study I present the complicated personal reality of an individual human being.

When I first heard reports about an "AIDS predator" in Chautauqua County, New York, on a television network news program in October 1997, my first reaction was, "Well, this is the last thing in the world that Jamestown needs." Jamestown is the largest city in Chautauqua County. It is also the town where I grew up, where members of my family live, and that I still reside relatively near. I've lived in several parts of the country since moving away in 1977, including the Midwest and Appalachia, as well as Eastern Europe. Traveling back to Chautauqua County, however, which I do relatively frequently, always seems like returning home.

All of us who were raised in this part of the country are used to a cer-tain marginal status. We take for granted the confusion of "New York" with "New York City." Most people outside the Northeast, and many no doubt within the region, have little idea about the vast rural and wooded areas that exist beyond the George Washington Bridge. Fewer still are aware of the numerous small to moderate-sized towns and cities that are located there. Upstaters in New York—not unlike, probably, upstaters in Michigan or downstaters in Illinois and Ohio—often have at least a modest inferiority complex. They are not residents of their state's cultural centers, and their economic power and demography do not elicit the same attention from state and national leaders as do more populous and wealthy metropolitan zones.

Due to their somewhat marginal status, folks from smaller towns and cities across the United States usually have had little experience with intense media coverage. When national media do converge, it is generally for only the worst kinds of events: serial murders, school shootings, environmental disasters, mine accidents, or train derailments. The Nushawn Williams story was that kind of news. The media represented it as a major national crisis. Although I eventually found the extent of the crisis to be exaggerated in important ways, I did not at first know that would be the case. As I observed the pictures of this young African American man that flashed across the television screen, along with millions of other Americans I couldn't help but be both fascinated and saddened—fascinated by the spectacle and saddened not only for the various participants involved but for the city of Jamestown itself.

The cities of upstate New York have suffered much in the transition from the "old" economy to the "new" one. The industrial infrastructure that once supported them remains largely abandoned, and in most cases it has not been replaced by a vibrant information-based or service economy. Aging populations and empty storefronts are good indicators of long-term economic and demographic trends. That does not mean that these communities have no economic or cultural life, however. Older brick buildings offer a refreshing aesthetic counterpoint to strip-mall America. Smaller towns, even economically challenged ones, maintain a soulfulness that is generally lacking in recently prosperous suburbs, with their proliferation of monster SUVs and grotesque McMansions. The arrival of immigrant groups from Latin America, Eastern Europe, and Asia, attracted by low costs of living, indicates an evolving diversity that may eventually rekindle the economic lives of such communities. In the meantime, people at the economic and regional margins of the country will no doubt suffer from greater health and environmental problems than will those in wealthy suburban areas. They will often be ignored by public officials, and then will almost never find their way onto the popular-culture radar screen unless they play host to specific disasters that can pique the interest of media producers on the prowl for the "next big thing."

Methodology

General Issues

In this book, I offer a multiperspectival approach to a set of events that became a sensational media story. In the chapters that follow, I engage the matter of what is "real" and what is spectacle in a particular case from a variety of angles. Given the complexities of the relationships between "actual" events and their representations through media, it is difficult to make definitive judgments distinguishing the two. Media images feed on one another, and the interpretations of even the closest participants are necessarily colored by them, as, of course, were my own interpretations even before I entered into a serious investigation of the case. Media spectacles, in other words, generate a kind of self-referential loop from which it is very difficult to break free. That does not mean, however, that it is not sometimes important to try.

Foremost in my thinking when I began this project was to "test" the veracity of media coverage of a particular episode in the life of a local community against data that I uncovered "in the field" from my own investigations. Our lives and consciousness are permeated with media representations and images, whether or not we are active or devoted followers of news and pop-cultural happenings. Very seldom do we have the opportunity to check a media story against the testimony of actual participants, to gain an understanding of context unavailable to most observers. Because of my own position as a one-time, longtime resident of Jamestown, I had access to the unarticulated understandings of identity and place that few other outside observers of this case had.[1] I was, I felt, uniquely situated as participant and observer to check media representations against my own interpretations of what "actually happened."[2] Although I would not presume to contend that I have determined the "real" in contrast to the sensationalized and imagined, I would hold that my own investigation has resulted in more complete disclosure of what occurred and why than have other narratives put forward to this point.[3]

Moreover, my intent from the beginning has been to do more than simply summarize and criticize media representations of the case, although that is an important part of the project. In this volume I also attempt to provide historical context, along with legal and political analysis. In other words, at the same time that I am very interested in how and why Nushawn Williams came to be cast as an "AIDS monster," I am also determined to view this story as the production of a particular place and time: Chautauqua County, New York, in a period following deindustrialization and within the context of a continually evolving network of globalization. Moreover, as a social scientist whose primary fields are law and public policy, I am interested in the legal and policy implications of the story. The legal aspects of the Williams case are theoretically compelling because the case raises issues of "intent" that go to the heart of the system of criminal law. Thus this case must be considered in relation to other legal cases involving HIV transmission. These, too, must be evaluated in historical terms—that is, in terms of the legal history of disease control and its transformations by the appearance of HIV and AIDS.

Finally, running through this study is the biographical narrative of a young African American man who has done many bad things, who has victimized others in a variety of ways, but who has paid a heavy price for his actions. Nushawn Williams is not Hurricane Carter. Nor is he Anthony Porter, who was freed in 1999 after sixteen years on death row owing to the efforts of the Illinois Death Penalty Education Project. That is, Williams is not just "a victim of the system." Still, his status as predator and monster has elevated him to something more than an ordinary prisoner, someone "doing his time because he did the crime." For one thing, he has been treated differently from the vast majority of the HIV infected who have had unprotected sex with uninformed partners—that is, unlike most of them, he is in jail. And his life in prison has been different from that of most prisoners, even those guilty of more severe crimes, because he was transformed from a person into a commodity for consumption by mass-media audiences. The media spectacle of Nushawn Williams has dominated and overwhelmed most attempts at serious, rigorous analysis of his case.

Data Sources

When engaging in a project such as this, I find that the best starting point is with media representations themselves. That is, what did the press say about the case? These representations become the benchmark against which I consider all other findings. The flurry of newspaper and television reporting that immediately followed the release of Williams's name to the public resulted in a highly charged and, in many respects, inaccurate rendering of the nature and scope of what had occurred. Often, reporters and commentators on the case seemed to have little understanding of the medical implications of HIV infection or of how and under what circumstances HIV might be transmitted. A detailed analysis reveals a whirl of sensationalized and often contradictory claims occasionally intermixed with more measured accounts that strove for greater accuracy. An important part of this project, then, has involved my own reading and interpretation of news coverage of the case. To that end, I surveyed more than 150 newspaper articles, including accounts from local and regional sources such as the *Jamestown Post-Journal* and the *Buffalo News*, national sources such as the *New York Times* and the *Wall Street Journal*, and international newspapers such as the *Guardian*. Additionally, I scoured transcripts of stories about the case from television network and cable news outlets as well as television talk-show discussions.

Interviews have also played an important role in this study. In all, I conducted twenty-four in-depth interviews. The interview subjects were not meant to represent a cross-section of the county's residents; rather, they were individuals who were closely involved with various aspects of the case, such as Dr. Robert Berke, Chautauqua County's highest-ranking public health official, and James Subjack, the county attorney who was responsible for prosecuting the case. I asked the respondents a variety of questions about their understanding of what occurred and their participation in various aspects of it. The interviews were open-ended, and I tended to follow the drift of the conversation.[4] Thus the nature of the questions differed depending on the person being interviewed and his or her position in relation to what occurred. Each interview also evolved into a dialogue with its own set of internal dynamics.[5] I recorded most of the interviews on audiotape, but for some that involved searches for background material, I simply took notes.

My interviews with Nushawn Williams, as will become clear, involved much more than simple taping in a formal setting. These interviews became conversations that stretched over the course of almost three years. They included letters, numerous phone conversations, a dozen prison visits, and Nushawn's own detailed written accounts of his life story. As one might imagine (and as I make clear in chapter 3), the participant/observer distinction became increasingly fuzzy as time went on and Nushawn and I developed a kind of friendship. I must leave it to the reader to judge whether this in some sense contaminates the current study to such a degree as to make it suspect. I can only offer that in the pages that follow I attempt to communicate my interpretations and reactions as carefully and as forthrightly as I possibly can.

An understanding of historical context is important for an understanding of any discrete event or set of events in time. The history one chooses and how one interprets it will by necessity shape one's understanding of contemporary social phenomena. History is a significant aspect of this study, and I draw on historical materials at a variety of points in the discussion. For instance, I treat Jamestown as a city with a history. One must understand that history in order to be able to grasp the meanings of what occurred there. Jamestown's history is connected, as all histories are, with various mythologies that help to place it within broad cultural trajectories. The history of Jamestown is, in other words, the history of many American small towns and cities. Although Jamestown has its own particular identity, its particularities partly define and are defined by a more generalized sense of what small cities and towns mean in American cultural history.

Diseases also leave their marks, and any discussion of Western history would be incomplete without reference to the various diseases that have ravaged European and American societies. More to the point with regard to the current study, the management of the diseased, through social practices and law, has in certain respects changed and in others remained the same over time. The use of the criminal justice system as a primary mechanism for controlling the diseased is a relatively recent development. Nushawn Williams's treatment is indicative of a trend away from a public health model for the treatment of the disease and toward a more punitive one. Attention to legal and social history helps to reveal the parameters of these changes.

Given the importance of law for controlling the spread of various diseases, especially HIV, the current study is permeated with various kinds of legal analyses, often involving examination of cases. My aim in introducing legal cases in this discussion is to show the conceptual problems that surround the criminalization of HIV transmission and the transmission of other diseases as well.[6] I introduce the legal cases to provide a particular kind of historical context, to provide points of comparison against which the reader may evaluate Williams's conviction, and to indicate evolving legal trends related to HIV.

In writing this book, then, I have drawn information from a variety of sources—newspapers, legal cases, historical materials, and in-depth interviews with various participants, including Nushawn Williams. As a result, I have borrowed eclectically from the methodologies employed by various disciplines: history, political economy, sociology, communications, law, and literary theory. The guiding methodological ethos that holds this work together is my intent to reveal the deep social and political structures that made the Williams case of such intense interest to the media, as well as my determination to consider carefully this case's wider political and policy implications.

Although my utilization of multiple data sources and research techniques might strike a strict positivist as disorderly, such an approach is recognized as entirely appropriate in the literature on qualitative research. As Yin notes: "Case studies need not be limited to a single source of evidence. In fact, most of the better case studies rely on a wide variety of sources."[7] The advantage of the use of multiple evidentiary sources is that it yields "triangulation," a commonly employed technique in qualitative analysis.[8] According to Cresswell, triangulation "provide[s] corroborating evidence collected through multiple methods, such as observations, interviews, and documents to locate major and minor themes." Researchers can achieve methodological legitimacy by "rely[ing] on multiple forms of evidence rather than a single incident or data point."[9] When an investigator is able to view a set of phenomena from multiple perspectives, the field and depth of his or her view are expanded. A project employing such an approach attempts both "understanding" and "explanation," but it can be (and in this case is) agnostic on definitive connections of interpretation to "truth."[10]

Overview

This volume consists of five chapters and a conclusion. In chapter 1, my focus is on media treatments of the Nushawn Williams case itself. I begin with a review and analysis of the notion of "moral panic." Drawing on the work of Stanley Cohen, Stuart Hall, and others, I argue that there is an underlying politics to the generation of moral panics.[11] Moral panics are nothing new in American cultural life. In fact, they can be traced back at least to the "white slavery" scares of the beginning of the twentieth century.[12] Although their character has evolved over time, they have continued as mechanisms for maintaining social discipline in advanced and potentially unruly capitalist societies. They tap into deep-seated fears of socially dispossessed elements, such as youth, racial and ethnic minorities, and the sexually ostracized. The Williams case provided an exceptionally compelling opportunity for the generation of panic, because it discovered (and then reconstructed) a politics of race, class, and HIV in the mythologically protected space of the American small town.

By comparing various news representations of the case with one another and with the responses I received in interviews with a number of key participants, I attempt to show how the reaction to what occurred spiraled out of control as the numbers of those depicted as potentially infected skyrocketed when media reports fed on one another. The demonization of Nushawn Williams intensified as the media drew on well-worn tropes of dangerousness associated with young black men, including fear of their sexual association with white women. Williams was an easy enough character to demonize, given his history of petty crime and participation in the drug trade. Any attempt at balance or depth was overwhelmed by a narrative of "good" versus "evil," "guilt" versus "innocence." Although there was solid evidence that Williams had sex with numerous teenage girls and women, none existed that he had deliberately set out to infect anyone with HIV. Yet that became one of the key elements of the story. Why else would such a story garner so much attention? Surely the motivations of the central figure must be truly evil and his actions thus particularly heinous if not downright monstrous. Nushawn Williams became the AIDS monster right before our eyes, even though the representations of his monstrosity are not entirely compatible with the actuality of who he is and what he did.

Chapter 2 begins with an investigation into the mythological place that small towns hold in the American cultural landscape, a place marked by a complex set of ambivalent idealizations. Americans have long had mixed feelings about the meaning of small-town life. Jeffersonian democrats applauded rural life and the New England town meeting as paradigmatic of democratic politics. They asserted that citizens need face-to-face interaction in order to recognize the value of community, which reinforces a sense of enlightened individual interest.[13] Yet small towns have also been portrayed in myth and literature as cramped and stifling, repositories of naïveté, intolerance, and ignorance.

This deeply embedded set of cultural understandings and expectations formed the background against which the events that unfolded in Jamestown were interpreted. Jamestown was a mythologically constructed virtual community, both a snow-covered rural paradise that had been violated by a postindustrial thug and a deindustrialized heap, so disintegrated and decayed that an HIV outbreak was entirely in keeping with any reasonable set of expectations. As the media represented Jamestown, the town did not perhaps "deserve" what it got, but there was little reason to believe that anything of a more positive nature might rise from its smoldering ashes.

Jamestown, however, turns out to be a real place with a real history. As in all American towns, the cultural mythology that surrounds it speaks to certain truths about the fabric of life there. The historical Jamestown reinforces expectations, but it also unsettles them in sometimes surprising ways. Jamestown, New York, like many towns in the northeastern United States, has struggled economically as a result of changes in the global economy. In certain respects its leaders and residents have responded well to the changing economic landscape, but the nature of the forces that surround them are often beyond their control, and they often acknowledge as much. It is interesting to note that Hillary Clinton's candidacy in New York in 2000 for a U.S. Senate seat spotlighted Jamestown and other similarly situated upstate communities in ways that had not previously occurred. Hillary Clinton, somewhat improbably it seemed, turned the attention of national leaders to upstate New York's economic problems, and upstaters took her seriously as a person who cared about their concerns and would attempt to get them help from public institutions.

Chapter 2 also includes a historical representation of the "real" city of Jamestown, in terms of industrial development and decline, the statistical increase in and perceived impact of crime (especially that associated with drug use) on the community, and a discussion of social problems, such as teen pregnancy and the spread of HIV. I argue that the gap between Americans' simplified idealizations (both favorable and unfavorable) and the actual complexities of life in small towns leads to a disjunction between media representations of places like Jamestown and the lived experiences of the actual citizens of such towns. There is a gap, in other words, between fantasized media creations and people's sense of what it means to live in the world. The presence and expansion of this gap has implications not only for folks in Jamestown but for citizens of the national community, no matter where they reside. Specifically, the continuing disconnect between media-projected experiences and ordinary lived ones reinforces cynicism, which undercuts people's constructive impulses to act politically. The popular news culture nourishes a sense of alienation.[14]

In chapter 3, I attempt to give some sense of who Nushawn Williams is as an actual living, breathing human being. The chapter is meant as an antidote to the caricatures of Williams constructed by various media, which consistently used the word *monster* to specify, categorize, and marginalize him. This term is a potent one, with deep-seated historical and literary resonances. I begin chapter 3 with an exploration of the cultural meaning of *monster* and ask whether Nushawn Williams deserves the appellation. Although I would hold that there are indeed human beings whose motivations and actions might be construed as truly monstrous—Timothy McVeigh, Jeffery Dahmer, John Wayne Gacy—I would also argue that Nushawn Williams isn't one of them. I have no particular interest in romanticizing the life of a small-time criminal, which is what Nushawn Williams essentially was when he lived in Jamestown. Nor do I see him simply as a victim of circumstances, although his background and life's circumstances certainly had much to do with the path that he chose. Still, it is important morally and politically that we distinguish as carefully as possible between those who do things that are unattractive and criminal and those who are so irredeemably evil that we essentially deny them a place in the human community by characterizing them as monsters. I don't believe that Nushawn Williams, or the many others like him who have not been entirely truthful with their sex partners about their HIV status, should be cast out of the moral universe inhabited by so many other deeply flawed human beings.

Nushawn Williams is, it turns out, a smart, in many ways likable street kid who can be self-centered, engaging, and demanding. Through the many conversations he and I had, I feel as though I did in fact get beyond the media's portrait of him. It is relatively easy to demonize an abstraction, a mug shot, or a disheveled man seen in a video clip on his way to and from a courthouse. A flesh-and-blood human being, however, is not abstract, and meeting an individual can influence one's understanding of that person in multiple and unexpected ways.

Williams, like many moderately successful drug dealers, was entrepreneurial. He "discovered" a previously untapped market in Jamestown for the crack cocaine that he sought to distribute. At the same time, he entered into the fabric of the community, or at least part of the community, a subcultural underground, the presence of which both frightened and attracted members of the more respectable middle class. Such marginal elements exist in most American towns of any size. In Jamestown, Williams became a "somebody," liked by many and sought out by others for the illicit pleasures he provided, welcome diversions from a hard life in a city whose economic and social fabric had been torn. Improbably, Williams, a street kid from New York City, found a kind of home in this small upstate community. He has often made it clear to me that he liked it there. He was attracted by many of the same things that appeal to middle-class residents: people were friendly and easygoing, the countryside was beautiful, the violence that had marked his life in New York City was mostly absent. Had he not been infected with HIV and become the object of a national media frenzy, he might likely still be living there, making money (probably illegally), hanging out, and courting young women.

Cornel West argues that apparently self-destructive actions on the part of the poor and disenfranchised in American society are evidence of the broader nihilistic tendencies of the consumer culture.[15] Americans primarily value financial success, sexual success, and material consumption. The poor covet these as much as do the rich and are as constantly bombarded with popular-culture messages conveying their significance for a happy life. Unfortunately, the poor simply don't have the economic means to achieve the same levels of consumption as their wealthy counterparts, and as a result they may feel themselves to be quite empty; they may feel that they literally have nothing. As a result, some, like Nushawn Williams, find ways to achieve success and status by whatever means they can. Sometimes those who take the illicit route eventually become successful and valued members of the community, like the Kennedys. Sometimes the lives of outlaws are celebrated in popular culture, as in films and television shows such as *Bonnie and Clyde*, *The Godfather*, and *The Sopranos*. Williams was both intelligent and ambitious, and he pursued a distorted but by no means incoherent version of the American Dream. This accounts in part, I think, for his demonization by the media.

In chapter 4, I turn my attention to the historical and legal context that provides the background for criminalization of disease. I offer a historical map of the evolution of the political in relation to the control of disease and the diseased, beginning with an examination of leprosy and plague, two diseases that helped to define the meaning of social life in Europe for hundreds of years. Negotiating control of the diseased was a singularly important matter in these preliberal societies. Without rights or other legal protections, the diseased had little recourse to the due process that we now associate with Western modernity. This did not mean, however, that a capriciousness ruled by fear defined the relationships of the infected and uninfected. Fear was certainly present, especially during the era of plague, but wholesale sequestration, imprisonment, and quarantine were not the primary practices for dealing with the diseased in these societies. Although some legal rules for dealing with the contagious were in place, there were many gaps, and enforcement was often sporadic at best. Customary and local practices provided individuated norms concerning control over the infected, so such control was far from complete.

With the advent of the liberal state, a tension arose between attempts to guard the community's interests through law (for example, through the imposition of quarantines) and attempts to protect the individual rights of the infected. Resistance to state attempts to impose quarantines came from more than just the individuals who would lose the right to move about freely if they were confined to institutions or excluded from particular cities. Business interests also often opposed quarantines, either by lobbying against their passage or by attempting to circumvent them once implemented. In the nineteenth century, scientific controversies about the nature of contagion often fed into and were influenced by political conflicts regarding the necessity of quarantines.

When AIDS became a public health threat, demands for quarantine were grounded implicitly in the understanding that in the past quarantine policies had been rigorously enforced. Yet a look at the social and legal history of infectious disease does not support this assumption. In the United States, a body of law developed in the nineteenth and twentieth centuries that balanced the individual rights of the infected with the community interests of the uninfected. Infected individuals were not, however, always treated similarly. The application of more formal approaches to the control of infection was inconsistent. Often rules were imposed against particular groups, such as Asians, on the basis of prejudice rather than on the basis of any careful weighing of potential health risks. Formal applications of quarantine rules reflected and continue to reflect the organization of political power. The association of the alien and the dispossessed with disease and infection has been crucial to the determination of the law's meaning in relation to public health.

Past practices in both the nineteenth and twentieth centuries were relatively free from the imposition of criminal sanctions against the infected. The Williams case and others like it represent a distinct change, if not an entirely new development. Criminal sanctions are now being imposed on persons who are HIV infected in a fashion that is without historical precedent. Quarantines and civil confinements, which involved complicated negotiations among the state, threatened communities, and individuals, have given way to an enforcement model. Many states have enacted HIV-specific laws under which an individual who knows he or she is HIV-positive can be charged with a felony for failing to inform any sexual partner of that status.

In chapter 5, I explore the implications of the trend toward criminalization of persons who are HIV infected. More than twenty states now have criminal statutes that expressly forbid sexual contact between those who are HIV-positive and partners who are not informed of that status. Other states, such as New York, employ existing statutes, such as those concerning reckless endangerment or even attempted murder, to bring charges, sometimes successfully, against HIV-infected persons who do not tell their sexual partners of their status. More than one hundred persons have been convicted of having unprotected sex while being HIV-positive. (Tens of thousands, however, have engaged in the same activities and have not been prosecuted.) In chapter 5, I examine the laws that now exist, constitutional challenges to those laws, and a variety of legal cases in which charges have been brought successfully in instances of HIV transmission.

There have been, I would argue, cases of HIV transmission in which criminal charges *should* have been brought. There have been instances, although rare, in which individuals have knowingly and deliberately attempted to infect others with HIV. In one particular case, a doctor injected a patient with a serum that contained HIV-infected blood.[16] There have also been cases in which an infected person has explicitly indicated a desire to infect others and has engaged in unprotected sex for the express purpose of transmitting the virus.[17] In most cases, however, the relationship between the infected and the noninfected is more complicated. Individuals may engage in sexual activities without a clear understanding of HIV or AIDS and the potential for transmission of the virus. Others may be in denial or simply caught up "in the moment." Given this complexity, attempts to respond to the AIDS epidemic by widening the reach of the criminal law seem misguided. Such efforts not only impose a penal model with serious equal-protection problems, they distort the criminal law itself, by extending it into the domain of public health. Establishing a health model of prevention and education is, in the long run, not only more effective than imposing a system of criminal sanctions but fairer as well.[18]

In chapter 5 I also consider the conceptual problems illuminated in and by the Williams case. As I have noted, I don't believe that Williams was the deliberate and knowing transmitter of HIV that he has often been characterized as. Although he may have been to some extent culpable, he was also in certain respects a victim of the criminal justice system, and certainly a victim of a media system that had spun out of control. Nushawn Williams was, in fact, used as a poster child for increased criminal sanctions. This was based on an incorrect reading of the facts of his case, to the detriment of both Williams as an individual and the criminal law as a whole, as many states passed HIV-transmission laws or increased the penalties for intentional transmission of the virus in direct response to the Williams case.

My concluding piece in this volume isn't a conclusion in the typical sense. This is deliberate, because I believe that it is virtually impossible to write a final chapter on a case such as this. Its many implications continue to evolve and resonate, and they will do so for quite some time. I do believe, however, that it is important to leave the reader with a sense of where I found the case leading in the end.

Nushawn Williams, as of this writing, remains in prison. He is currently seeking an appeal for part of his sentence. He was denied parole on his first attempt, and the attempt itself led to a flurry of media activity.

Jamestown, New York, has progressed as its leaders have attempted to find avenues for revitalizing the community's economy. Sam Teresi, who was the city's director of development when I began this project, is now Jamestown's mayor. Since he was elected, a very impressive multimillion-dollar skating arena has been constructed in the middle of downtown. Jamestown has been a national center for the training of figure skaters for many years, and the completion of this state-of-the-art training facility is expected to reinforce the area's presence in the field and to generate business activity. Political and business leaders are optimistic that Jamestown may be turning an economic corner.

AIDS, of course, continues to be the world's primary public health threat. The wisdom of turning public health matters, such as transmission of HIV, over to the criminal justice system has not been the focus of a major national debate in the United States. Although thousands of new cases of AIDS are reported each year, no one HIV-infected individual has captured the national media spotlight in the way that Nushawn Williams did.

1

Moral Panics and Media Politics

If this were a movie, it might be called "Media Behaving Badly."
Chris Bury, reporter, ABC News Nightline, October 31, 1997

On October 27, 1997, legal history was made in New York State. For the first time, an exception to the state's HIV confidentiality law was invoked so as to allow public identification of a person believed to be knowingly transmitting the virus to his sex partners.[1] The person eventually identified at a press conference in the small Chautauqua County town of Mayville, New York, was a twenty-year-old African American man from Brooklyn named Nushawn Williams. As the announcement was made to a roomful of reporters from the local and national press, Williams was in jail at the Rikers Island Correctional Facility, having been arrested for selling twenty dollars' worth of crack cocaine to an undercover police officer.[2] The following June, Williams would be arraigned and indicted in a Chautauqua County courthouse on two charges of statutory rape, both involving the same thirteen-year-old Jamestown girl. He eventually pled guilty to the drug charge, the two charges of statutory rape, and one count of reckless endangerment. He is currently serving a sentence of four to twelve years in the New York State prison system.

For a brief moment, a bright media spotlight was focused on Chautauqua County, and a variety of media narratives were generated. Various members of the community were subjected to intense scrutiny, including the public health commissioner, Robert Berke; various other public officials; several of the girls who were involved with Williams; and, of course, Nushawn Williams. As is often the case, the media then vanished as quickly as they had arrived. But the impacts of the media attention to this case have lingered. On June 18, 1998, in the final flurry of the last day of the legislative session, the New York State Legislature passed a major revision to the state's public health law. This revision requires physicians and laboratories in the state to notify public health officials whenever a person tests positive for HIV. It also authorizes local health officials to notify those persons who might be at risk of contracting HIV from those who have tested positive.[3] A good argument can be made that the Williams case and the media's attention to it were crucial to the passage of this legislation. Moreover, in Florida, state legislators cited Williams as they revised the Florida criminal code to make knowing transmission (or attempted transmission) of HIV a class I felony punishable by up to thirty years in prison. In August 2000, *Poz* magazine reported on 101 "AIDS criminals," individuals who had been convicted of various crimes involving, in one way or another, the reckless or deliberate transmission of HIV.[4] This all marked a watershed in strategies for dealing with HIV, as policies shifted toward criminal sanctions.

One cannot understand the Williams case, and the media attention to it, without connecting the various facets of the case to wider histories and cultural contexts. The reasons this case received the intensity of attention that it did are not immediately self-evident. According to the Centers for Disease Control and Prevention (CDC), as of December 2001, more than three-quarters of a million AIDS cases had been reported in the United States. The number of deaths attributed to AIDS so far in the United States is approximately 450,000. Worldwide, more than 36 million people are estimated to be living with AIDS, and 21.8 million have died of the disease since the beginning of the pandemic.[5] In South Africa, where many lack access to drug therapies, nearly one-fourth of the nation's adult population is now estimated to be HIV-positive.[6] Why would a case that involves what amounts to a relatively small number of new cases generate so much attention, anger, and even hysteria? This is not an easy question to answer, but it is an important one to raise, because such media events map our sense of meaning and cultural identity. Not long after the event, JoAnn Wypijewski wrote, in a seminal *Harper's* article, "In the story of Williams, pop culture's

▼ Moral Panics and Media Politics

2

trinity of sex, race, and danger was perfectly realized."[7] Although, as I will make clear later, I have some reservations about Wypijewski's portrayal of a number of aspects of the case, I believe that in this one pithy statement, she squarely hit the mark. In a word, the media were attracted to this case because it was *lurid*. It frightened and repelled, enticed and fascinated, shocked and reassured. White middle-class audiences, the demographic targets of so much media strategizing, are used to titillation. In fact, they expect it. The most prized news stories are those that threaten the boundaries of social safety while encouraging feelings of moral superiority in the audience. Such stories set the parameters of what has become known as a "moral panic."

The Concept of "Moral Panic"

The phrase *moral panic* can be traced to British sociologist Stanley Cohen's book *Folk Devils and Moral Panics*, which was published in 1972.[8] Cohen gives a pathbreaking account of the appearance of stories about "mods" and "rockers" in the British press in the 1960s. The two groups clashed in the seaside resort of Brighton, the result being what might be characterized as a small riot. According to Cohen, however, the British press sensationalized the incident far beyond the boundaries of what was warranted based on any actual threats to public order that the mods and rockers may have posed. Cohen interprets the press reaction as a form of deviance management. "Youth" and its culture were increasingly viewed as a potentially subversive social element in 1960s Britain. Press accounts of the Brighton incident reflected that unease and at the same time reinforced a sense of social crisis. This in turn led to demands for the reassertion of social control. According to Cohen, the Brighton incident revealed a general set of dynamics at work in modern social systems.

"Societies appear," Cohen states, "to be subject, every now and then, to periods of moral panic." Moral panics, he contends, follow a consistent pattern in relation to different circumstances. First is the emergence of a "condition, episode, person or group of persons" as a "threat" to "societal values and interests." Second, this threat is portrayed by mass media in a "stylized and stereotypical fashion." In reaction to these media reactions, "editors, bishops, politicians and other right-thinking people" "man the moral barricades." As "experts pronounce their diagnoses and solutions," coping mechanisms evolve. Eventually the condition "disappears, submerges or deteriorates." Moral panics are produced sometimes by "novel" phenomena and sometimes by something that "has been in existence long enough, but suddenly appears in the limelight." Moreover, although panics are often forgotten or pass into "collective memory," at other times they have significant impacts on public policies and on "the way the society conceives itself."[9] Groups of young people have often been the inspiration for moral panics: teddy boys, mods and rockers, Hells Angels, hippies, skinheads, and gangs of "wilding" black youths have all been the subjects of such episodes.

Historical Precedents

Cohen's work invites us to consider a variety of occurrences as moral panics of one kind or another. Since the publication of Cohen's book, scholars have characterized an array of historical events as moral panics, including seventeenth-century witch-hunts.[10] It is easy to see how this could happen. The notion of moral panic is intuitively appealing as a means to describe a diverse array of social phenomena. Prohibition, for example, could reasonably been seen as a kind of panicked response to the crime, poverty, and social dislocation that marked Gilded Age industrialism in the United States. Yet the broader the application of the concept of moral panic becomes, the less powerful it would seem to be as a heuristic. Seventeenth-century witch-hunts, nineteenth-century social movements, and twentieth-century health campaigns are not equivalent, although they may have certain attributes in common. Overuse of the concept of moral panic, in other words, has sometimes had the unfortunate effect of erasing historical and cultural distinctions.

In my view, what is most important about Cohen's work is its emphasis on mass communication as a mechanism for encouraging panic and the political effects that flow from that. The particularities of the panic are less important than what they tell us about the emergence of new and evolving forms of media culture. The speed with which communication now travels across an array of geographic regions and social groupings generates the potential for confusion between perceived and actual social threats on a very wide scale. Thus I prefer the term *media panic* to *moral panic*.

In the United States, the "white slavery scare" of the first part of the twentieth century is an early example of this kind of media-generated panic. It stemmed from the belief that young girls from farms, hamlets, and small towns were being lured by unscrupulous conspirators into large cities, where they were ultimately forced into lives of prostitution. The scare was promoted by the Hearst and Pulitzer newspaper chains, which shrewdly viewed it as a business opportunity. It also generated an early form of literary pulp. From 1909 to 1914, twenty books were published about "white slavery," both fictional and nonfictional accounts. Journalist George Kibbe Turner asserted that prostitution was being organized "with all the nicety of modern industry" and compared prostitution districts to Chicago's stockyards, where "not one shred of flesh is wasted."[11] Reginald Wright Kauffman's *The House of Bondage* became a bestseller, with more

▼ Moral Panics and Media Politics

than a dozen editions published by 1912.[12] Movies with titles such as *The Traffic in Souls* reinforced the anxiety. Grand juries were convened, Senate hearings were held, and the Mann Act was passed in 1910, making it a federal crime to aid or entice young girls across state lines for purposes of engaging in prostitution.[13] Yet investigations in New York, California, Illinois, Wisconsin, Massachusetts, and Minnesota turned up no evidence of the existence of white slavery. In fact, not a single case of white slavery (i.e., a case involving a young girl's kidnapping and sale into prostitution) during the period has ever been verified.[14]

Media panics dredge up feelings of fear and shame as they reveal real or potential social disorder. Politicians both stoke and assuage such fears. The stimulation of a media panic allows conservative politicians (who are often then joined by their "liberal" brethren) to lament societal decline and to call for a return to traditional moral prescriptions and practices. Thus, even though media panics may constitute fairly brief episodes, their recurrent appearance creates an atmosphere that makes behavioral restrictions and repressions more politically palatable.

Media Panics and the Instabilities of Capitalism

The dynamic relationship that exists between the appearance of a media panic and social and political repression is indicative of a structural feature of postindustrial capitalist economies. Capitalism, like any functioning social system, needs discipline and control to operate successfully over time. Both capitalists and workers must be willing to forgo some gratification for the sake of future compensation, whether that be in terms of return on investment for capitalists or the promise of access to new opportunities for workers or their children. Max Weber famously proposed that the religious ethic that undergirded capitalism's early development was grounded in a fearsome asceticism.[15] The hard work that generated the capital accumulation that made the industrial development of the West possible was not intended to create luxury or material comfort for capitalists. Rather, the accumulation of wealth indicated the personal virtue of male breadwinners and commitment to family, community, and church. Over time, however, as wealth grew, it became more difficult to channel the energies of the affluent toward only such ascetic commitments. The temptation to indulge—to consume—became overwhelming, and the fostering of a consumption ethic became a structural necessity for growth.

Economic growth initiated a consumer culture that both supported and undermined the system of capital accumulation. Mass consumption was necessary to keep the system functioning, but as more aspects of life became incorporated into the universe of commodities, the underlying rationale for sacrifice, the principles and values that launched the system in the first place, became more difficult to sustain. Moral systems tend to weaken, in other words, in the face of advancing capitalism. Capitalist ascetics, such as H. L. Hunt, the fabled billionaire, who was said to have brought his lunch to work every day in a brown paper bag, have few successors in today's business world. Today we are more likely to encounter Kenneth Lay, who cashed in his billions in Enron stock while encouraging his employees not to, thus maintaining his vast stores of wealth while the company's workers lost their life savings.

Capitalism is after all a dynamic system that holds little respect for "values." Communities, the repositories of social values, are routinely undermined by changes in modes of production. Work and the desire for wealth, as well as unemployment and the dislocations of poverty, can destabilize communal commitments and social bonds. In infinite ways, the social glue that sustained capitalism's early growth has weakened over time. The "Protestant ethic" has diminished, and the social bonds that justified the sacrifices made in the pursuit of economic success have loosened. Under these circumstances, media panics conveniently reassert the significance and power of those social repressions that were loosened by capitalism's dynamism. In other words, libertarian desires for more freedom, individuality, and consumerism need to be both cultivated and controlled in stable capitalist economies. Their cultivation is necessary to make the system function and grow, but too much individuality, too much self-indulgence, undercuts the system's stability. Media panics provide a mechanism for reasserting the power of the state and society while generating profits for media. Members of the public are induced toward acquiescence as a sense of "community" is reestablished along the parameters of "us" against "them."[16]

In *Policing the Crisis*, Stuart Hall and his colleagues explore these patterns in Britain so as to explain authorities' reactions to certain kinds of crime problems.[17] The perception of and control over crime exist, they argue, within an ongoing "crisis of hegemony" that pervades the postwar capitalist state. Stimulated panics involving crime represent attempts on the part of various institutions to maintain their power and authority in the face of contradictions that threaten them. In particular, Hall et al. focused on the crime of "mugging," which represented in British society not the appearance of a new crime (mugging had existed for at least a century in British life) but the appearance of new social groups, immigrants, often of color, who threaten to undermine the stability of the social order.[18] The panic that coalesced around mugging in England in the 1970s became a mechanism to alert the white English working class to a potential threat "from outside," so that they could mobilize energy and resources against it while at the same time reasserting their loyalty to the state as the enforcer and protector of national (and class) interests.

In the United States, "crime" has long had a similar political reso-nance. Beginning with the 1968 presidential campaigns of Richard Nixon and George Wallace, the word *crime* took on an expansive meaning and became, in essence, a code word used to mobilize the "silent majority"—white middle- and working-class elements, traditional constituencies of the Democratic Party—against "hippies," desegregationists, black nation-alists, rioters, "bra burners," and students who were cast as out of control and in need of discipline. Neoliberalism, neoconservatism, and indeed Clintonism can all be seen as heirs to this legacy.

Stuart Hall and his associates argue that the nature of media panics in-volving crime has evolved over time. They note a "spiraling" effect evident beginning in the 1970s. In the period before World War II, panics started as fairly localized events and took time to permeate the culture as a whole. Partly this was due to the relatively decentralized and diversified nature of the mass media of the time. Newspapers took longer to disseminate information than do radio and television today, and the dispersed nature of news media ownership was a barrier to concentrating the attention of a national public on particular events. Class and regional distinctions were also more important during this period. Over time, consolidation oc-curred, local identities weakened, and a consumer society emerged, held together by a loosely organized, semicoherent set of signs. Consumerism and "pop" essentially became the dominant culture. "Communities" trans-formed into "audiences."

Audiences are not passive receptacles of media images, but are primed for and, in fact, demand a role in participating in and shaping the meaning and power of pop-cultural events. In some cases, such as "Beatlemania," the results are benign or even "fun." With media panics, however, "the public" is provoked and demands that its leaders act to protect it. As Hall et al. note, "There begins the regular, immediate escalation of *every* con-flictual issue up the hierarchy of control to the level of the state machine." "The public" acts in concert with the state as "popular moral pressure from below and the thrust of restraint and control from above *happen to-gether*." As a result, media panics proliferate, and state authorities are "sen-sitized to the emergence of the 'enemy' in any of its manifold disguises; the repressive response is at the ready, quick to move in, moving formally, through the law, the police, administrative regulation, public censure, and at a developing speed."[19]

Research findings have supported the hypothesis that the mass media have tremendous influence on the public's sensitivity to specific crime problems. Fishman, for example, found that a spate of news reports in New York City about crimes against the elderly generated great public concern that translated into demands for action and resulted in public officials establishing new policies aimed at protecting elderly persons, in spite of the fact that no detectable increase in such crimes had occurred, and some types of crimes had even decreased in frequency.[20] Voumvakis and Ericson examined media reporting on sexual assaults and found a similar disconnect between media depictions of crime and actual crime rates in Toronto, Canada.[21] Surrette conducted a comprehensive study of media representations of crime, and he concludes that crime coverage (1) presents violence to an extent disproportionate with crime data, (2) provides explanations that are nearly always "simplistic" and "individualistic," (3) encourages exaggerated fears of victimization, and (4) exacerbates racial divisions.[22]

Media "Realities"

Since Hall and his colleagues published *Policing the Crisis,* media panics have proliferated, to the point that they have become one of the defining features of media culture. The presence of the mass media now permeates domestic and international cultures to a startling degree. The ubiquity of media is not in itself a sufficient condition for panics to multiply and intensify; rather, it is the ways the media are organized institutionally within global markets that provide the conditions that make further proliferation and intensification of panics not only possible but perhaps inevitable.

Profit continues, of course, to be a primary motivating factor: the media produce stories that media executives believe will garner a large portion of the market. Crime panics—whether arising from mass shootings in Littleton, Colorado, or local coverage of drug busts and gang shootings—sell. Often, media coverage is inconsistent with the existence of actual threats, but nowadays coverage may reinforce the likelihood that threats will occur (as with, for example, "copycatters"). Both the style and the subjects of coverage create a sense that the social world is collapsing. As in the Williams case, stories appear suddenly, receive tremendous attention for short periods of time, and then disappear as quickly as they arrived to make room for the next "big story." The impression many people get is that they are threatened by one catastrophe after another. The media abhor a vacuum, and media organizations are involved in a never-ending search for the next sensation, whether it be shark attacks, child abductions, or the emergence of multiple forms of domestic terror activities.

Profits drive not only the cycles of news coverage, but the choices of subjects as well. Audiences are not treated as one "mass" of potential subjects. Rather, coverage is slanted toward the perceived interests of those in the more affluent demographic ranges. "Drug" coverage tends to portray local street dealers and small-time hoods. Drug abuse is portrayed as primarily a problem of the urban poor—more often than not, black and brown men. Such portrayals match the deep prejudices of the people who make up the affluent demographic that most television news programs are attempting to reach. They reinforce the sense among viewers that not only is social disintegration occurring, it is being caused mostly or solely by deviant elements in the population. At the same time, powerful institutions, such as banks, are immune from careful scrutiny, as attention is deflected to less powerful segments of the population.

Embedded within the concept of a media panic is the idea that it results from a partially false or exaggerated understanding of the nature of a particular social problem. The term *panic* implies that people are reacting irrationally to a perception, and that if they only understood more clearly the nature of the supposed threat, their panic would subside.[23] Of course, the line between "appearance" and "reality" is never very clear, and in our media age it is increasingly difficult to make the distinction. "Crime" is a social reality, and real people are injured by it in multiple ways. How is it possible for us to know when its representations are inconsistent with actual existing threats? There is no easy answer to this question. In the case of the "white slavery" scare of the early twentieth century, there seems to have been little or no evidence of any actual threat that girls and young women were being kidnapped and sold to prostitution rings, although prostitution itself was of course a concrete reality. Schools shootings are a definite threat to children, although the likelihood of any child actually being shot is almost infinitesimally small.[24] The same is true of shark attacks and child abductions. In the 1990s, as crime rates declined, media caricatures of crime continued unabated. As Krajicek notes, crime still accounts for "one-third of the content of a daily newspaper and up to half of many local tv broadcasts."[25]

One of my primary aims in this volume, then, is to reveal the hysterical and often superficial nature of media and expert constructions of a particular case, the Nushawn Williams case. In examining the case, I bring a variety of data to bear as a means of criticizing these constructions. In the end, I make no claims that I have uncovered *the* "reality" of what occurred, although I would contend that I offer alternative perspectives that are more thoughtful, nuanced, and detailed than those that have heretofore been available. In other words, although I cannot claim to reveal the "real" of what "happened," I do provide synthesis and critical analysis of existing media reports, along with historical background and the perspectives of numerous individuals involved with various aspects of the case.

HIV/Race/Media

The HIV pandemic is not a media panic, but reactions to it have often resulted in panics of various kinds. Estimates of the nature and scope of the transmission, etiology, and progress of the disease, as well as the numbers of infected, have been politically charged from the start. The early association of HIV with gay men's sexuality led to the encoding of HIV/AIDS as a problem of "morality" rather than simply one of public health. Voices on the religious right, from Jerry Falwell to Patrick Buchanan, labeled HIV/AIDS as a gay plague—divine retribution for promiscuous and "unnatural" lifestyles. As Falwell so graphically put it more than ten years ago, "AIDS is God's judgment on a society that does not live by His rules."[26]

In this atmosphere, most of those who tested positive for the virus were blamed for contracting the illness. They were not only responsible for their fate, and thus unworthy of sympathy and sometimes even medical care, they were a moral and physical threat to the rest of "us." Thus, from the beginning, representations of HIV transmission have been laced with a discourse of "innocence" and "guilt." Some "victims" of the virus—hemophiliacs like Ryan White, for example—were deemed to be innocents. Others, the "guilty," needed to be identified and then monitored or isolated. Conservative columnist William F. Buckley, for example, proposed that those who test positive be given two tatoos, one on the forearm and another on the buttocks, as a warning to potential drug and sex partners.[27] Calls for leper colony–style quarantines were not unheard of.[28]

The demonization of HIV-infected persons, however, went beyond attacks on gay sexuality. HIV's association with other marginalized groups—including West Indians, Africans, and intravenous drug users of all races, genders, and classes—allowed the then "new right" to use the HIV/AIDS epidemic in the service of its full-scale cultural "war" on the remnants of 1960s left-liberalism. HIV/AIDS came to symbolize, for the right, the dangers not only of sexual "deviance," but sexual freedoms, and indeed pleasures, of all kinds, as well as any politics that favored the extension and/or protection of race and gender equality.

The HIV crisis was then perfectly suited for the Reagan era, a period in which human bodies (and minds) were being (re)disciplined (morally and economically) for participation in a newly deregulated capitalist state. In a process that continues to unfold, the denizens of this world order would be required to renounce unproductive and socially disruptive politics of equality and pleasure in the service of restoring and restructuring transnational capitalist institutions. If HIV had not appeared, in other words, the architects of the new global economy would have had to invent it.

Simon Watney was, then, exactly right when he wrote in 1989 that "AIDS is not only a medical crisis on an unparalleled scale, it involves a crisis of representation itself, a crisis over the entire framing of knowledge about the human body and its capacities for sexual pleasure."[29] The political battles over the meaning of HIV/AIDS represented broader cultural confrontations over how pleasure, work, and economy would be written on and through human bodies. There is little doubt that dominant Western representations of sexuality were not (and are not) well equipped to deal positively with the HIV crisis.[30] The increasingly heterosexual character of transmission is clear evidence of that. Although AIDS has generated a plurality of discourses and responses, in the "mainstream" it is still too often reduced to a simple morality play in which "innocents" and "victims" are continuously threatened by moral reprobates and evil pleasure seekers.

HIV has been imbued with racial constructions since the beginnings of the epidemic. The notion of its supposed origins in Africa has, for example, been important to various constructions of its meaning. Black people were immediately proposed as the source of the epidemic. AIDS, as Susan Sontag has written, "illustrated the classic script for plague. . . . [It] is thought to have started in the 'dark continent,' . . . spread to Haiti, then the United States and to Europe. . . . It is understood as tropical disease . . . and a scourge of the *tristes tropiques*. . . . Africans who detect racist stereotypes in much of the speculation about the geographical origin of AIDS are not wrong."[31] As Richard Chirimuuta and Rosalind Chirimuuta put it, "It was almost inevitable that, once AIDS appeared in black people in any numbers, they would be attributed with its source. Haiti was the first unfortunate victim. Africa would soon follow."[32] It was not simply that AIDS had originated in Africa, but *how* it originated that was important to its racialized meanings. The widespread notion that AIDS "jumped species" from green monkeys to humans further reinforced racist stereotypes. As Chirimuuta and Chirimuuta note, "Such ideas cohabit easily with racist notions that Africans are evolutionarily closer to sub-human primates, or with images gleaned from Tarzan movies of Africans living in trees with monkeys."[33] Refutations of the "green monkey" thesis—first proposed by Robert Gallo on highly speculative grounds—were mostly ignored by the "mainstream" press, and the residue of this theory is no doubt still embedded in the popular-culture consciousness.[34]

The constructions of AIDS in relation to Africans, African Americans, and other people of color followed a script that has been used frequently by major media sources in the United States. Media representations of black people in American society have often reflected the racism that has marked U.S. national history. In the early days of television, African Americans were mostly invisible on-screen, and when they did appear, they were represented as stereotypical minstrels and buffoons. As Gray notes, "Black characters who populated the television world of the early 1950s were happy-go-lucky social incompetents who knew their place and whose antics served to amuse and comfort culturally sanctioned notions of whiteness, especially white superiority and paternalism."[35] In the later 1950s and the 1960s, some television producers made attempts to "universalize" (or "whiten") black entertainers, such as Nat King Cole, by "sanitizing" them. Cole, for example, was carefully disassociated from any connections to culturally rebellious figures such as Charles Mingus, Billie Holiday, and Miles Davis.[36] In the 1970s, a search for "authenticity" yielded television programs about urban ghetto life *(Good Times, Sanford and Son)* in which characters were infused with solidarity and good humor in the face of economic disenfranchisement and racism, as they ultimately supported middle-class values of "family, love, and happiness."[37]

Representations of African Americans in mass media have not, of course, been wholly negative. The 1977 television miniseries *Roots,* for example, although it in certain respects simply borrowed the mythology of the struggling European immigrant for its story about slaves, thus oversimplifying the complex and continuing story of racism in the United States, at least publicly acknowledged the oppressions and legacies of slavery and portended the significance of an African American television audience. And in the 1980s and early 1990s, the *Cosby Show,* in spite of criticisms that it ignored the economics of racism, also reflected the growing significance and economic power of a black middle class.[38] The celebrated PBS documentary series *Eyes on the Prize* showed the complexity of the civil rights struggles of the 1950s and 1960s. The emergence of the black-owned Black Entertainment Television network on cable in the 1990s helped to provide a more diverse set of program options, but since its sale to Viacom in 2002, BET is no longer owned by African Americans.[39]

Although cultural representations of African Americans have achieved some diversity over time, they have continued to be haunted by racist and stereotypical imagery. A cultural politics is in place that the media draw on when necessary to place black images into the white mainstream public consciousness so as to instigate implicit (or explicit) racist fears. The media construction of the "drug epidemic" provides ample evidence of the long-term association of blackness with images of crime and violence. The very meaning of the term *crack* has been highly racialized, with important legal consequences.[40]

The infamous Willie Horton campaign ad, broadcast during the 1988 presidential campaign, is still the classic example of how racial messages can be encoded into popular culture through media images. (The pictures of Williams that were posted in Chautauqua County after his name was announced to the press were reminiscent of nothing so much as the Willie Horton ad campaign. He had became the "Willie Horton of AIDS.") Media coverage of the O. J. Simpson trial reflected the capacity of white-dominated media to focus on images of blackness/whiteness and violence to mobilize racist attitudes and generate viewership. Specifically, *Time* magazine's decision to darken Simpson's face in the mug shot photo it featured on the cover provides graphic evidence that editors have few scruples when it comes to using racism to solidify or broaden a share of the weekly newsmagazine market.[41]

The Nushawn Williams case, then, must be considered in relation to media stereotypes of African Americans historically. That Williams is African American and was having sex with teenage white girls, transmitting HIV to some of them, in a small-town subculture that was infected with drugs, was simply irresistible to the media given the narratives, symbolisms, and representations that were (and are) in place. The results were perhaps entirely predictable in terms of the framing of the case.

The Numbers

The justification for the invocation of emergency public health measures in the Williams case, as well as the intense media attention, was, and in fact had to be, based on the *numbers* of women and girls potentially infected by Williams. The original "cluster," uncovered by Commissioner Berke, was made up of four young women. The number of Williams's sexual partners, or possible partners, however, continued to escalate as the "crisis" unfolded. The problem of determining the number of people involved was heightened by reporters' and columnists' apparent inability to distinguish among primary and secondary exposure, HIV positivity, and actual AIDS. Public officials further exacerbated the problem by making vague or exaggerated statements to the press.

Commissioner Berke was initially quoted as suggesting that there were seventy primary or secondary exposures to HIV resulting from Williams's sexual activity.[42] Later, he said that "as many as 100 people may have been exposed to HIV."[43] Given that there were only fifty cases of AIDS reported in the county up until that time, people in the area were understandably alarmed. The state health commissioner, Dr. Barbara DeBuono, then suggested that Williams had given the names of fifty to seventy-five women "who he claimed to have sex with" to New York City officials.[44] Another unnamed state official then suggested that Williams had kept a "list" of seventy to eighty women "extending from New York City to Rochester . . . with whom he had claimed to have sex."[45] This assertion, never verified, led to Berke's suggestion that Williams was a "scorekeeper."[46] In a CNN interview, county attorney James Subjack stated, "This could geometrically grow by leaps and bounds."[47]

The figures were explosive enough that they were picked up by the *Guardian*, which ran a short article that included the vague and highly inflammatory assertion that Williams "may have infected up to 98 people."[48] It is not clear where that number came from, but it was eventually featured in a *U.S. News & World Report* article that reported Williams "may have infected as many as 98 people in the state."[49] Some commentators then began to suggest that the stated figures would themselves turn out to be too low. *New York Newsday* reporter Shirley Perlman wrote that, based on her interviews with health department officials, she could conclude that "the total number of people exposed to HIV is expected to increase *exponentially*, depending on how active Williams's partners are and whether they practice 'safe sex.'"[50] (This was, of course, true in the strict sense, but the implications of this statement were completely disconnected from the reality of what was unfolding.) One news service reported that "*hundreds* of people may be at risk of HIV infection through direct or indirect contact with Nushawn Williams."[51] Conservative *Orlando Sentinel* columnist Kathleen Parker undoubtedly made the most exaggerated (and least responsible) claim when, abandoning the language of "risk," "exposure," or "contact," she projected that "the final tally of those who may wind up with AIDS as a result of Williams' charm may number in the hundreds."[52]

On rare occasions, public officials were more circumspect. Fred Winter, a spokesman for the New York City Health Department, questioned State Commissioner DeBuono's claim that Williams had given city officials fifty to seventy-five names. Winters stated that the number of names was "far smaller," and he was, laudably, and somewhat uncharacteristically for this case, unwilling to attach a specific number to his statement.[53]

Authorities eventually concluded that Williams had had direct sexual contact with forty-eight people. Thus Berke's initial claim that Williams "had sexual encounters with at least 100 females" more than doubled the actual number.[54] Of these, thirteen eventually tested positive for HIV, and these women in turn named eighty-five other contacts (including individuals living in Rochester, where Williams resided briefly, and New York City).[55]

When all was said and done, it seems that the total number of persons who could credibly be said to have had a reasonably high chance of being infected through either primary or secondary contact with Williams was fourteen—a much lower number than was originally suggested. Thirteen young girls and women both had sexual contact with Williams and tested positive for HIV. Eleven of the total lived in Chautauqua County and two lived in New York City. Three of the thirteen had been contacted previously as a result of information that Williams gave when, in jail for automobile theft, he was first notified that he was positive for HIV infection. (He gave authorities a total of twenty names at that time.) Seven other cases were part of the HIV "cluster" that originally drew the attention of county health officials. Three cases turned up after Williams's name was released. There was one secondary contact, a child born to an HIV-positive woman with whom Williams had been involved, but apparently not his child.[56]

It should be noted that some of the infected women were drug users and had multiple sexual partners, making it virtually impossible to point the finger at Williams with certainty.[57] (In the general hysteria that followed the release of Williams's name, more than fourteen hundred people sought HIV tests in Chautauqua County. When the results of these tests were released to the public, it turned out that only one had yielded a positive result.)[58] In any event, although Williams's actions were highly irresponsible and eventually deemed criminal, Williams was not, it turned out, "the source of a near epidemic."[59] Nor was he, as Ted Koppel asserted, a "super transmitter."[60]

Constructing Nushawn

"Tragic" cannot, of course, begin to express what it means to be thirteen years old and positive for HIV. This discussion should not be mistaken for an attempt to minimize the impact on each of those fourteen people, most of them quite young, of discovering that they have been infected by a virus for which there is no cure and that leads, it seems even now, almost inevitably to a slow and horrible death. But on a daily basis, around the world, many dozen times that number contract HIV, and their personal tragedies seem to warrant little attention from American media outlets. The media frenzy and local panic that accompanied the Williams story were caused in part by those who bandied about large unsubstantiated numbers from the beginning of the case. Other matters came into play as well, which I will discuss later, but these numbers took on a life of their own as the story developed a momentum that carried it across the country and around the globe.

Eventually, as test results came in and the numbers of HIV-positive individuals connected to Williams turned out to be much smaller than had been suggested in many media reports, few spoke up to criticize either the media or the health officials involved. Rather, the narrative turned to a renewed sense of calm and reassurance in Chautauqua County. As one report put it, "A nearly audible sigh of relief drifted through the snow-covered hills."[61]

The *Washington Post*, in noting that the numbers were much lower than many had assumed, reported that "fear [had] spread that hundreds of people may have been infected through direct or indirect contact."[62] This article gave no indication that this fear had been the result of overstatements, misstatements, and exaggerations by newspaper reporters, columnists, and public health officials. And although it was clear by mid-November that the early numbers had been overstated, not everyone got the message. William F. Buckley wrote in the November 24 issue of the *National Review* that Williams had "apparently" infected twenty-eight women "directly through heterosexual contact," and fifty-three others "may have been infected indirectly." "Billy the Kid," he noted, "killed only 21 people in the course of his legendary career."[63]

In a sense Buckley could not be blamed. He was simply following the standard of evaluation earlier put forward by Dr. Berke, who described Williams as "a guy who came in and shot a number of people with a different kind of bullet."[64] But sloppy journalism aside, the numbers had taken on a life of their own in the first week after the story broke, and these numbers became a crucial aspect of Williams's vilification. To the many aliases and nicknames that were attributed to him ("Face," "Shyteek," and so on) were attached new ones: "20-year-old sexual predator," "modern Typhoid Mary," "one-man HIV epidemic," "latter-day patient zero," "lethal Lothario," "an individual with no regard for human life," "maggot," "would-be serial killer," and "dirtbag."[65] One *USA Today* writer called him "the bogeyman incarnate."[66] In the *Buffalo News,* commentator Donn Esmonde called for punishment "involving devices not used since the Middle Ages" and compared Williams's actions to those of the Oklahoma City bombers.[67] CNN legal correspondent Greta Van Susteren predicted that Williams would be charged with "first degree assault, which is a 25 year offense," or even first-degree murder.[68] Attorney Wendy Murphy, interviewed by Geraldo Rivera on *Rivera Live,* stated, based on no direct knowledge of the case, "I don't have any doubts whatsoever that he should be charged with at least attempted murder, and, if people die from this disease, absolutely charge him with murder. His intent is crystal clear to me."[69] Dr. Berke himself compared Williams to a mass murderer, stating: "I liken this in many ways to me waking up in the morning and turning on some program, news program, and seeing that somebody's walked into a McDonald's and shot 5 people in a community. This is very similar. It shouldn't happen here. Why did it happen in that community? This is a guy who came in and shot a number of people with a different kind of bullet."[70] Public officials such as New York Mayor Rudy Giuliani jumped on the bandwagon, calling for Williams to be charged with attempted murder although they knew virtually none of the facts of the case.[71] One young man from Jamestown, when interviewed on *Rivera Live* about what should happen to Williams, stated, "Death sentence. I mean it seems only fair."[72]

The characterization of Williams as a sexual predator went beyond the media's simply casting him as irresponsible or even callous. He was depicted as a true bogeyman. Berke said that Williams "liked to lurk around the edge of schools and parks maybe where kids would be playing basketball."[73] County Executive Andrew Goodell, apparently picking up on published comments made by Berke, stated that Williams "preyed on school girls he met in the park." County legislator Joseph Trusso, expanding on

Goodell's scenario, stated, "He'd go to dances all around the county and look for some girl standing against a wall, some wallflower type, and sweet-talk her and have his way with her."[74] *New York Daily News* "critic at large" David Hinckley colorfully transformed this fantasy into a portrayal of Williams as "a character straight out of 'Reefer Madness,' hanging around playgrounds going, 'Pssstttt! C'mere little girl,' and all the while little girls are lining up not only to take his drugs, but also to have unprotected sex with him."[75] Williams was presented as diabolical and ingenious in his capacity to seduce young girls, but at the same time as one who had no self-control. Surprisingly, even the otherwise responsible *Poz* magazine stated in July 1999, in a short article on Williams's sentencing, that he had "been diagnosed as schizophrenic."[76] This was untrue. Williams had undergone a psychiatric exam, on the recommendation of the Bronx district attorney, but he was never diagnosed as mentally ill.[77]

At first glance, it might be difficult to imagine how someone as purportedly unattractive as Williams—someone who "was scary" and had "a nasty mouth"—managed to have "a steady stream of girls coming by at all hours."[78] What strange charm did this postmodern Rasputin possess? Sexual prowess was the (racial) subtext, but the ready answer was drugs. Williams was by all accounts a heavy marijuana user, and he was consistently described as a "crackhead" (a charge that turned out, as far as I can tell, to be untrue).[79] Thus he was easily cast as a pied piper who used drugs to attract and corrupt the innocent teenagers of Jamestown. Health Commissioner Berke was apparently the first to make a "sex for drugs" allegation in the Williams case when he stated at the initial news conference that "sex for drugs appears to be implicated in at least some of the contacts." This comment was apparently picked up by Mike Striver, policy director for the National Association of People with AIDS, who was quoted as stating, "This is clearly a man who was allegedly preying on young women and trading sex for drugs."[80] CNN also reinforced the charge by leading its report on the case on the CNN.com Web site with a sentence describing Williams as "an HIV-infected man suspected of trading drugs for sex."[81] CNN reporter Martin Savidge asserted in his lead-in to a Williams story that "police say Williams admitted to having traded drugs for sex with as many as 75 people."[82] Buffalo attorney William Gardner (who deals with AIDS issues) asked, "Why are these girls having sex for drugs anyway?"[83] ABC News found a man from Brooklyn, Rodney Prior, who claimed to have been a lookout for Williams when Williams was selling drugs in the neighborhood. On camera, Prior said that Williams was "messing around with crackheads," but reporter John Miller went a good deal further in his voice-over, stating that Prior had told him that "when he [Williams] went from selling to smoking crack, Williams degenerated into a homeless addict trading crack for sex."[84] In truth, however, Williams was neither homeless nor a crack addict.

When Dr. Neil Rzepkowski, a physician who treated four of the infected girls, described one of them as a "typical good-looking, middle-class kid" who had told him that she did not take drugs, the scenario began to unravel.[85] Some officials were also not inclined to see the sexual activity as a quid pro quo arrangement, given that there was virtually no evidence to that effect.[86] County Sheriff Joseph Gerace conceded that there may have been some drug use, but asserted, "In no way should we be saying this is a drugs-for-sex case."[87] The youngest girl who slept with Williams, who harbored no love for him and who eventually testified against him at his preliminary hearing, also denied the sex-for-drugs allegation. On *CBS This Morning,* she told interviewer Jacqueline Adams, "I smoked weed with him sometimes, but that's not what got me in bed with him. He was nice, I trusted him and he was there for me."[88] And by the time of Williams's sentencing in February 1999, the *Buffalo News* was no longer reporting that Williams traded sex for drugs; instead, reporters Lou Michel and Charity Vogel stated that his "methods of seduction" were "compliments, dinners, [and] trinkets."[89] The sex-for-drugs images were by then firmly embedded, however. An Associated Press story reporting on Williams's guilty plea stated that "among Williams's partners were teens he allegedly seduced with crack before he was jailed on a drug charge."[90]

Lost completely in all of the media coverage of the case was any indication that Williams had been cooperative with health officials each time he had been questioned.[91] When he was originally approached by an official of the Chautauqua County Health Department and asked to take an AIDS test, he voluntarily, according to authorities, gave the names of twenty sexual contacts. When he was again questioned after he was located in the Rikers Island jail, he again gave the names of his contacts, for which he was condemned as a "scorekeeper."

The characterization of Nushawn Williams as a malicious predator perhaps helps to account for the threats he has faced since he was arrested. ABC News reported that Williams was transported to his first sentencing hearing on drug charges under "heavy guard" because prison officials were "worried about death threats."[92] While in prison, Williams has been held in the protective custody unit because of various threats against him. On one of my trips to the state prison to talk to Williams, I asked one of the guards why he had been in protective custody. The guard said that it was because of what Williams had done. "You know," he said, "he's a rapist." I was somewhat surprised to hear this, given what I knew about the case, but a survey of some of the early news stories about Williams helped to explain things. CNN, for example, reported on its Web site when the story first broke that Williams "faces rape charges." Williams did face charges of *statutory* rape, but the CNN story on-line reported that he faced charges of "second-degree" rape, clouding (perhaps even deliberately) the distinction between sex with a minor who consents and forcible rape.[93] *CBS Morning News* also reported early on that "officials here [in Jamestown] have charged Williams with rape."[94] When Williams was sentenced, the *New York Times* stated that "Mr. Williams could receive 2 to 6 years in prison for each count of raping a 13 year old girl."[95]

Williams was also accused in the press of willfully and intentionally exposing his partners to HIV, long before the facts were fully known. For example, the following exchange took place on *ABC News Nightline*:

CHRIS BURY (reporter): Do you think that Nushawn Williams intentionally infected people?

JOE GERACE (county legislator): Yes.

BURY: Why?

GERACE: He knew that he was HIV positive. He slept if indeed accurate in his numbers, he slept with many, many women and he had to know that he was infected.

BURY: He knew exactly what he was doing?

DR. ROBERT BERKE: There was no question about that. That is well documented as to the risks, the potential risks he posed to everybody else that he came in contact with.[96]

The assertion that Williams infected others not only knowingly but deliberately and with malice seems to have been triggered by a comment from his sister, Mikka. A reporter asked Mikka, "Do you think he would have sex with those girls knowing he was HIV positive?" She responded, "Yeah. Because he felt he don't have nothing to live for."[97] The highly speculative question elicited an ambiguous answer (yeah *would have* or yeah *did*?), but in any case the portrayal of Williams as someone not only with knowledge but with malice persisted. ABC News reporter Lisa McRee stated on *Good Morning America* that "this really was a case of a predator. He knew he had HIV, and his sister, at least, has said publicly that he knew he was going to infect people, and that he did it on purpose and almost with malice" (which is not of course what she said).[98] On another *Good Morning America* segment, Williams was highlighted as a man who "purposely infected dozens of teens with HIV" (although the follow-up interview with James Subjack did not live up to that billing, as Subjack discussed "reckless endangerment" charges involving "depraved indifference").[99]

Having unprotected sex with others when one knows oneself to be HIV-positive is not responsible behavior, and Williams's guilty plea is legally determinative that he was informed of his HIV status when he had been in jail previously in Chautauqua County. But given the media's re-action to the Williams case, one might think that this sort of activity is virtually nonexistent among the HIV-positive population as a whole. In fact, the media often seemed to use the supposed uniqueness of the case as an implicit justification for the amount and intensity of the coverage it received. It is at least questionable, however, whether most HIV-positive individuals tell their sexual partners about their status. It is also not easy to determine whether there are numerous HIV "clusters" in the United States. The CDC does not keep records of such phenomena, and they would be extremely difficult to detect in larger population centers with relatively high concentrations of HIV cases. Anthony Fauci, former direc-tor of the National Institutes of Health, noted, "This whole thing would have been missed if it happened in New York City."[100]

Somewhat similar cases have elicited nowhere near the same amount of media coverage. In 1996, Darnell "Boss Man" McGee was alleged to have had sex with a hundred women or more, and thirty of his sexual partners later tested positive for HIV. The case received little national media atten-tion, however. The *New York Times,* for example, carried only one article about McGee, and CNN carried a story on him only after the Williams story broke, although the circumstances of the McGee case were, in many respects, more sensational than those of the Williams case.[101] For instance, more partners were involved in the McGee case, and McGee was eventual-ly shot and killed by one of his lovers.[102] All of McGee's lovers were African American women.

In April 2002, a twenty-year-old man from Chicago, Nikko Briteramos, who at the time was attending SiTanka Huron University in South Dakota, was charged with three counts of exposing his girlfriend to HIV. Briteramos had apparently been apprised of his HIV status when he at-tempted to give blood in late March 2002. On April 23, when Health Department counselors went to see him in his dorm room, he appeared in his underwear, and the counselors determined that a young woman had been with him in the room and had slipped out when they arrived. Briteramos admitted to having had unprotected sex with her. Although this case garnered nothing like the national attention that Williams's case did, it did elicit two *New York Times* articles, a flurry of wire service stories, and a brief segment on *Today.*

At first, as happened in the Williams case, the media speculated about the potential HIV exposure of large numbers of people. One Associated Press reporter suggested that "one of the people tested gave the names of 70 others who were in contact with Briteramos, and the chain would run into the hundreds."[103] As it turned out, however, Briteramos was not espe-cially promiscuous. He had had only three sexual contacts while in South

Dakota, two before he had knowledge that he was HIV-positive. Still, prosecutors stated that he could receive up to seventy-five years in prison if convicted under the state's two-year-old criminal HIV-transmission statute, which the state was invoking for the first time.[104] The young woman with whom he had had the contact for which he was being prosecuted was not infected with the virus.

Some of the same themes emerged in Briteramos's case as had in Williams's. The media and health officials presented the incident as a wake-up call to South Dakota, which has one of the lowest HIV infection rates in the country (1.1 cases per 100,000 residents).[105] The state's governor, Bill Janklow, used words that were almost an exact match to Dr. Berke's regarding Williams's actions, stating, "This is no different than pointing a gun at somebody and pulling the trigger."[106] Yet the press did not portray Briteramos as a "monster." The most inflammatory language offered came from his father, who suggested that his son was neither a "monster" nor a "viral terrorist."[107] In fact, his lawyer's statement that he was a "sincere young man" who was "baffled by the charges against him" seemed to set the tone. Brad Smith, the interim chancellor of Huron University, characterized the school as "supportive" and "concerned," and Briteramos as "a kid who made a mistake."[108] The *New York Times* described the young basketball player as "lanky" and "personable," and an Australian newspaper labeled him the "sporty lover-boy."[109]

With his bail set at ten thousand dollars, Briteramos pled guilty at the end of August to three counts of knowingly exposing someone to HIV. He received a five-year suspended sentence, with 120 days of jail time and 200 hours of community service. As part of his sentence, he was allowed to continue at Huron University during his incarceration. Things soon, however, took a turn for the worse. On the day that he was sentenced, Briteramos was given two hours to go to the campus, register for classes, and then return to the jail. He apparently had some difficulty registering because his student status was unclear, and he took more than five hours to return to the jail, having made a detour to his apartment and the apartment of a friend before going back.[110] Later, his blood tested positive for trace amounts of marijuana (levels so low that they were likely caused by secondhand smoke).[111] The judge was not pleased. In early October, he un-suspended the young man's sentence and sent him to prison; he will be eligible for parole in 2004.[112]

Briteramos was never demonized as Nushawn Williams was. Had he not foolishly gone to his friend's apartment, he most likely would not have served any time in prison. South Dakota officials did, however, send a clear message that they would join other states in pursuing criminal prosecutions in HIV-transmission cases.

The Setting: Small-Town America

If a dyadic relationship between "innocence" and "guilt" has tended to be a dominating feature of the popular-culture construction of HIV/AIDS, the Williams story lent itself quite easily to that narrative. But if the "guilty" party was easily identifiable as a young, "predatory," oversexed black man, the notion of "innocence" was more problematic. This was evident in the treatment of both the town involved—Jamestown, New York—and the girls and women who were Williams's sexual partners. Both were presented as injured, yet somehow culpable.

The Girls

It is tempting to think that the young women who were involved with Nushawn Williams were cast as innocent victims, and that it was their innocence that justified the vitriol that was heaped on Williams himself. But that was clearly not the case. In truth, very little was written about them. They were for the most part silenced by various media depictions. When one of them did surface, the sight was generally not a pretty one. The girls and women involved with Williams were cast as a "bunch of rural waifs" or as "the AIDS monster's victims."[113] They were seldom given credit for agency, as the popularity of the "sex for drugs" scenario illustrates.

When they did speak, however, the women showed an understandably complex set of reactions to Williams. One of the young girls who was infected by and eventually testified against Williams was quoted numerous times as saying that she thought he should "die." After he was sentenced, another was quoted as saying, "I hope he rots in jail and dies of AIDS."[114] But others were more circumspect. "Shanequa," who was also most likely infected by Williams, said, "I'm just as guilty as he is. We all knew what type of man he was—very sexually active, basically a nymphomaniac.... I hope the other women realize it was just as much their fault.... They could have asked him to put on a condom."[115]

It wasn't until eighteen months after the story broke that a more nuanced depictions of "Nushawn's girls," as they were sometimes labeled in the press, began to emerge. For one thing, most continued to be sexually active, sometimes informing their partners of their status and sometimes not. Some were in heavy denial, with at least two not taking their medications. Six were pregnant with the children of other men. But perhaps most important was the dim recognition that these young women were not simply "white trash." As Dr. Neil Rzepkowski, who treated most of them, put it, "These girls are not all the same. Some had bad childhoods, but not all. Some are upper middle class, some are not.... Some are low intelligence, others are very smart and going to college. There's a lot of variety. You can't classify them."[116]

I was able to interview only one of the young girls personally. Andrea Caruso had lived with Williams in the winter of 1997, a time when he was moving back and forth between Jamestown and New York City, selling drugs. She had, she explained, moved in with him because people had told her he was a "nice guy." Amber Arnold may have wanted to declare to the world that she still loved Nushawn Williams, but Caruso would have none of it. She was now HIV-positive, more than likely as a result of her sexual relationship with him. She told me that he kept her as a virtual prisoner in their apartment and forced her to have sex with him. She also claimed to have no knowledge that he was selling drugs. She was convinced that Williams knew that he was HIV-positive when they were together, and she had heard rumors around town to that effect after he left for New York, which prompted her to seek a blood test. She refused to accede to any suggestion that he may have been "in denial."[117] Denial's insidiousness, however, resides in its implacability. Caruso has had three children since testing positive. Two are HIV negative, but the youngest is HIV-positive, the result, apparently, of Caruso's not properly following her drug regimen.[118]

The Town

Media representations of a given community, or a given story, cannot be treated as monolithic. Newspapers have different constituencies and are driven by different economic imperatives. Yet, although there is some diversity in viewpoints among different kinds of media outlets, it would be a mistake to consider media presentations of nationally significant events as a diverse "marketplace of ideas" in the John Stuart Mill sense.[119] In the Nushawn Williams case, a fairly consistent picture of Jamestown and Chautauqua County emerged, and this depiction or representation carried through even small press sources, such as *Harper's*. Variations in the story resulted usually from the resistance generated by local reactions to the national media blitz. Some citizens of Jamestown understandably began to see themselves as living in a town under siege, not necessarily from HIV, but from the widespread media representations of the town.

The media gaze on Jamestown was, albeit short-lived, extremely intense. One Buffalo television station devoted thirteen minutes to the Williams story on the day of Robert Berke's press conference.[120] The *New York Times* published more than a dozen stories related in one way or another to the case. Wire stories and regional newspaper analyses resulted in dozens and dozens of articles spread out across the United States. Both cable and broadcast television networks covered the story on their national newscasts. National Public Radio sent a reporter. Montel Williams and Geraldo Rivera both did shows featuring some of the key participants. When a news story receives such intense attention, the coverage starts to circulate into itself, so that the distinction between "reality" and "coverage" tends to converge. People in places like Jamestown follow the news that is reported, and they incorporate their reactions to the news stories into their perspectives. As a result, it becomes increasingly difficult to locate and reveal "facts," because everything comes to be shaped by media-generated representations.

One of the things that made the Williams story a "go" was the contrast—the bipolarity, really—between the media's representations of Williams and their representations of Jamestown and Williams's "victims." Two themes, at times contradictory, emerged from media representations of the local area. First, the county's rural character and isolation led to its media presentation as idyllic and nostalgic, a place of past innocence, a (white) world violated by a (black) big-city thug.

At first, many reporters mistook Mayville, New York, for the place where Williams operated (apparently because it was where Dr. Berke held the initial press conference).[121] They described Mayville as being situated "in a rural county famous for its annual snowfall," a place "primarily known as a beautiful resort area."[122] A reporter for *USA Today* described Chautauqua County as "mostly bucolic and normally placid," and a *Philadelphia Inquirer* reporter described it as a "community of rolling hills and cornfields."[123] People there were "staggered . . . by the realization of what one man from New York City may have done to their communities," and at a school in Fredonia, "girls with pigtails and clear-faced boys with braces gasped in unison as they heard about Williams' sexual history."[124] Drawing on the history of the Chautauqua movement, a *Washington Post* reporter posed the highly dubious proposition that "there is no name more redolent of old-time American values than Chautauqua." Regretfully, however, he suggested, "time has passed Chautauqua by," in that old manufacturing had "gone the way of long-winded speeches and oratorical grandiloquence."[125] In a column for the *Indianapolis Star* headlined "Story of Sick Stranger Tarnishes Memories of Safe Small Town Life," Celeste Williams, who had grown up in Jamestown, described the town in the most idealistic terms imaginable. She remembered it as the place where she had had a "deep infatuation with Wendell Kibler, the boy down the street—Main Street. His father fixed the wings of injured birds. We never even held hands." Jamestown was where she would ride her bike through the local cemetery and where she saw her first big-screen film. Her father, a minister, worked three jobs, and the family wore secondhand clothes, but they somehow "never, ever felt poor. Not in Jamestown."[126]

A peek under the idyllic surface, however, revealed a different story. The second theme that emerged more forcefully as the "crisis" unfolded was one of economic decline, poverty, and "hopelessness." Chautauqua

County wasn't just "white," it was white trash. Jamestown became a "fad-ing industrial town," a "small beaten down city where for years drugs and homelessness have made their mark."[127] One schoolteacher was quoted as saying, "Things are on the skids here, and they have been for a long, long time."[128] The county as a whole was described as "working-class."[129]

New York Daily News reporters Tara George and Patrice O'Shaughnessy described Jamestown as a city "frozen in the 1970s, almost lifeless," where "too many children look toward bleak futures" and "clotheslines and junk piles surround houses with peeling paint." They called Jamestown a "drab world," where Williams was "a bit of a novelty"[130] A *New York Times* re-porter described the ride from Mayville to Jamestown on a "bleak byway" as a "scene from another century."[131] *People Magazine* reported that "many of [the] factories and mills closed before the birth of Lucille Ball, the area's most famous former resident."[132] (Lucille Ball was born in 1911.)

JoAnn Wypijewski's *Harper's* article was excellent in many respects. Her understanding of the complexities of the HIV crisis, particularly in terms of the role of denial in it, was exceptional. She never condemned Nushawn Williams. She interviewed a number of Jamestown's most dis-possessed kids and presented their stories in a way that remains unsur-passed. Still, even Wypijewski's otherwise admirable reporting was tainted by sensationalism. Part of this was in the presentation. The article was hawked with a bright yellow attachment to the magazine's cover promis-ing an "American Tale" of "Small Town Sex, Big Time Trouble." It was set off from the rest of the issue by having been printed on sepia-toned paper. The faded look had the effect of highlighting a sense of bleakness and despair. This was further accentuated by *Harper's* decision to include fifteen black-and-white photographs: graffiti, for sale signs, and distressed individuals.[133] Unfortunately, the images overwhelmed the positive things that Wypijewski said about the area. Moreover, some of her statements were extreme. Jamestown was a place, she wrote, where "some people, high placed people, pride themselves in provincialism; where police are known to harass and judges known to issue one-way bus tickets to kids who come from out of town."[134] She found "year round cottages off dirt roads hard by the water that recall nothing so much as Mississippi."[135] Jamestown, Wypijewksi wrote, "is the kind of place that can make a person's hate pure." And she "pray[ed] that every kid [she] met could get out."[136]

Few media stories represented the town in any more nuanced or com-plicated fashion. Only *Buffalo News* reporter Donn Esmonde noted that Jamestown High School had only a 2 percent dropout rate, and that 50 per-cent of the students graduated with regents diplomas. Esmonde also noted, however, the presence of "about 50 streetwise kids" whose involvement with hard drugs and highly promiscuous sex brought them into contact with Nushawn Williams. "The streets they live on are not blighted slums," he noted, "but tough, predominantly white, working-class neighborhoods."[137] Esmonde was heading in the right direction, but the U.S. media are, by and large, no more equipped to deal with the nuances of class than they are to address the nuances of race or of HIV infection. The media most often reduce working-class people to caricatures such as those found in the TV sitcoms *Laverne & Shirley, Roseanne,* and *Married . . . with Children.* The increasing corporatization of media ownership makes it difficult, if not impossible, for television and other major media outlets to deal in a serious way with the complexities of the lives of U.S. workers in a global economy.[138]

Public officials in Jamestown attempted to voice their objections to the one-dimensional picture of the community that was being generated in the national press, but when they did so, they were often presented as naive, foolish, or simply disingenuous. County Executive Andrew Goodell, for example, asserted that Jamestown was not "down-and-out" or "depressed," pointing to a strong growth rate and relatively low unemployment (5.2 percent) (this was not, of course, an adequate response, but it did at least problematize such figures in relation to the national economy). Obviously exasperated, Mayor Kimball asked people in the city to write to national news organizations and tell them "what is good about this city and this county and why we think we got a bad rap."[139]

Apparently angry, John Goodell, a local lawyer and father of Andrew Goodell, asked reporter Wypijewski, "Have you seen our ghetto? . . . I bet you'd be happy to have our ghetto in New York." In response, she quoted a line from a Billy Preston song, "Nothing from nothing leaves nothing."[140] Certainly there is naïveté in the expression of such sentiments, and it is possible even to ridicule them. But it is also possible to hear in them a pride of place that often exists for people even in dire circumstances. Moreover, poverty, deindustrialization, racism, and the deterioration of public health are complex, multifaceted problems. With the exception of a highly informative analysis of "rust belt" economics that the *Buffalo News* ran coincidentally with the Williams story, virtually none of the reporting on Jamestown at the time went beyond caricature of the community, its people, and its political economy.

Local Evaluation of Media Coverage

In my own interviews, local people later provided thoughtful critical judgments about what had occurred, in striking contrast to the many media oversimplifications. The locals with whom I spoke reacted with skepticism and sometimes hostility toward the media representations of Jamestown, but their reactions were not uniformly negative. Russ Tilaro, an HIV-positive gay man and president of the Chautauqua County AIDS Coalition, had been quoted in several articles and had been the subject of a *New York Times* profile. When I interviewed him, he expressed a mixed view. Although he felt the *Times* had done a good job of getting at some issues involving AIDS in rural areas, he also suggested that the newspaper coverage, as a whole, tended to racialize the story, and he asserted that if Williams "had been a white kid from our community, they wouldn't have done it." Tilaro, like a number of other folks, singled out the talk shows as especially worthy of criticism. He thought that he had arranged a "responsible show" with Jenny Jones, one in which the American Red Cross would show the education that it gives to kids about HIV/AIDS. In the end, however, "they went after the girls."[141]

District Attorney James Subjack said that the national media acted "fairly responsibly," but he also singled out the TV talk shows, "the Montels of the world, who got these people to essentially divulge their personal life, then not recognizing I think the ridicule and scorn of most of the people that watched it." Subjack was one of a number of people who suggested that Montel had "lured [people] to New York with the promise of a limo ride there and back, a McDonald's on the way, and a McDonald's on the way back. And maybe a new dress if you wanted to wear one." "They," he said, "were the irresponsible ones."[142]

A number of interviewees were highly critical of Wypijewski's article. Subjack was particularly incensed, stating that it was "grossly irresponsible" and that "she must recognize at this point that what she wrote was so biased and so slanted and so really inappropriately misleading that it was just that." The most intense responses to Wypijewski concerned her portrayal of the town. "It's not the garden spot of the world. You got a lot of closed businesses," Subjack said. "But it's not as she portrayed it. . . . You take pictures of the houses without paint with the screen doors open, windows broken. That's supposed to be a cross-section of Jamestown. . . . There's a subculture [of poverty here]. Jamestown has its share like everyplace else. But I think it was unfair to portray Jamestown as a cauldron of seething drug activity and illicit sex. I think the real take on that is: It's happening everywhere."[143]

Neil Rzepkowski, or Dr. Neil, as he is affectionately known in the community, HIV-positive and the man responsible for treating most of the AIDS patients in the county, was among the least charitable toward the national media. "They sensationalize everything," he said. "It was so funny. The press were crawling over everybody trying to scoop each other. It was just ridiculous. ABC was crawling over NBC. We got him first. It's ridiculous. But that's showbiz."[144]

Dr. Rzepkowski related a previous experience he'd had with the national press. In the early 1990s, when it became public that he was HIV-positive, he was forced to resign from his position as an emergency room doctor at Brooks Memorial Hospital in Dunkirk, New York. The incident generated a fair amount of press attention.[145] He had already agreed to an interview with CBS when ABC called, wanting him to appear on *Good Morning America.* He refused to talk to ABC first because of his prior commitment to CBS, and when he refused, ABC dropped the story entirely, as though the "scoop" was what made the story important. "Because ABC couldn't get it, it was now no longer news. It was amazing, just amazing. It sure gave me insight into how the news manipulates the American people." His animosity toward the press in the Williams case was based on the sex-and-drugs angle that the press played up. "With Nushawn too. It didn't fit. And so to make it fit into everybody's thinking, well he was trading sex for drugs. That's not at all what it was. He happened to take drugs and he happened to have sex, but the two didn't go together, like they're supposed to in the classic case."[146]

Matt Milovich, a youth services worker who runs a local shelter for out-of-home teens, was one of the most hostile toward the press among all my repondents. Milovich was also a common source of quotations used by the media in the early stages of the crisis. Although he praised the *Buffalo News* for some of its reporting, his "impression" was that "the folks that have come in here already had their story written in their head, already knew the spin they were going to put on it, then they came to find enough facts to back their theory. It was like a self-fulfilling prophecy, something like that. I don't know if there was really much honest journalism." Milovich said that he had been misquoted by the *New York Times,* and so called the paper up and "read them the riot act for what it was worth." The reporter had included a long quotation, attributed to Milovich, about folks from New York "with gold chains and dreadlocks . . . made me sound like Goober or something. Never said it. And that was that. . . . That was the take that she wanted. Small pastoral Jamestown gets hit by big slick you know guy from the big city thing. That was her take and so she just created that story from there. Yeah, it really pissed me off." Milovich was much more charitable toward Wypijewski, however. He didn't think that "she offered an accurate picture of Jamestown. . . . The pictures were black-and-white. The smokestack. That shit. She had her own spin." But on the other hand, "She did her homework. . . . She got in places where I can't go. She hung out at some of the drug houses and that type of stuff."[147]

Sheila McCarthy, the news director of local radio station WJTN, suggested that although the local newspaper did a reasonably good job in its coverage, the town was "raked over the coals by the networks." She ridiculed network stories that showed Mayville High School as a backdrop (twenty miles up the road from Jamestown), "just because they came out of the county health department office for a news conference and saw a high school there, and put it up on the networks. . . . He [Williams] was never in Mayville, except in jail."[148]

Joan Patrie, who works as the public relations officer for the local chapter of the Red Cross, noticed the same thing:

It was comical, the news trucks from the networks that were lining outside the high school shooting footage of kids going to high school, when nothing of this story really happened in the high school, the shots of the high school, the shots of the town park in Mayville. There wasn't a single case in Mayville. The news release came out of Mayville, so the media grabbed onto that and with no understanding of Chautauqua County showed this bucolic downtown Mayville scene which really had nothing to do with the story. But the initial suggestion in the national news was that this outbreak was in Mayville. We were most of us pretty much in the dark when it broke, and we're thinking, how could this be? Why would an urban drug dealer be in Mayville? And we were as baffled as anybody else. It was really our local media who sat on the story for a little while until they got it straight and then they straightened it out. But you're swimming with sharks. They're coming here for a big story. They're going to collect that story and then move on to the next story. And that's all they cared about.

Patrie also noted that banks of news cameras were set up outside the county health department's offices, "so that anybody wanting to go in for confidential HIV testing would be on national television, to say nothing of the person who wanted to go in there for an unrelated reason who suddenly realized he or she was on national television, just by walking in front of them. I mean phalanxes of cameras. And an irony I found most distasteful." Patrie also objected to the treatment of Nushawn. "I think," she said, "they completely missed that this was a public health threat. They demonized Nushawn as a serial killer. . . . See this man and run."[149]

Perhaps the most disturbing thing that I was told, however, came from Donna Vanstrom, director of the Red Cross chapter. She told me that a

gentleman from CNN came in and tried to get me to say that our blood product was compromised, because of this. And he must have tried ten different ways to get me to say that. It was just incredible. He didn't want facts. He wanted me to say something that he could broadcast. Needless to say I thought my job was on the line, so all I needed to say was, yeah that's a possibility, and that would have been it for me. . . . He asked the questions a lot of ways, and have we seen a drop off in blood donations, which we had to that point, honestly, because people were concerned about giving blood. Is there even a remote chance that you know the blood supply can be tainted? And the interview went on for about an hour, and he just always, periodically, just interjected a real quick question there to see if he could catch me to say something that he could report. It was quite an interesting experience dealing with the national media—not a pleasurable one, I'll tell you.[150]

Even Dr. Robert Berke, in some ways the darling of the media in this set of events, was highly critical of media representations of the case. Although he singled out *New York Times* reporter Richard Peres for doing serious work, he also contended that some of the coverage was "awful." He called the *Jamestown Post-Journal*'s reporting "awful" in terms of the inflation of the numbers involved. "The first day, we hand out a press release, to tell them look we've got this many contacts, this many positives," he told me, and that turned into "hundreds may be involved." In the end, he had a mildly cynical view of the press. "They're in it for whatever they can get out of it. Friday that week the nanny story broke. They were gone. Out of here. You looked out, and they're gone."[151]

(Re)constructing Rights

Although most of the heavy coverage of Williams and Chautauqua County dissipated within a couple of weeks, there is little doubt that it will have long-term impacts on the people who live in the area. Jamestown has been indelibly etched into the popular consciousness as that place where the "AIDS predator" made his dubious mark. What this might mean for the community in the long run is certainly open to speculation. The *Jamestown Post-Journal* ran a story in July 1998 suggesting that the media attention would hurt the area's potential for economic development, a proposition that, at the time, seemed valid (although Jamestown is now undergoing a revitalization that may belie these predictions; see chapter 2).[152] On a wider scale, the concrete impacts of the constructed panic in the case are discernible in terms of new social policies in New York State and beyond.

The construction of Nushawn Williams as a lethal sex predator created an atmosphere in which newspaper columnists and public officials could credibly call for significant changes in legal rules related to HIV. First, demands for criminal sanctions were forthcoming, not only for Nushawn Williams, but for any HIV-positive person who might put other persons at risk. Second, there was a clamor for changes to the confidentiality rules related to HIV in the state.

Criminalization

First came demands that Williams be punished. A *New York Daily News* editorial was typical, asserting, "It is hard to understand why the state could prosecute a stalker with a gun but not someone who knowingly spreads a lethal disease," and urging that Williams be charged with murder.[153] Governor George Pataki was quick to jump on the bandwagon, contending that "Williams violated felony laws and should 'never see the light of day again.'" He promised to appoint state Attorney General Dennis Vacco as a "special prosecutor" in the case, should the need arise.[154] Chautauqua County Attorney James Subjack, however, had already stated that he would bring charges of reckless endangerment against Williams, felony charges that could bring up to fifteen years in prison. Subjack said that he had considered an indictment on attempted murder but decided not to pursue it because it would involve proving that Williams had actually planned to kill his partners by giving them HIV. "As much as people hate him," he asserted, "I don't think jurors would buy that."[155] It eventually became apparent, however, that even the lesser charge of reckless endangerment would be difficult to pursue. It was not designed for, nor had it ever been applied to, such a purpose as was being proposed, and the conceptual and evidentiary issues involved seemed difficult to surmount.

On May 22, 1998, Williams was indicted in a Chautauqua County courthouse on two counts of statutory rape (twice having sex with a thirteen-year-old girl). At that time, Subjack was indicating that he was still pursuing charges of endangerment and assault, although it looked increasingly unlikely that the latter indictments would be brought forward by the grand jury. They never were. Instead, Williams accepted a plea bargain, agreeing to plead guilty to three charges (statutory rape, reckless endangerment, and drug possession) in exchange for a prison term of four to twelve years.

As it became clear that New York's criminal laws were not adequate to generate the kinds of punishments for Williams that many were hoping for, calls went out from Pataki and others for increased criminal penalties in cases where HIV-positive persons put uninformed sexual partners at risk. State Assemblywoman Nettie Mayersohn charged that "the laws in New York State border on insanity."[156]

Bills were introduced in the legislature. One would have required HIV testing of any prison inmates who attack guards. Assemblyman Daniel Feldman of Brooklyn, a Democrat, was quite explicit that he believed the Williams case increased the potential for legislators' passing such bills.[157] State Senator Joseph Holland also believed that the Williams case would give a "boost" to two bills that he had previously proposed, one that would make it a felony to fail to report an HIV infection to a sex partner, and

▼ Moral Panics and Media Politics

one that would increase the penalties for HIV-positive people who were convicted of rape and other sexual abuses. Holland asserted that the virus was as "deadly" as a "handgun," and he stated that Williams had engaged in a campaign of "biological warfare."[158] Determined to outdo Holland, a Democrat, State Senator Jim Alesi, a Republican, argued that knowingly putting someone at risk should be treated as "no less than attempted murder."[159] Attorney General Dennis Vacco, a Republican, seemed less enthusiastic, saying, "We don't need a law we can't enforce."[160]

The New York State Legislature did not ultimately act on any of the criminal sanctions bills in the 1998 session, choosing instead to redraw the boundaries of confidentiality in relation to testing. The impact of the Williams case was nevertheless felt across the country. As noted previously, Florida increased the maximum penalties that individuals could face for not informing sexual partners of positive HIV status, from a stiff fifteen to an extraordinary thirty years. The lawmaker who sponsored the measure cited the Williams case as an impetus to making the change. The author of a *Kansas Law Review* article also referred to Williams in making a case for establishing hefty criminal penalties for knowing HIV transmission in Kansas (a state with among the lowest number of reported cases in the United States).[161]

Today, twenty-seven states attach criminal penalties to knowing HIV transmission, ranging from misdemeanor charges to major felony charges, but in those places that have such laws, they are enforced inconsistently and sporadically (I discuss this point further in chapter 5). There are several reasons for this. In any given case, it is very difficult to prove the facts of transmission, knowledge, and intention, and no doubt many prosecutors have reservations about devoting considerable resources to the prosecution of such cases. So although there has been a tremendous proliferation of formal rules regarding the knowing transmission of HIV, the application of these rules has been somewhat random and thus highly inequitable.

Confidentiality

New York State did make substantial changes in the laws governing the confidentiality of those who test positive for HIV. New York had passed a strict confidentiality law in 1988, which guaranteed anonymity to anyone whose HIV test yielded a positive result. Public health officials and physicians kept neither names nor other records on those who tested positive (although they did keep counts of those who were diagnosed with AIDS). The rationale behind the confidentiality legislation was that it would encourage people to be tested. The stigma that had been attached to AIDS from the beginning, that it was a "gay plague," could (and still can) have serious consequences, including the loss of health insurance, employment, and housing.[162] Fear of these consequences, it was reasonably argued, would discourage people from being tested. The New York State Legislature put in place one of the strictest confidentiality laws in the United States.

The consensus among most New York lawmakers, physicians, and activists that privacy is a public good held together remarkably well until the Williams case was publicized, but that consensus was "shatter[ed]" thereafter.[163] On January 13, 1998, the Gay Men's Health Crisis released a statement supporting the reporting of the names of HIV-positive people to the state by New York doctors.[164] This helped to pave the way for passage of a version of the Mayersohn confidentiality bill in the state legislature. The bill was a "name" bill, meaning that actual names would be used to identify those testing positive. (A "coded" system would have been more acceptable to privacy advocates.) Before passage of the bill, New York and California were the two states with the most HIV-infected persons that did not make such identifications.

New Jersey is the state with the most HIV cases that has name identification. There a full "HIV registry," with the names and demographic characteristics of each person who has tested positive in the state, is kept in computer files.[165] The New Jersey system has been offered as a great success story, in that it has provided detailed information on age, gender, and ethnic characteristics of HIV-positive people in the state. The tightly controlled and monitored system has not been breached. Although more than thirteen thousand names are now recorded in the registry, it has been estimated that there are twenty thousand more people in the state who are HIV-positive and untested.[166] We cannot know definitively whether significant numbers of these people have not come forward out of fear that their information will not be protected or simply due to ignorance that they are at risk. Florida's reporting system was breached in 1996 when a public employee anonymously mailed a computer disk with the names of HIV-positive people to two newspapers.

There is an important difference between the New Jersey system and the one adopted in New York. The New York statute requires that those who test positive for HIV identify those whom they may have put at risk. The required revelation of one's sexual history and one's history of drug use carries more than a whiff of the punitive, especially in an atmosphere where the criminalizing of transmission may become an important part of the equation. Ironically, of course, Nushawn Williams volunteered information to public health officials that made him the subject of both vilification and prosecution. There is an additional irony here: when the Williams case first came to light, Dr. Richard Berke encouraged at-risk individuals in the county to be tested. At that time, he made explicit guarantees that their anonymity would be protected. In the aftermath of the legislature's actions, such guarantees were no longer valid.

Conclusion

With rare exceptions, media representations of the Williams case ignored or effaced the complexities of poverty, race, HIV, and drugs, and how these elements intersect with one another in the new global economy. Reporters, editorialists, and public officials reinforced one another in their zeal to present an unfolding drama that pitted "good" against "evil." In a sense this is unsurprising, given the history of the social construction of HIV in American popular culture. Whatever Williams's culpability in the infections that have been attributed to his actions, it is most dismaying that more than twenty years into this epidemic, it is still difficult for the media to report it as a public health problem rather than as an indicator of moral decline or apocalypse.[167] When HIV issues are inflected with race, the anxieties generated seem to be virtually uncontrollable. The Williams case is disturbing for many reasons, but one of its most disturbing features is that there has been so little criticism of the media's role. Unfortunately, there is little doubt that, given the right circumstances, the media will represent other such cases in the future in similar ways.

2

Small-Town Mythologies and the History of a Place

A s a highly provocative news story unfolds, it takes on a life of its own. It feeds on itself, creating a vortex, the center of which spawns sensation and hyperbole. Distance and perspective are easy victims, as the "real" becomes further enmeshed in the "imagistic," as the intensity of "the story" increases, peaks, and fades, leaving its cultural residue. In the end, one may have the vague sense that something important happened, but even the most devoted news junkies are no doubt left exhausted as well as perplexed after they scrupulously sort through all the mediated noise of a given story's cycle in a futile attempt to garner truths that may lie obscured within. Monica Lewinksy, Columbine, O. J. Simpson—although we may have our viewpoints and interpretations, they must always be tentative and provisional, given our positions as consumers of news generated and shaped by large corporate structures over which there is little accountability or control. Moreover, symbolic references that allow news producers and consumers to make sense of given events are deeply embedded in our histories and mythologies. The meanings that we attach to media representations are derived from cultural tropes about which we may have little conscious understanding.

In the Williams case, the narrative lines of the story were connected by the notion that something new and deeply disturbing was occurring in small-town America. Nushawn Williams had violated a sacred space, a place that many of us "remember," whether or not we have ever experienced it. Jamestown, New York, represented a lost nineteenth-century innocence contaminated by a diseased other. Simultaneously, however, Jamestown was a broken-down remnant of twentieth-century industrialism, the quintessential "factory town" with closed factories and little to offer of relevance for the ascending cyber age. Jamestown—and, by implication, the industrial infrastructure of the northeastern United States—was symbolically dying, infected with HIV, crack cocaine, and economic irrelevance. Such representations, although in some ways particular to this story, invoked cultural understandings of small-town and city life that can be traced to early and continuously evolving self-definitions of American identity. In this chapter I examine the symbolic and sociological meanings of small-town and city life and investigate the actual histories and political economies of Jamestown and the surrounding regions. My purpose is to show how towns like Jamestown are symbolically constructed while also offering an account of a "real" town that both challenges and confirms media constructions.

The Small Town as Symbol and Subject

The small town holds a complex and ambiguous place in American cultural life. On one hand, small-town life is often viewed as egalitarian, democratic, and virtuous, with the small town the repository of what is best in American cultural and civic traditions. A small town is a place where people know one another's names and take the time to help their neighbors. At the same time, however, small towns are often seen as stifling, as inhabited by the pinched and narrow-minded and suffused with cliquishness and intolerance. Small towns are perceived to be cut off from the widening influences of urban cosmopolitanism, and so are viewed as cultural backwaters, places from which the best and brightest flee to seek creative challenges and economic fortunes.

The ambivalence that marks today's perceptions of small-town life was already visible at the earliest stages of the American republic's development. It was epitomized in the conflicting positions of Alexander Hamilton and Thomas Jefferson regarding the relative merits of rural and urban ways of living. Jefferson did not visit a town of any size until he was nearly eighteen years old, and he maintained that "rural people are the wellspring of civic virtue and individual vitality."[1] Jefferson associated large cities with the corruptions of European society. He believed that the United States was different and democratic because of its agrarian foundations. Jefferson thus opposed the development of manufacturing, because factory work would tend to degrade the lives of individual workers, in part by removing them from the soil. He also associated a manufacturing society with centralized government, which he understood to be antithetical to democracy. Jefferson believed that the best form of political organization consists of loosely connected sets of "ward republics" in which intensive face-to-face interaction provides the basis for participatory democracy.[2] The kinds of virtues that Jefferson associated with rural life eventually became enfolded into a mythology, not only of agrarian society, but of the hundreds and eventually thousands of small towns that sprang up within it as it matured. Small-town and rural life were seen as the antidote to the alienation and impersonality that marked urban industrial centers.

Hamilton, on the other hand, fervently believed in the importance of manufacturing, which he associated with economic and political power that could both protect Americans from European encroachment and eventually challenge the system of European nation-states. Political scientist Everett Carl Ladd Jr. has characterized Hamilton's "Report on the Subject of Manufactures," issued while Hamilton was Washington's secretary of the Treasury, as an "extraordinary issuance in an agricultural society." It was extraordinary because it took aim at the heart of American economic arrangements as well as cultural self-definition. In this report, Hamilton criticized the nation's economic dependence on agriculture, called for government support for and investment in manufacturing, and stated his support for the use of child labor.[3]

Although Hamilton's motive was to support the advancement of American political, economic, and military power, he also hoped to nurture a class of cosmopolitan and sophisticated Americans who could compete culturally with Europeans. Hamilton neither saw nor wanted to see virtue in farmers or townsfolk. They were, in his thinking, simply fuel to drive the machine that was the expanding American republic.

The perceived virtues of rural life were, over time, transferred, at a symbolic level, to small-town life. Small towns personified the virtues of hard work, personal responsibility, and civic obligation. As industrialism advanced, the significance of small-town mythology moved with it, offering a nostalgic counterpoint for those who were fearful of and displaced by encroaching modernity. Towns or settlements, as Robertson notes, "carried virtually identical visions and expectations, of physical shape and boundaries, of the working of a specific land, and of the integrated cohesiveness of people. . . . The expectation was that they would survive and prosper—if they did—because they completely integrated these aspects of life into one undifferentiated whole."[4] As industrialism fragmented work, family, and community, Americans responded with utopian experiments in ultimately failed attempts to recapture the increasingly threatened world of quilting bees, church socials, and barn dances.

Yet a deep ambivalence remained as to whether the "loss" of small-town and rural life meant the end of "real community," whether urban life represented servility and impersonality or freedom, diversity, and opportunity. The image of Mark Twain's Hannibal, Missouri, is still etched into American cultural consciousness, but in 1920, Sinclair Lewis published *Main Street*, a novel that depicts a midwestern prairie town in the most frightening terms. Gopher Prairie's Main Street is a vision of "unsparing, unapologetic, ugliness." Lewis's Babbitt became the model of the small-town bigot whose main purpose in life seems to be mindless boosterism. Lewis was not alone in his suspicious view of small-town life. H. L. Mencken characterized small-town folk as the genus *American boobus,* whose primary values were Yahooism and Rotarianism. During this time, "the city," as Robertson notes, "more and more became the symbol of freedom, opportunity, and diversity as opposed to the rural community. Urban life was an escape from small-town America."[5]

Sociological analysis confirmed many people's suspicions that small towns are not as idyllic as sometimes imagined. At first, Robert S. Lynd and Helen Merrell Lynd had difficulty finding a publisher for their anthropological study of what was an unidentified small midwestern city, but on its publication *Middletown* became an immediate best-seller.[6] It is now widely held to be one of the most significant works of twentieth-century American social science.[7] For their study of Middletown (which was soon discovered to be Muncie, Indiana), the Lynds borrowed from the tools of cultural anthropology, specifically the work of W. H. R. Rivers, applying his method of studying "primitive societies."[8]

The Lynds deliberately sought a setting without racial or ethnic conflict, because they desired to understand the culture of settled white Protestant America. Middletown definitely fit the bill. At the time of the study, the town's population included less than 2 percent immigrants and only 6 percent African Americans. This "middle-of-the-road quality" of Middletown—its lack of "extreme" social problems or conflicts—is what made it appropriate, in the Lynds' thinking, for the study.[9] Their findings were thus particularly disturbing. Middletown, it turned out, was a deeply divided community, divided along lines not of ethnicity or race but of class. Those in the "working class," who were primarily engaged in the making of "things," had a very different social experience from those in the "business class," whose activities revolved mostly around "people" in such activities as banking, law, sales, education, and government.[10] The largest proportion of the city's inhabitants, 71 percent, were of the working class, whereas 29 percent were members of the business class. The Lynds concluded that this division was the "most outstanding cleavage in Middletown." Moreover, they found relatively little movement between classes, noting, "The mere fact of being born upon one or the other side of the watershed roughly formed by these two groups is the most significant single cultural factor tending to influence what one does all day long throughout one's entire life."[11] The presence of a rigid class structure in the heart of "middle America" seemed to run directly contrary to fundamental American assumptions regarding the presence of economic opportunity and class mobility.

The class system in Middletown was reflective of industrial development in the town. Middletown's economy, once organized around agriculture and skilled trades, had come to be dependent on routinized and monotonous industrial labor. This work—specialized, repetitive, and boring—was low paying, of precarious duration, and offered little in the way of economic advancement. It was also physically debilitating. On-the-job injuries were common, and most workers were "used up" by the time they turned fifty.[12] Yet unions had lost strength in Middletown, and the dominant ideology, embraced by the business class and acceded to by the working class, was oriented toward individual acceptance of responsibility for one's place in the world. One reached the place in life that one more or less deserved. Both workers and businesspeople tended to be somewhat "mystified" by the larger national and international forces that shaped their economic lives, and neither seemed settled, in that all were "running for dear life in this business of making the money they earn keep pace with the even more rapid growth of their subjective wants."[13] The harder they worked, it seemed, the less they had, or at least the less they felt they had.

The place of the small town in American mythology thus began to change in important ways after World War I. A general recognition seeped into the national culture that rural life was indeed passing, and that older, agrarian lifestyles were being displaced by modern industrial modes of economic and social production. The small town could offer only a limited refuge, if that, from these forces. In fact, it seemed to incorporate the most banal aspects of modern life, yet without the color and cosmopolitanism of the great metropolis. Middletown may not have been, as one contemporary critic of the Lynds' book remarked, a "stopping point along the way to Dante's Inferno," but neither was it the kind of wholesome, friendly, naive place represented by, say, Andy Griffith's Mayberry.[14] A placid surface masked anxieties and conflicts churning just beneath.

The Lynds continued the saga of Middletown through a second book,

Middletown in Transition, which tracked the impacts of the Great Depression and the New Deal on the community.[15] In 1982, a neoconservative revisionist analysis of Middletown appeared. The authors of *Middletown Families* contended that the community had remained intact in spite of the changes of the postwar era, that class antagonisms had weakened if not disappeared, and that the town offered evidence that the "decline" of American families was simply a "myth."[16] Middletown was also a reference point for Robert N. Bellah and his colleagues when they wrote *Habits of the Heart.*[17] Middletown again mirrored the political and social conflicts of the wider society when Xerox pulled its sponsorship of a PBS film series about the town due to sexually explicit content in one of the segments.[18]

Over time, Middletown became a kind of indicator of the psychic health and conflicts taking place in American small towns and cities. It set the tone for "realistic" appraisals of small-town life that lifted the veil of nostalgic idealizations and recognized the impacts of broader social and economic forces. The Lynds helped to embed in the American psyche the notion that alienation and consumerism were eating into the heart of the American experience. Yet when the first study of Middletown was completed, the lives of American in small towns and cities could still be considered characteristic of the lives of most Americans. As the twentieth century unfolded, however, it became clearer that this particular mode of social organization was on the decline. Many of the social scientists who followed in the footsteps of the Lynds noted not only the decline but its impacts on the overall structure of American community life and political economy.

J. F. Steiner's 1928 study of "Tipton" revealed the coherence of American small town life, even in an industrial age, before the trauma of the Great Depression.[19] By 1945, however, James West's study of "Plainville" indicated that the wider world was indeed having significant impacts on the life of the community, mostly in terms of its children, about half of whom left the town as soon as they graduated from high school.[20] West, like the Lynds, refused to idealize small-town life. He found in Plainville a highly developed class system, the existence of which was firmly denied by the town's residents. In fact, Plainville's suffocating social hierarchy, along with the residents' hypocrisy, encouraged many of the town's young people to leave.

In the postwar era, with the increasing popularity of the automobile, the growth of suburbs, and the internationalization of the American political perspective, social scientists began to note, again with mixed feelings, what seemed to be the almost complete disappearance of small-town America. In a spate of books, sociologists and political scientists examined the cultures, economies, and distribution of power in small towns. The most renowned of these books was perhaps Arthur J. Vidich and Joseph

Bensman's *Small Town in Mass Society*. Operating under the aegis of the Cornell Studies in Social Growth, sponsored by the university's College of Home Economics, Vidich and Bensman set out to examine various facets of the life of a small community they called "Springdale." The actual town was Candor, New York, located about twenty miles from Ithaca, the small city where Cornell is located.

Vidich and Bensman posed the mythology of small-town life against the realities of what they called "mass society," which they associated with secularism, universities, large corporate businesses, mass communication, and urban life. The mythology was largely created and reinforced by the Springdalers themselves, who harbored an ideology in which they perceived themselves as "just plain folks." They asserted that social relationships in Springdale were characterized by "neighborliness" and equality, yet they distrusted those who lived in "shacks in the hills." They treated introverts and intellectuals with suspicion, because "book reading and studying all the time . . . shouldn't be carried too far."[21]

Although Vidich and Bensman admitted their respect for Springdalers' commitment to local democracy and qualified egalitarianism, which they deemed "representative of almost all of the American past," they asserted that these ideals were "based on the period from 1810 to 1860," and thus hopelessly out of tune with postwar America. Springdale and, by implication, communities like it around the country were, accordingly, entirely at the mercy of forces beyond their control. Interventions from mass media, national business corporations, and federal programs (such as milk price supports) had all worked to undermine the autonomy of the local community. Vidich and Bensman went so far as to assert that "almost all aspects of [the] town were controlled by external forces over which they [the townspeople] had little control; the idea of democratic self-determination had no basis in fact." The external controls were all the more effective because the town's residents denied their existence. Vidich and Bensman concluded: "Despite our attempt to find original and indigenous sources of the community's culture and values, we were unable to find any. Instead we found external sources and origins for everything that the community cherished as being most genuinely representative of its own spirit."[22]

In other words, Springdale had already been overwhelmed by mass society. The town's residents were unequipped even to see this, so they lived with the illusion that they could and did resist the incursions of the outside world. Public life was, in fact, "dominated by a system of illusions." The system was reinforced by a local attitude of respect and awe for the very "mass society" whose influence was denied. Quite simply, the denizens of Springdale, in spite of overwhelming evidence of their cultural irrelevance, believed that "the American heritage is better preserved in the small town because it can resist bad city influences and thereby preserve the best of the past."[23]

The study, which is now considered to be something of a classic, at the time generated considerable controversy. Vidich and Bensman were accused of invading the privacy of Springdale residents, and Cornell University itself became a platform for lectures in which the study was condemned. The residents of Candor hanged the authors in effigy and put on a theatrical display portraying them as manure spreaders.[24]

In the United States the scholarly analysis of small-town life began in the 1920s, and analysts approached the work with a firmly held belief that these entities, for good or bad, would be a permanent part of the American landscape. In the postwar era, as industrialization reached its peak, the decline of small-town and rural life was considered to be an important historical occurrence. In essence, Vidich and Bensman announced the end of the political, cultural, and economic autonomy of the American small town, even though, as they noted in the preface to a later edition of *Small Town in Mass Society,* "Springdale still exists as a territorial entity and it is absolutely certain that it will continue to be there . . . no matter how many epitaphs are written for it by sociologists."[25]

More epitaphs for the small town were indeed written. Joseph B. Lyford's *The Talk of Vandalia,* published in 1962, questioned whether the town of Vandalia could survive at all.[26] Lyford depicted Vandalia as entirely at the mercy of forces outside of its control, even though most of the residents were unwilling to see this. Factories were vanishing and, along with them, the jobs that supported the community. By the mid-1970s, it became clear that small towns and small industrial cities in the United States were indeed facing economic catastrophes of enormous significance. The problems were not confined to the smallest cities; larger ones were affected as well, especially across the Northeast and Midwest. Youngstown, Ohio, and Pittsburgh, Pennsylvania, were hit particularly hard, as the steel industry, faced with high labor costs and international competition, began the process of shutting down its largest factories, often moving their operations first to southern states and then overseas.

The impact of this new "deindustrialization" on American cultural understandings and the imagery of the small town was enormous. In his 1989 film *Roger & Me,* Michael Moore, with more than a touch of irony, seeks out General Motors CEO Roger Smith to ask him why he closed the GM plant in Flint, Michigan. Popular songwriters also commented on the changes. Billy Joel's "Allentown" documents the decline of the steel industry in Bethlehem, Pennnsylvania, and Bruce Springsteen's "My Home Town" laments the loss of community and jobs in what was formerly working-class America.

The harbingers of the 1950s and 1960s became clearer and more immediate as industrialized small cities seemed to collapse under the weight of
global competition and the shift to an information economy. Deindustrialization did not affect only small towns, and it did not undermine all small
towns, but its effects on the Northeast and Midwest were often devastating. There was little that politicians or business owners were willing to do
to stem the tide. Today, as David Plowden has noted, "the old order, which
began to crumble before the tides of change after World War II, has been
almost swept away. Ever fewer fragments of what used to constitute the essence of small town life have survived."27

An understanding of the ambiguous place of the small town in
American cultural mythology is important to a full understanding of the
cultural construction of the Nushawn Williams case. Nostalgia for a past
that probably never existed in quite the way it was remembered pervaded
the media's depictions of Jamestown when the Williams case broke. The
town's economic difficulties were at first ignored and then magnified.
Jamestown was represented through a haze of symbolic associations. As
is often the case with such media depictions, those who reported on Jamestown conducted little historical or economic analysis. Rather, they relied
almost entirely on first impressions and their expectations. Jamestown
became a mythical locale with an idyllic past and a dubious future. The
contradictory messages conveyed followed a path well trodden in works
of literature and sociology: "This is anywhere, U.S.A. This could happen
to you." And, "This is nowhere, wounded and decrepit, entirely removed
from the experience of most Americans."

The small town is now fragile and durable, everywhere and nowhere,
valued and despised. As globalization advances, its symbolic importance
is more deeply embedded and increasingly unstable. David Morley and
Kevin Robins note the deepening sense of "homelessness" that has been
endemic to modernity, saying, "Places are no longer the clear supports to
our identity, even though we may want them to be such." Sociologists and
cultural critics have long noted this, but the contradiction between what
we want and what we have is escalating as globalization accelerates. As it
"progressively erode[s] territorial frontiers and boundaries," it provokes
"more immediate confrontations of culture and identity." As "fluidity and
impermanence pervade our consciousness . . . there is a desire to be 'at
home' in the new and disorienting global space."28

As the Williams case unfolded, Jamestown captured and represented all
of these trends. On the one hand, it was indicative of the "old" industrial
economy and its failures. Towns like it had already been laid to rest in the
collective consciousness. On the other hand, however, it inspired nostalgic
yearnings for a place that time had forgotten, the illusive Currier and Ives

portrait of a snow-covered small-town paradise. Jamestown had become a kind of "virtual community."[29]

A Little History

Jamestown sits on the southern tier of the westernmost part of New York State. Four or five miles from the Pennsylvania border, it is geographically isolated from most of New York's urban centers. It is more than four hundred miles from Jamestown to New York City; the closest city of any size is Buffalo, some seventy-five miles away. This isolation became a common theme in newspaper reports regarding the Williams case.

Although Jamestown and Chautauqua County as a whole have long been peripheral to the centers of economic, political, and cultural power in the state, historically the area was important because of its location between Lake Erie and the rivers and streams of the eastern Mississippi watershed. The Portage Trail, the shortest overland route (about twenty miles) between any of the great lakes and navigable waterways to the south, ran from the southern shore of Lake Erie to the northern tip of Lake Chautauqua. Small cities sprang up along the trail, which eventually became an important trade route; Westfield (originally "the Crossroads") on Lake Erie and Mayville on Lake Chautauqua were two of these. Jamestown benefited from its position at the south end of Lake Chautauqua along the Chadakoin River.[30] Economic development, especially in the northern part of the county, was also encouraged by the expansion of railroads that occurred in the middle part of the nineteenth century. In 1851, the New York and Erie Railroad completed a line from the Hudson River to Dunkirk, New York, in the northern part of the county. As Paul A. Spengler notes, the completion of this line had "a decisive impact on the county. [It] reduced the price of imported goods and increased the profits on exports. Real estate prices rose, the old plank roads and stage lines became obsolete and agriculture became more market-oriented."[31]

The French made incursions into Chautauqua County as early as 1739, but settlements did not take root until late in the eighteenth century, after the War of Independence. The land, which had originally been within the territories controlled by the Iroquois nation, was purchased in the 1790s by the Holland Land Company, which sold it relatively cheaply to people who had few assets. As a result, attempts to collect debts that were owed sometimes resulted in violence, such as the burning of the Mayville land office in 1836.[32] The inns, trading posts, and post offices that had dotted the area became the villages of Westfield and Barcelona in 1802, and Fredonia, Silver Creek, and Mayville appeared on maps in 1804.[33] The county had almost 2,500 residents by 1810, before Jamestown, which eventually became the county's largest city, even had its first house built.[34]

Most of these earliest settlements were located along the shoreline of Lake Erie.

With the founding of Jamestown in 1815 by James Prendergast, rudimentary manufacturing began in Chautauqua County. Prendergast's father, William, had been a participant in a revolt against the tenured land system in the 1760s in the Hudson Valley. He was originally sentenced to be hanged for the role he played, but was eventually pardoned; perhaps as a result of this leniency, he remained a Loyalist during the American Revolution.[35] Four of William Prendergast's sons decided to move Westward. They traveled first to Tennessee but found it not to their liking, and eventually all four settled in various parts of Chautauqua County.[36] James, so the story goes, discovered the rapids of the Chadakoin River while attempting to recover horses that had wandered. Recognizing the river as a potential source of power, he bought one thousand acres of land and built a dam, a sawmill, and a gristmill.[37] The village of Jamestown was incorporated in 1827, with a population at that time of four hundred.[38] (In 1836, Prendergast sold his thousand acres, originally purchased for two thousand dollars, to a group of businessmen for eighty thousand dollars.)

Chautauqua County was originally a farming area, but the presence of the railroad spurred the development of manufacturing. Jamestown's history and economic fortune became tied to the manufacturing sector that dominated the industrial belt of the Northeast and the Midwest. Early industry in the city revolved around timber. Pine trees were cut and floated down the Chadakoin to Pittsburgh, and hardwoods (which would not float) were burned and used to make potash or "pearl ash," giving Jamestown its nickname, the "pearl city." (Potash was used to make lye as well as saleratus, which was used as a baking powder.)[39] Potash was a relatively profitable commodity to make, and in the early years, the Holland Land Company accepted it as payment on land debts.[40] Early manufacturing often relied upon resources that were locally available. In Jamestown, artisans made pottery with clay found in Chautauqua Lake, and textile makers drew on locally grown wool and the fur of indigenous animals.[41] Eventually, the main industry that developed in Jamestown was the manufacture of furniture. The furniture factory workers were highly skilled, and made most of the furniture by hand. The earliest factories were small and often family owned, and the owners sometimes took an interest in their workers that went beyond simple economic imperatives. In 1873, for example, the Jamestown Cane-Seat Chair Company went bankrupt as a result of a national depression. Unwilling to close down, the company's owners issued scrip to the workers, which they then accepted as payment for groceries in a store that they bought for that purpose.[42]

By 1900, Jamestown had fifteen furniture factories, and by 1911, the city was the second-largest furniture manufacturing center in the United States.[43] The wood furniture industry attracted Swedish immigrants, who were often skilled workers, and Swedes eventually became one of the predominant ethnic groups in the city. In 1904, Jamestown resident Charles Dahlstrom developed the first practicable fireproof door, a hollow metal door that became extremely popular for use in public buildings and railroad cars.[44] In the 1940s and 1950s, metal manufacturing increasingly took its place alongside the wood furniture industry as Jamestown became a center for metal furniture, machinery, and parts and tools. The furniture factories of Jamestown were all locally owned. (This tended to be the case with "light industries," whereas "heavy industries"—those involved in the basic manufacture of steel and so forth—were often under the control of conglomerates, the ownership of which was more dispersed.) Marlin Rockwell Corporation, American Voting Machine, and Crescent Tool Corporation all began in Jamestown.

Unlike larger manufacturing centers such as Flint, Michigan, Jamestown does not have a colorful history of labor unrest. The organization of labor came relatively late to the area, and it tended to be most complete among skilled laborers. The primary labor union active in Jamestown was the conservative AFL, which organized typographers, cigar makers, and other skilled laborers in the late nineteenth and early twentieth centuries. In 1913, when the street railway workers went on strike, rioting broke out in Jamestown. In response, the mayor deputized 600 citizens, who helped to restore order and eventually ended the strike.[45] In 1919, the Machinists Union struck, and sympathy strikes resulted in the closing of fifty-six factories; several thousand workers were affected. Although the furniture factories settled with their workers, the metalworking plants held out and eventually broke the strike.[46] This failure of a major strike no doubt contributed to the relatively docile character of labor in the city until the postwar period. In 1931, "Communists and their sympathizers stormed the City Hall," demanding "cash payments from the city for all unemployed persons."[47] The mayor, Samuel Carlson, expressed sympathy with the workers, but "did not indulge in any gallery play, either in support of the Communists nor in attacking them as Russian allies." He is reported to have told the workers that their demands were unreasonable, that the city had no power to grant their demands, and that unemployment was a national problem, not merely a local one.[48]

Although the role of labor unions was important but somewhat muted in the history of Chautauqua County manufacturing, the city of Jamestown had a markedly progressive tradition. Mayor Carlson, who led the city for twenty years (1908–28), was a pacifist who expressed tolerance for, perhaps even sympathy with, certain aspects of the Russian Revolution.[49] Under the Carlson administration, the city of Jamestown built the first municipally owned electric utility in the United States, which still operates as the largest publicly owned utility in New York State.[50] Carlson, although not a socialist, was a pragmatic political Progressive who took the notion of the public good seriously. After the electric utility was successfully established, he proposed to construct a publicly owned milk-processing facility to collect, inspect, and distribute all milk that would be sold in the city.[51] It was this proposal (never adopted by the city) that earned him the moniker "Milkman Carlson."[52]

Workers in Jamestown followed the national trends in the 1940s and 1950s, demanding their share of the increasing national prosperity. The resulting series of strikes benefited the workers to the point that the average wage for production workers in the city was consistent with that in New York State as a whole.[53]

Economic Decline

It is difficult to pinpoint exactly when Jamestown's economic decline began. Some of the county's previously flourishing lakefront villages, such as Celeron, never completely recovered from the Depression of the 1930s. One city Planning Commission report released in 1980 argued that Jamestown itself had never recovered economically from the Depression, when the furniture industry had been "flattened."[54] In 1973, a local historian described Jamestown as follows: "Bordered by factories and railroad, the [Chadakoin] River reflects signs of sporadic and slightly faded industrialization. Graying, deserted factories sit in shuttered silence beside still-active railroad and lumber yards. . . . remembrance of an energetic and purposeful past seems to pervade the area."[55] In the 1950s, Jamestown had been the largest supplier of metal office furniture in the world. But in the mid-1970s, Art Metal Furniture, the company that had been responsible for this status, went bankrupt.[56] Like other large and small cities across the country in the 1960s, Jamestown went through a process of "urban renewal" during which weathered gothic buildings were turned into fast-food restaurants, discount stores, and parking lots. Although economic decline had clearly settled in by 1980, the city's Planning Commission was still upbeat that a new city hall, replacing the old "tired, shabby structure," had been built and that urban renewal would provide space for new industrial development.[57]

Today, the signs of economic decline are clearly evident in Jamestown. When I was growing up there in the 1960s, in what was even then an economically marginal neighborhood, numerous working- and middle-class families lived on our street. In the mixed-race, mixed-class elementary and junior high schools that I attended, some of the least well-off students in town shared classrooms with the children of the most affluent. In this regard, Jamestown in the 1960s was no doubt a fairly typical northeastern manufacturing town. I remember lying in bed at night and listening to the steady rhythm of the Crescent Tool stamping machine, even though the factory was located about a mile away from our house. Perhaps it wasn't Norman Rockwell, but poverty did not seem endemic to the economic life of most Jamestown citizens, and the size of the town, along with the fact that it had just one high school, generated a democratic ethos that, although perhaps not universal, was fairly pervasive.

Nowadays, however, even though my former grade school is still intact, refurbished with new windows, and looking much better than it did when I attended, and the junior high has been replaced by a newer, more modern facility, signs of wear and tear are evident. My family's house is one of the few single-family dwellings remaining on the street. Most others have been purchased by local landlords and turned into multiple-dwelling units that have not, as a general rule, been kept in the best condition. Residents on the street seem to be divided between aging retirees who raised their kids there and have not, at least yet, succumbed to the temptation to move to warmer climes, or even to very affordable homes in nicer sections of town, and folks with subsistence incomes supplemented by public assistance. As a local undercover cop told me with reference to my old neighborhood, "Yeah, we do a lot of business up there."

This does not, however, mean that the neighborhood is a terribly dangerous or even unfriendly place. When I visit Jamestown, I still see kids playing touch football out in the street, in almost exactly the same way my friends and I did when we were kids. I have never felt physically threatened in the neighborhood, in daylight or after dark. In truth, none of Jamestown's neighborhoods seems particularly threatening, even those showing the greatest signs of economic distress. Although there have been some high-profile incidents related to the drug trade in town, including the severe and very tragic wounding of a local undercover police officer, street crime is not endemic, and few people would probably feel unsafe walking any of the city's streets. The town has not been overwhelmed by violence. It has the look and feel of a dozen other upstate New York towns of roughly similar size.

In other words, Jamestown, like other "rust belt" communities, is struggling economically because of changes that have occurred in national and international economies. It is not an idyllic winter wonderland, a nineteenth-century haven in a heartless world, but neither is it a war zone, a disaster area. For many people, in fact, Jamestown is still a pretty good place to live. The cost of living is low. There is access to recreation on Lake Chautauqua. Upscale patrons make their way to Chautauqua Institution each summer for classical music, scholarly lectures, and evening potluck suppers. The active local pop music scene was once famously led by the band 10,000 Maniacs.

What has happened in Jamestown, and in Chautauqua County in general, is that income inequality has sharpened. This phenomenon is not confined to Jamestown—income inequality has been increasing in the United States as a whole since the late 1970s—but it is more pronounced in Jamestown than in some other places. In this respect, Jamestown is not an aberration but a reflection of broader social and economic trends. In Jamestown, as a result of the Williams case, a series of ever-present public health and social problems endemic to American life became more graphic and visible than is generally the case. This is partly because what happened subverted a set of cultural expectations. In large metropolitan areas and in Appalachian coal regions, the juxtaposition of wealth and poverty seems "natural"; it goes unnoticed because of its historical persistence and prevalence. Poverty's ubiquity decreases its visibility. Such places are representative of "the way things are."

When transitions occur in places like Jamestown, however, there are moments of clarity because expectations are challenged. "How could this happen there?" so many of the media accounts of the Williams case seemed to ask, as though poverty and disease are not woven into the fabric of most American communities. The events in Jamestown disrupted the cultural mythologies surrounding the once-sturdy manufacturing town as stable home to European immigrants whose persistence and hard work provided the foundations of American affluence. Images of disease and decline in the heart of "middle America" disturbed many people deeply and spread the flames of panic. Moments of crisis such as these can provide opportunities for self-examination and teaching. Unfortunately, those opportunities were largely lost, replaced by calls for retribution, purgation, or escape. In the meantime, the very real problems and potentials of places like Jamestown remained for the most part unexplored.

Structural Problems and Comparisons

The media's focus on Jamestown as a symbol of small-town life and Nushawn Williams as an evil character who had invaded it allowed a denial of the real structural problems that many cities in the formerly industrialized Northeast face. In truth, manufacturing towns in the Northeast and the Midwest began losing key employers in the mid- to late 1970s, although this trend continued through the 1980s and into the early 1990s. The recessions of the 1980s piled on top of regional trends to reinforce the intertwined problems of unemployment, population loss, and poverty. The "real" Jamestown experienced structural changes that were endemic to many northeastern and midwestern communities. In certain respects it was better-off than other similarly situated regional centers, and in others it was slightly worse-off. Jamestown's economic problems are undeniable, yet the city still nurtures a viable community where many people find interesting work and live satisfying lives.

From 1980 to 1990, the Northeast experienced a 21.2 percent drop in employment in the manufacturing sector. Some metropolitan areas in western New York and Pennsylvania were especially hard hit; Buffalo, for example, had a 12.2 percent unemployment rate in 1992, and Niagara Falls had a rate of 13 percent. Erie, Pennsylvania, was not far behind with a rate of 9.7 percent. The rate for the nation as a whole in 1992 was 7.5 percent.[58] Jamestown's levels of unemployment have, in fact, been significantly below those of some of these larger cities and the national average. In 1993, Jamestown's unemployment rate was only 4 percent. In other words, Jamestown was not in especially dire straits in terms of unemployment in this period compared with other northeastern cities, but it was not an island of prosperity either. Many higher-paying, lower-skilled industrial jobs had left the area, displaced by lower-wage, low-skilled positions.

Long-term declines in good-paying industrial jobs have had significant impacts on population figures in both the Midwest and the Northeast (in fact, the central cities of the Midwest have experienced greater population losses than those in the Northeast). From 1980 through 1998, thirty-eight northeastern cities had significant population losses (5 percent or more). Utica led the way among the fifteen New York cities that experienced such losses, with a 21.5 percent population decline. Buffalo lost 16 percent of its population; Erie, 13 percent; and Niagara Falls, 10 percent.[59] These figures are somewhat deceptive, however, in that they often indicate movement from urban areas to suburbs. Jamestown is a good example of this. The 1990 population figure of 34,681 represents a 17 percent drop over a thirty-year period, but Chautauqua County's population dropped at a much lower rate (from 145,377 in 1960 to 142,339 in 1993, and then to 139,750 in 2000).[60] As in other places, relatively affluent people account for most of the movement to suburban areas outside of Jamestown. As a result of this movement, the city has experienced the physical and economic deterioration that led to the media's presentation of Jamestown as a lost paradise. As in other parts of the country, the distinct differences between the city of Jamestown and its and suburbs indicate structural economic inequalities.

Yet there is little doubt that many people have left the Northeast entirely, no doubt accounting for some of the population growth seen in the South. Many of those who have left are young and well educated, resulting in a loss of the human capital necessary to generate economic growth. This creates one of the great ironies of economic hardship in the Northeast. Although unemployment remains stubbornly persistence, labor *shortages* have undermined potential economic expansion. At the same time low-skilled manufacturing jobs have departed, high-skilled positions remain unfilled. Kodak in Rochester has trouble finding engineers. Syracuse has a shortage of machinists and welders. In Buffalo, a business survey found that 67 percent of employers had difficulty finding employees with specialized skills.[61]

The same is true in Jamestown. In 1998, Sam Teresi, former director of development (and now mayor) of Jamestown, told me, "There're good jobs available, but the local labor pool cannot fill those. So in many cases, the engineering jobs for manufacturing . . . they're having to recruit people from outside. . . . The excess labor pool is typically not walking around with chemical or engineering degrees."[62] The tech economy, in other words, has had strong impacts on the Northeast (Rochester and Poughkeepsie are among the most prolific patent producers in the United States), but the region has remained organized around processes of material production rather than "information."[63] In fact, in Jamestown, as of the 1990 U.S. Census, 27 percent of those in the labor force still reported themselves to be employed in the manufacturing sector.

Another important irony emerges here. The lack of an educated workforce remains a significant problem in an area of the country that has the greatest concentration of colleges and universities in the United States. The Northeast is home to 40 percent of the nation's institutions of higher education (489 total) and only 19 percent of the nation's population.[64] Yet graduates do not stay in the Northeast to fill the available jobs. Only one-third of University of Buffalo graduates stay in western New York, and only 15 percent of SUNY Albany graduates stay in the Albany area. As one upstate New York demographer has noted, "For years, New York's leading export has been talent and brains."[65] Moreover, a number of public educational institutions in New York State were hurt by budget cuts in the 1990s. New York had one of the premier state university systems in the 1960s, but its position has steadily eroded over time due to reductions in public support, especially under the administration of Governor George Pataki.

Two kinds of potential workers tend to remain, then: older ones who have lost jobs in what was once a vibrant industrial economy but do not have the requisite skills to fill vacancies in the tech economy, and younger unskilled ones who never had a place in the industrial workforce. Teresi described the former as "a guy or a lady in their forties that for the first time in twenty years find themselves without a career, without a job, without an income. In some cases [they need] retraining. In some cases, [they lack] basic skills."[66] Although older workers may not have specialized skills, they do have experience with the day-to-day realities of working. The pool of younger workers may face more intractable problems. The manager of a

▼ Small-Town Mythologies

51

large job training center in Buffalo told a reporter that one-third of the center's clientele is functionally illiterate. He noted: "We have to start with the basic stuff. We tell them to get an alarm clock."[67] Teresi reported the same problem in Jamestown. "A lot of industries," he said, "are reporting that they would be able to bring people in to train them if they were trainable. A lot of folks walking around this community have a lack of basic skills, literacy, computation, and so forth." In fact, in 1990, 30 percent of Jamestown residents over age twenty-five had not graduated from high school, and nearly 10 percent had never completed the ninth grade. Teresi wanted to be clear, however, that his comments were "not an indictment in any sense of the local school districts." In fact, Jamestown High School has a very high graduation rate. The problem is that "the economy, the society, the socioeconomic makeup of the community is changing faster than any of the institutional players can keep up with it."[68] Those who do graduate from high school often leave for college and simply don't return.

What Jamestown represents is the decline of the working middle class. Affluent residents, who work in health care, the professions, services such as insurance and banking, and education, remain in the area, but they have in many cases left the city itself for the suburbs along the lake. One can see how these changes in Chautauqua County have evolved by comparing median household income figures over time. In 1969, the median household income in the United States was $26,707; that same year, it was $29,168 for residents of New York State and $24,149 for residents of Chautauqua County. By 1979, the median household income was $28,220 for U.S. residents, $27,895 for New York residents, and $24,971 for Chautauqua County residents. During the period when factories began to close down in the Northeast, national household income increased, New York state household income decreased, and household income in Chautauqua County remained stagnant.

By 1989, after the United States had moved through and then recovered from a period of recession, the national median household income increased to $30,056, New York State's median household income rebounded to $32,965, and median household income in Chautaqua County fell to $24,183. Thus there was a modest but steady increase in median household income nationally from 1969 to 1989, but a small decrease in Chautauqua County, which, at this point, seemed to be detached from the upswings (but not the downswings) in the national economy. In real terms, the median income in Chautauqua County had fallen 3.2 percent from 1979 to 1989, while the national median had risen 6.5 percent and New York State's had risen 18.2 percent.[69] By 2000, the county's median income had risen to $31,051, reflecting that the area had participated to some extent in the "Clinton boom," but it still remained below the national figure of $35,000 and New York State's $36,369.[70]

What median income figures do not capture, however, is how the rest of the income numbers are distributed. To get a real sense of how unequal the distribution of economic assets is in the Northeast in general, and in Jamestown in particular one needs to look at poverty rates. In 1989, twenty-five cities in the Northeast had poverty rates of more than 20 percent. By 1993, as a result of the recession of the late 1980s and early 1990s, the number of northeastern cities with poverty rates of 20 percent had climbed to thirty-six. By 1995, although each of these cities had experienced a decline in poverty rates, not one had a rate that had fallen to pre-1990 levels.[71]

In 1994, Jamestown received a rare bit of national attention when *U.S. News & World Report* ranked the city as fifteenth nationally in a list of cities with significant "white" poverty, as measured by numbers of single-parent families. The magazine's study, conducted using 1990 census data, created a bit of a stir, because it challenged the "culture of poverty" thesis that African American families are uniquely susceptible to the problems of single-parent poverty.[72] Eugenicist Charles Murray, coauthor of *The Bell Curve*, predicted "social disintegration" in these communities, given his belief that poverty, crime, drug addiction, and homelessness can all be traced to the prevalence of single-parent households.[73] Jamestown just barely qualified for the list with the discovery of a concentration of 306 female-headed households in a particular part of the city (45 percent of all households in the area). Still, this demographic earned the city the dubious honor of being named as home to one of the nation's "white slums."[74]

Although Jamestown had a high poverty rate in 1995, it was only twenty-fifth in rank among the thirty-six central cities in the Northeast with high poverty rates. Jamestown's rate was less than half that of Camden, New Jersey, which had the highest rate (44.2 percent).[75] That 8 percent of Jamestown's population was living at less than 50 percent of the poverty level was indicative of a city with significant economic problems, but in this Jamestown was simply representative of larger regional trends.

Some northeastern cities have been characterized as "doubly burdened" because they have had high population losses along with high unemployment rates, high poverty rates, or both. In 1998, there were fifteen such cities in the Northeast. These included old factory towns such as Lawrence, Massachusetts, and Johnstown and Wilkes-Barre, Pennsylvania, as well as the two largest cities in New York State: New York City and Buffalo.[76] Jamestown, because of its relatively low unemployment rate (5.8 percent in 1998), was not one of these. In fact, when compared with other northeastern cities of similar size or larger, Jamestown does not stand out as being in particularly bad shape. It ranked twenty-eighth among the thirty-six central cities in the Northeast with significant population losses; its proportion of population lost was only a third that of Johnstown, Pennsylvania, the city with the greatest losses (28.5 percent).[77] This is not to minimize the economic difficulties faced by a place like Jamestown, whose manufacturing base had gone through dramatic alterations. But, in comparison with other economically challenged cities in the Northeast, Jamestown was far from the worst-off.

One reason Jamestown was in less dire circumstances than other cities was the relative diversity of its local economy. Unlike Youngstown, Ohio, with it its steel plants, or Flint, Michigan, with its GM works, Jamestown had a variety of local manufacturers. Although furniture was the lifeblood of the local economy, tool and die making and appliance manufacturing were also important. Unlike a "company town," where all subsidiary businesses are dependent on one large employer, Jamestown had a number of moderate-sized firms that operated more or less independent of one another, although many responded similarly when larger structural forces began to operate on them. A number of manufacturers have remained in the area, but changes in ownership have affected both how these firms act and how they are perceived.

Robert Reich, a Harvard business professor who became President Bill Clinton's first Labor secretary, argued in his book *The Work of Nations*, published in 1989, that the national identity of business ownership is irrelevant to a country's economic development and prosperity. According to Reich, no matter who owns them, high-quality businesses supply jobs, pay taxes, and generally contribute to the economic and social lives of the communities where they are located.[78] Sam Teresi offered a contrary view, when I interviewed him. Jamestown's banking sector is one place where there has been a significant shift in ownership. For most of the twentieth century, Jamestown's banks were, Teresi told me, "all locally owned and operated banking institutions with decisions that were being made here. The front-office, the back-office operations were here." Starting in the 1970s, these relatively small local institutions were gobbled up by large multinationals. Local banks, Key Bank and Bank of Jamestown, were bought out by HSBC (Hong Kong Shanghai Banking Corporation), Chase Manhattan, and Fleet. Today, Teresi said, "basically, what we have is bank operations of international banking conglomerates." Although it is true that such huge corporations have tremendous capital resources, their directors follow bottom-line criteria that are generated in distant financial centers. The resulting "one size fits all" set of business practices affects everything from auto loans and mortgages to investments in local businesses. Given their investment strategies, such institutions are unlikely to adjust their risk analyses for the sake of local communities. Contrary to Reich's contention that foreign-owned firms are as likely as American ones to be "good corporate citizens," contributing to local charities and other worthy causes, Jamestown's experience showed otherwise. According to Teresi, international ownership of the banks in town negatively affected contributions to the United Way, support for the city's Little League, and other giving "right on down the line."[79]

A city's banking sector can be particularly important because it is the basic source of capital for investment. In Jamestown's case, however, banking was not the only part of the local economy in which business ownership changed hands. As Teresi told me:

> Banking is only one industry in which this is occurring . . . every major manufacturer has gone through the same type of change. . . . First, the operation is purchased and made a wholly owned subsidiary . . . independent subsidiary . . . of the parent banking organization or manufacturing firm. Then slowly but surely functions started to be shifted to other locations, whether it was payroll or accounting or other back-office functions. . . . Decisions started to move out of the community. . . . Those decisions can no longer be controlled locally here.[80]

Teresi provided a list of the ownership changes that had occurred: Cummin's Engine, which makes diesel truck engines, is based in Columbus, Indiana; Marlin Rockwell Corporation, once a local company that manufactured bearings, is now the bearings division of SLF International, a Swedish company, and the largest bearing producer in the world; Blackstone Corporation, which makes home appliances, "no longer exists"—it became part of Valeo, USA, a company controlled from Paris, France. Two other manufacturing concerns, Weber-Knapp and Chautauqua Hardware, are owned by British conglomerates. Moreover, at the time that I spoke with Teresi, he was concerned about other potential changes as well. Bush Industries is a producer of ready-to-assemble furniture (a far cry from the handcrafted furniture manufactured by Swedish immigrants in Jamestown in the 1950s and 1960s) that provides largely unskilled work that pays low-end wages. It had been a family business and one of the only companies in town with its corporate headquarters still there. But Teresi was concerned because the company had just built a large plant near Erie, Pennsylvania, and had transitioned to public stock ownership. "Now that they're a publicly traded company [their] corporate offices could potentially be leaving Jamestown at some point in the future." He emphasized, "I'm not going to say that it's going to happen. I'm just saying it's a possibility. It's on the radar screen out there." Such are the insecurities generated when control of a local economy shifts to forces that are beyond its control. The bonds between community and business, never tightly woven in advanced capitalist economies, become increasingly tenuous as ownership shifts nationally and internationally. As Teresi told me, this is a "traumatic type of thing to happen to a community." But he was careful to stress that Jamestown is simply a representative case in a broad set of trends. "I'm not suggesting for one minute," he noted, "that this is something that's isolated here in Jamestown. It's happening around us. It's becoming more, to use the hackneyed phrase, the global economy, global society that we're living in. [It's just] something that you have to deal with here."[81]

Observers, especially conservatives, often cite taxes as one of the chief reasons business fled New York State in the 1970s and why New York has had difficulty attracting businesses back into the state. In fact, in a *Buffalo News* series on the upstate New York economy titled "Upstate Downbound," taxes were a consistent theme. *News* writer Jerry Zremski reported that state taxes were 25 percent higher than the national mean in 1994, and 19 percent higher in 1998. Property taxes in the Buffalo area are twice as high as property taxes in most parts of Ohio.[82] New York is generally considered to be a poor place to do business, so the argument goes, because of the state's high taxes, high utility rates, and complex regulatory structure. The solutions to the state's economic woes, then, are a reduction in taxes, especially taxes on businesses, and deregulation. This was, in fact, pretty much the platform on which George Pataki ran for governor in 1994, and he has done his best to implement these changes since assuming office.

Sam Teresi is not convinced. When I asked him about the tax issue, he said, "I think that's an element. I don't put too much stock in it. . . . I do not believe that businesses make decisions exclusively on taxes. They make decisions on the cost of doing business, of which taxes is one part." He stressed, however, that there were important intangibles involved. Businesses, he argued, make decisions on "where they want to be." Managers ask, "Is it the stimulating type of environment I want to have my family in?" Employees need to be pleased with the community. "They need to have the people that are going to help make it a productive business. . . . Where do they want to be?" What Jamestown needed to do to attract and keep business, in Teresi's view, was to "build that environment here," a place "where people want to live." "It's stimulating. It's rewarding for people. Let's build the environment that businesses will find a reason to stay or even when people get displaced, they'll find a reason to stay."[83]

In the 1980s, cities began bidding wars to bring new manufacturers into local communities. Companies like Toyota were offered large tax breaks, publicly funded infrastructural improvements, and other amenities. Teresi did not view this as an effective development strategy for Jamestown. It was expensive and the odds of success were slim. Given that ten thousand communities were courting the next Toyota or Daimler-Benz and that only a hundred large manufacturing facilities are built in the United States in a given year, "the chance of bringing in a big fish is not very good." His first priority was to retain the existing facilities in Jamestown; his second was to encourage their expansion. Most jobs come from the expansion of existing industries, and downsized managers sometimes want to stay in an area and attempt to buy into existing businesses or start new ones. "Entrepreneurship," Teresi argued, is "a big part of what is happening in this community to hopefully lead to its continued revival."[84]

"Quality of life" issues are important, Teresi told me, because "most companies are selecting places where they want their workforce, their employees to be, that will be a good safe, clean, productive, stimulating environment . . . to enhance the productivity and the company's performance." Managers themselves are looking for decent places to live. At that level, perception is important. National publicity of the kind associating a city with drugs and HIV could have a potentially negative economic impact.[85]

Teresi did not put much faith in free-trade agreements. The promise of NAFTA was that facilitating international trade would help all the participating nations. Export markets would open up to American products, thereby spurring growth in U.S. manufacturing. At the same time, jobs requiring low-end, unskilled labor would shift to Mexico, and Americans would also benefit from lower-priced consumer goods. Although the impact of NAFTA on the nation as a whole remains the subject of intense debate, there is fairly compelling evidence that it has hurt the upstate New York economy. No boom transpired in response to NAFTA. New York State ranked fourth in the country among states with NAFTA-related job losses, and the bulk of those were distributed to upstate counties.[86] In 1998, the *Buffalo News* reported that "between 1994 and 1997, 6,528 workers in upstate metro areas qualified for federal job training aid after losing their jobs because of the trade agreement."[87] Moreover, the extent of the job losses was probably greater than shown by Labor Department figures, which include only those workers who apply for benefits as a result of unemployment directly attributable to the trade agreement. When reverse multiplier effects are taken into account, the actual numbers may be four or five times those reported by the Labor Department.[88]

In 1996, Mattel cut seven hundred jobs at Buffalo's Fisher-Price plant and increased production in Mexico.[89] However, although moving plants to Mexico gives companies important advantages in terms of reduced labor costs, in the case of upstate New York, most of the jobs are shifting to Canada. The strength of the U.S. dollar compared to the Canadian dollar makes Canada an extremely attractive location for production. Heinz Bakery Products, for example, closed its Buffalo plant and moved to Trenton, Ontario. Amsco-Basil, which makes industrial washing machines, moved all of it operations to Quebec in 1995.[90] In 1999, an Ontario printing plant was awarded the contract to print the state's "I love NY" bumper stickers.[91] One good example of how trade in itself does not translate into jobs is Buffalo's Ford stamping plant. Exports from Buffalo doubled from 1993 to 1996, in part because of increases in production and shipping from the stamping plant. But the assembly of parts produced at the plant is now being done in Canada, so few area jobs are being generated. At the same time, however, few jobs are moving from Canada into upstate. From 1994 to 1997, the total number of jobs lost due to Canadian trade was 4,775, whereas the total lost to Mexico was 1,753.[92] Upstate New York is one of the regions suffering the most negative impacts of NAFTA. It seems apropos that the Buffalo Peace Bridge became a key site for demonstrations against the Free Trade Agreement of the Americas. If history is a guide, passage of that agreement will reinforce negative economic trends already occurring in the upstate area.

Hillary Loves (Upstate) New York

The 1990s will no doubt be remembered as the period of the Clinton boom (or perhaps the Clinton "bubble"). Huge economic transformations occurred as the irrelevance of the old industrial economy seemed ever more apparent. With hindsight, we can see that much of the hype associated with the Internet economy was overblown. The Dow would not be reaching forty thousand, as one author predicted, anytime soon.[93] Yet it was within the context of then still-expanding Clinton prosperity that the upstate New York economy took on national significance in the 2000 election. The state of this older industrialized economy and what to do about it became a central issue in the country's most-watched senatorial campaign. Hillary Clinton, recognizing that the key to her victory would be a strong upstate showing, focused much of her campaign on revealing the upstate economy's problems and developing proposals for addressing them.

At a Chamber of Commerce meeting in Hamburg, New York, near Buffalo, Clinton is reported to have garnered applause with the statement that "no grown child should ever have to tell a parent that he or she is leaving their hometown because they can't find a good job in upstate New York." Noting that 170,000 young people had been estimated to have left the area, she said, "I don't think you can meet a challenge unless you acknowledge that there is one to meet."[94] Clinton was speaking in direct response to her opponent Rick Lazio's statement that upstate had "turned a corner" economically and that it was not an "economic wasteland."[95] Lazio's decision to portray upstate as a region on the verge of economic resurgence constituted one of the most damaging mistakes of his campaign. Clinton took full advantage of the opening that this provided. Lazio, she declared, was "out of touch" with the upstate area.[96] Her campaign ran an effective ad portraying Rick Lazio as an ostrich with his head in the sand, denying upstate New York's economic problems.[97] Buffalo Mayor Anthony Masiello piled on, stating that Lazio had a "profound misunderstanding of upstate New York."[98] Through this very clever portrayal of Lazio as an insensitive downstater, Clinton was able to neutralize depictions of herself as a "carpetbagger."

Attacks on Lazio were only a part of the strategy. Clinton spent a good deal of time traveling through various upstate cities and towns, including twenty-six visits to Buffalo. She traveled across the southern tier, visiting Jamestown and Elmira several times. As a result, she was perceived, even by her opponents, as someone with a work ethic.[99] She became "the one who put so much faith in old-fashioned shoe leather that she would turn up in tiny counties that are accustomed to seeing major political figures on TV."[100]

Hillary Clinton, also, quite brilliantly, portrayed herself as the bearer of the new economy. Her campaign proposals included a series of targeted tax cuts and economic aid packages. Although some observers character-ized these as "so complicated that the experts don't know what to make of it," that did not seem to matter.[101] In electoral politics, symbols are important. Clinton was able to overcome many of her political liabilities by portraying herself as someone who cared deeply, if somewhat improb-ably, about the citizens of upstate New York and who was prepared to help them make the transition into the global cybereconomy. As a result of her efforts, she was able to minimize her losses in traditionally Republican up-state counties, winning 47 percent of the vote there to Lazio's 50 percent.[102] After the election, she continued the push, proposing a series of tax credits for small businesses, technology bonds for high-speed Internet access in small towns and rural areas, and funds for businesses to acquire new tech-nologies.[103] This won her accolades from both upstate Republicans and Democrats and cemented her image as the one major national politician who cares about upstate New York.[104]

The Politics of Crack

The term *crack* was first used in print in reference to a form of cocaine in 1985 by the *New York Times*. By 1986, crack had made its way into the national consciousness. Both CBS and NBC produced documentaries on the subject, both suggesting that crack had become a major social problem. *Time* and *Newsweek* also hyped the crack scare, as some compared crack's effects on the nation with the effects of the Vietnam War.[105] Crack was labeled as a "plague" and an "epidemic" that was eating away at the core of American society and "killing a whole generation of children."[106] Crack became the justification for and focal point of an intensification of the "drug war." In fact, annual federal spending on antidrug efforts escalated from two billion dollars in 1981 to twelve billion dollars by 1993.[107]

Drug addiction is an extremely complicated cultural phenomenon, although it is almost never presented as such by mainstream American media and politicians. Although there has long been a subcultural romanticization of addiction, especially heroin, in the literary works of authors such as William Burroughs and in films such as *Drugstore Cowboy,* for the most part, the media present drug use, like many social and public health problems, in the starkest and most moralistic terms. Crack was, of course, no exception to this rule. In fact, crack has been perhaps the most demonized drug in American history.[108]

There are historical reasons for this extreme reaction. Crack arrived at a politically opportune moment. The social dislocations that resulted from deindustrialization, which were exacerbated by Reagan-era economic policies, especially cuts in social welfare spending in urban areas, were becoming increasingly apparent by the late 1980s. Crack served as a scapegoat for the more complex causes behind the crime, violence, and unemployment that were affecting inner-city youth. For example, William Bennett, President Bush's "drug czar," stated that "crack is responsible for the fact that vast patches of the American urban landscape are rapidly deteriorating."[109]

To demonstrate the breadth of the epidemic, George Bush gave a presidential address to the nation from the Oval Office, during which he held up a plastic bag containing crack that had supposedly been seized in front of the White House, in Lafayette Park. It turned out, however, that the whole display was nothing more than an elaborate hoax. Federal agents could find no one dealing crack in Lafayette Park, so they had lured Keith Jackson, an eighteen-year-old black high school student, there in order to make a purchase to support a line that had already made its way into the president's speech. DEA agents bought the drugs from Jackson for twenty-four hundred dollars and then let him go.[110]

According to the National Household Survey on Drug Abuse, cocaine use among the young (ages twelve to seventeen) peaked at 4.2 percent in the period from 1979 to 1982, during the height of its fashionability as a white middle-class drug. During the height of the crack epidemic, the figure ranged from 3.9 to 2.9 percent of all teenagers. By 1991, the figure was down to 1.9 percent.[111] Crack, in other words, although perhaps a particularly potent form of an already potent and addictive drug, did not cause more overall drug use among the young. Its impacts were felt primarily in areas that were suffering from long-term secular economic decline—it was not a cause of economic deterioration so much as an *effect* of it.

Users and sellers of crack are distinguishable from each other in terms of their goals and their values. The hard-core crack user is interested in the pursuit of pleasure, sometimes to the exclusion of all else. Although the stereotype of the "crackhead" is of someone who smoked the drug a few times, perhaps even once, and became dangerously addicted, the reality is more complicated. The materialist and determinist models that dominate discussions of drug use in the United States are simplistic. Not every person who smokes crack becomes a user, and not all users become addicted. The road from use to addiction is often circuitous, depending on a complex interplay of social and individual factors. [112] Patterns of crack use in Canada, Australia, and the Netherlands are very different from those found in the United States, causing fewer of the social dislocations associated with addiction. [113] There seems little doubt, however, that those Americans addicted to crack, especially the denizens of "crackhouses," have renounced, either willingly or under the duress imposed by addiction, the middle-class values of work, discipline, and social success. Ethnographer Terry Williams characterizes this as a "culture of refusal." "The young people in the crackhouses," he says, "refuse to be part of the system, refuse to obey their parents, reject school or any adult-controlled education or training, spurn prevailing social values and most authority. In the crackhouses, teenagers and adults refuse to engage in safe sexual practices—even though this refusal leads them to behaviors that are manifestly harmful both physiologically and psychologically."[114] Yet it would be unfair to say that crackheads reject *all* American cultural values. Their intense interest in pleasure is hardly antithetical to American mores. Crack use may be an extreme instance of pleasure seeking, but the American consumer economy is organized around the manufacture and delivery of pleasurable pursuits. In a capitalist economy, however, responsible consumers must find an appropriate balance between work and pleasure, something that crack users seem incapable of negotiating for a variety of reasons.

Crack dealers are different than users in that they do not renounce work in the pursuit of pleasure. Phillipe Bourgeois has argued, based on his ethnographic studies of inner-city drug dealers, that street dealers embrace many American cultural values. As he puts it, "Street participants are frantically pursuing the American Dream."[115] To be successful, crack dealers privilege economic success over the not-so-simple pleasures of the drug itself. In fact, in the cocaine economy, successful dealers are, for fairly obvious reasons, generally not consumers. The crackhouse itself is usually geographically separated from the place where the drugs are sold. Dealers don't want consumers around who are simply going to mooch and steal from them while drawing the attention of the police with their undisciplined behavior.[116] Bourgeois argues that crack dealers offer counterevidence to "culture-of-poverty theorists" who contend that the problems of poverty stem from a lack of socialization of the poor into the work values of the middle class. Rather, "ambitious, energetic inner-city youths are attracted to the underground economy precisely *because* they believe in Horatio Alger's version of the American Dream. . . . In fact, they often follow the traditional U.S. model of upward mobility to the letter: aggressively setting themselves up as private entrepreneurs. They are the ultimate 'rugged individualists,' braving an unpredictable free-market frontier where fortune, fame, and destruction are all just around the corner."[117]

There is a long American tradition of using the underground economy as a springboard to middle-class respectability. The Kennedy family was famously involved in the illegal alcohol trade during Prohibition. Business success there led to political success and eventual acceptance as America's "royalty." Las Vegas has overcome its early association with gangsters to become America's premier adult theme park. The success of the *Godfather* films is partly attributable to their close retelling of the Horatio Alger story. The same success has more recently been replicated in the television series *The Sopranos*. Even winsome Tom Hanks has portrayed a hired killer seeking fulfillment of the American dream in the film *Road to Perdition*. Crime as mechanism for economic and social advancement is not an aberration; it is a deeply embedded feature of national cultural identity.

Crack in Jamestown

Crack arrived somewhat later in Jamestown than it did on the coasts, largely because of Jamestown's geographic separation from large metropolitan areas. The city's police chief, William MacLaughlin, told me that 1995 was when "we started to see the explosion, what we call our 'explosion' in the drug culture in Jamestown. Before that we certainly had our little bit of this and little bit of that. We heard about crack cocaine . . . [but] when we were inundated, we were inundated big time. . . . I took over as chief in 1995. My first year as chief was 'hell on wheels' as you call it."[118]

Jamestown is approximately seventy-five miles from Buffalo, but, unlike other smaller upstate cities, such as Utica, it doesn't sit on a major cross-state expressway. To reach Jamestown from the north, one must leave the New York State Thruway and travel south on secondary roads for about twenty-five miles. One does not, in other words, pass through or stop in Jamestown on the route from Albany to Cleveland or Detroit; finding it from the north requires a traveler to make a deliberate decision to head south. On the other hand, State Highway 17 (now Interstate 86) provides a link between Jamestown and New York City and other larger cities to the west. This road doesn't have anything like the same usage as I90, the main cross-state highway. In fact, as one drives (as I often do) across 17 from midstate to Jamestown, the traffic thins out to little more than a trickle in the last hundred or so miles along the southern tier westward. There are vast open stretches of farmland there, with small towns such as Cuba and Olean dotted in between. The highway provides a real but relatively unobtrusive connecting link between Jamestown and larger metropolitan areas where the drug trade has flourished. Its discovery was somewhat belated.

Chief MacLaughlin has a theory as to how crack began to move into Jamestown. He attributes its appearance to policies established by New York City Mayor Rudy Giuliani, who developed a policy of "displacement" of drug dealers. He encouraged police to harass them enough that they would leave the city. This policy was successful with what MacLaughlin labels the "sublevel drug dealers." The policy did not, however, drive them out of business; rather, it drove them to "Binghamton and Elmira and then Utica [until] some of these folks started to get over this way—that is, into Jamestown."[119]

Once they found Jamestown, they discovered an extremely fertile market. As the chief put it, "You know there's a market here. It transcends all social and economic boundaries." A local undercover narcotics officer whom I interviewed confirmed this. "Lots of people use it," he told me. "Not just kids and folks down on Washington Street [where many of the city's poorer residents of color live], but all kinds of people, including teachers in the high school."[120] As MacLaughlin put it, "Some of [the dealers] found their way here, and said 'Hmmm, we got something here.'" Once the potential of the market was uncovered, MacLaughlin believes, "there are certain people in New York City that [started] sending people here." The diversity of the crack market in Jamestown made it especially lucrative. "They could come here with two thousand dollars worth of crack, and in an afternoon they turn it around and make five, six thousand dollars. Very profitable bus ride." In the space of a year, the crack economy went from being nonexistent to the point where the police were confiscating "kilos of crack" in drug raids.[121]

At first, the city police department was simply unprepared for what followed. The Southern Tier Drug Task Force operated mostly out of Buffalo, and Jamestown had a difficult time getting the attention it needed from higher state and federal authorities. People who were midlevel drug dealers in places like New York were, initially at least, unknown in Jamestown. They had an advantage against an overwhelmed police department that was unfamiliar with the "players."

"The drug dealers," MacLaughlin pointed out, "see that as an opportunity. And I think they took advantage of it." As the dealers see it, "'We got a place where we can go. We're making big money. We're not known there.'"

Down there [in New York], they're known." As a result, crime rates and violence increased in Jamestown. In 1995, the crime rate was the highest it had
been "in a long time." These increases were directly related to increases in
drug usage, according to the chief. Violence also increased. "Violence went
up," he told me. "Robberies went up. Jamestown experienced homicides."
One was attributed to an eighteen-year-old New York kid, involved in the
drug trade, who had already been convicted of murder twice.[122]

Some of the increases in violence in Jamestown resulted from turf
battles between established local drug dealers and newcomers. Up until
the newer element arrived, the known local dealers went without guns. But
as different dealers came in, "the two clashed," according to MacLaughlin.
"That's when we were having the problems," he told me. The violence did
not necessarily spill over into the civilian elements in the community,
although burglaries often did. Understandably, Jamestown's citizens' perceptions of increased danger from violence and crime were reinforced by
the exchanges between drug gangs and by increases in property crimes.[123]

A Traveler

Nushawn Williams's account of why he came to Jamestown differs from
that imagined by Chief MacLaughlin. According to Williams, he was not
driven out of New York by Rudy Giuliani's drug policies. In fact, he didn't
move directly from New York to Jamestown, but slowly made his way
across upstate, living for periods in Rochester and Dunkirk.[124]

Nushawn dropped out of school and left home when he was fifteen
years old. He was bored and frustrated. His mother smoked crack and
he had been living with his grandmother, Elenora McCrae, in Brooklyn.
Accounts differ as to why he left his grandmother's home. He told me that
he "wanted to see what the world looked like" and wanted "to make the
journey more exciting." McCrae told a writer for *Poz* magazine that she
kicked Nushawn out because he was dealing drugs.[125] This is something he
adamantly denies.

In any event, when he left Jamestown, he moved to Rochester. There
he met a woman named Charlene, who lived with a boyfriend who abused
her. She told Nushawn that if he could get rid of the boyfriend, she'd offer
him a place to stay. One day when the boyfriend came home from work,
Nushawn told him that he was no longer welcome. When the boyfriend
called the police, Charlene stood by Nushawn. Charlene was the first of
many women who offered Nushawn somewhere to stay. Having found a
place, he began "making money and hanging out," selling "weed" and
"crack." He had plenty of girlfriends, three or four of whom let him stay at
their apartments or houses. But he was arrested by the Rochester police for
drug possession, so, while free on bail, he left town and moved down the

New York State Thruway to the smaller city of Dunkirk, an old Lake Erie port town that sits in the heart of Welch's grape country.

In Dunkirk he set up shop again. He met plenty of girls there, and life seemed pretty good. But his friend Jabbo suggested that they go to Jamestown, because they could make more money dealing drugs there. In Jamestown, Nushawn moved into an apartment on Barrows Street, in a rather run-down section still referred to as "Swede hill" because it was once home to the city's first Swedish settlers. Life in Jamestown suited him. He met many young women. He was, he told me, a "communicator" with women. Having grown up with many women around, he believed he "understood" them. He met Jennifer while shoplifting chicken from a grocery store. He met Amber Arnold, who eventually became infamous for going on national television to say that she still loved Nushawn, in a bar while playing PlayStation. They were immediately attracted. They "hit it" (they had sex in the bathroom). He had a special fondness for Amber, and she, he told me, was the only one of his girlfriends that he took to New York. Going to New York was living the high life, like a "trip to Honolulu," all expenses paid. Still, Williams didn't want women to "lock him down," as Jo Lynn once had tried to do. He "wanted to be free." He didn't object to his girlfriends' sleeping with other men, and he didn't want them objecting to his sleeping with other women. Jamestown, he said, "was like an orgy every day."

Life in Jamestown was not without its problems, however. Jabbo was arrested for robbery and Nushawn had to post his bail of five hundred dollars. Jo Lynn's mom put up her house as security, so Nushawn couldn't flee back to New York because Jo Lynn's mom might lose her house. He didn't like such commitments and the restrictions they imposed. Jamestown also held the potential for violence. At one point Nushawn was stabbed outside a bar. The weapon used was a very small knife, a penknife, but he was stabbed and there was some blood. His friend Malik had a sock with a brick in it, and he hit the guy who had stabbed Nushawn in the head with the brick.

Yet, although the gangster life in Jamestown presented certain challenges, the streets there were nowhere near as mean as those of New York City. That was an important part of the appeal. The Jamestown drug trade was very lucrative. What would have been a nickel bag in New York could be sold for forty-five or fifty dollars. A gram of crack (an "eight ball") could bring in as much as twelve hundred dollars. And not only were the profits good, the cost of living was low. Living in the marginal sections of town was cheap—Nushawn rented an apartment for ten dollars a month. With the extra cash he was making, he had spare time to pursue some of the good things available to more affluent members of American society.

Nushawn and his friends would "rent" cars from local crackheads and tool through the small communities around Jamestown.[126] Although Jamestown is no longer the thriving factory town it once was, many of the surrounding towns are quaint, and the countryside, with its small farms and woodlands, is quite beautiful. It is a bit hard to imagine New York street kids like Nushawn and his friends ordering beers in the local juke joints after a day out touring the countryside in a car on loan from a neighborhood crackhead, but it is easy enough to see why he stayed in the area. Kennedy, Sinclairville, Busti, and Sugargrove are a long way from the noise and danger that confronted him in Brooklyn.

In an earlier day, gangsters like Legs Diamond would head up to the Catskills when the heat in New York became too intense. Nushawn and his cohorts may have moved farther, but they found many of the same charms that upstate has to offer. They would go snowmobiling through the forests and fields of Chautauqua and Cattaraugus Counties. Nushawn was even learning how to ski. He was, in fact, a classic example of the drug dealer who attempts to live his version of the American Dream. The version is distorted, perhaps even nihilistic, but it has precedents in the dreams of previous immigrants who set up bootlegging enterprises and other activities that became the basis for organized crime.

Organizing a drug-trade operation is not an easy task. It requires some of the same skills as do many traditional business enterprises. One must find reliable employees and establish a method for keeping accounts. One must develop and maintain mechanisms for buying and distribution. In addition, one must deal with a whole set of considerations that are not a part of normal business practices, such as making one's operations known to potential buyers while also keeping them secret from the police. Moreover, one must keep on top of competitors, who may be willing to use violence to maintain their markets. This might, in turn, require one to use violence as well.

Jonathan Law, an undercover police officer with whom I spoke in Jamestown, expressed some admiration for the very people he helped to put in prison. One dealer in particular, originally from Detroit, now serving a twenty-year prison term, elicited Law's respect. This dealer had divided the city of Jamestown into a grid and had subcontracted out responsibilities for each of the sections. "It was a remarkable operation," Law said. "He was a very intelligent man." The dealer ran into difficulties when one of his subordinates became ambitious and informed on him to the police in an attempt, ultimately failed, to take over the entire operation. Such are the vicissitudes of the drug trade.[127]

Nushawn Williams did not run such a high-level operation. He was, according to Chief MacLaughlin, a fairly typical character in the drug economy, a lower- to midlevel dealer. Before the HIV story broke, the police just considered him to be another drug kid from New York they had to keep an eye on, not an especially bad character, but not an especially good one either. He had a moderately long rap sheet that included arrests for marijuana possession and automobile theft.

Nushawn told me on any number of occasions that he liked to "smoke weed," but that he did not consume crack. Having seen what it had done to his mother, he wanted no part of it. Yet he had no compunction about dealing it to others, and he suffered no sense of moral contradiction. His reasons for selling the drug were simple: he needed and wanted the money that crack made available to him. And he never forced anyone to take it—customers came to see *him*.

Although he never used the drug, Nushawn told me, crack dealing was an "addiction" for him. He liked having the money, but he also began to crave the attention. It boosted his ego. It seemed that everywhere he went in Jamestown, he was known. People liked to see him and they were interested in the products that he had to offer. People would stop him on the street. He attracted a crowd. One of the attractions of being a small-town dealer was the glamour attached to it. Moreover, he "knew the whole town in and out." He had, in an odd and perhaps unfortunate way, become a member of a community. He had escaped the alienation and violence that seemed endemic to his life in New York City.

Community Responses

Although the crack economy thrived in Jamestown, it was still a distinctively underground phenomenon. It flourished beneath the surface of the respectable lives of most working people. The vast majority of the city's residents had no direct contact with the use or sale of the drug. Crack had a large effect on the lives of a relatively small number of people, but for most the impact was indirect, found in the recognition of rising crime rates, increasing violence, and a recognizable deterioration of the fabric of some parts of the community. Jamestown was portrayed in press accounts of the Williams story as a town that had almost entirely collapsed, yet, even as the story unfolded, various institutional structures were being organized in response.

According to Chief MacLaughlin, even before Williams's actions became the subject of media scrutiny, Jamestown had made moves to put community policing into practice. The city had applied for and received some federal grants for programs to fight street-level drug dealing, and officials had conducted community surveys to determine citizens' perceptions of crime problems. Neighborhood Watch groups had grown in number from six to twenty-six, and a community policy advisory board had been set up to "empower the neighborhoods in the community."[128]

Both MacLaughlin and Teresi emphasized that working with neighborhoods was an important part of the process of revitalizing the town. "We try," Teresi said, "to do our day jobs of dealing with protecting the conditions and the integrity of the neighborhoods, to make it a decent place to live in. We work with other city departments, like the police department, in trying to track down funding to help them introduce new neighborhood-based-type programs. We work to try to improve the appearance of neighborhoods, by rebuilding streets, housing rehab programs."[129] Although many of these efforts began before Nushawn Williams became a public figure, MacLaughlin suggested that the attendant publicity raised awareness about police department activities and encouraged cooperation on the part of local residents:

> People in the community were more understand[ing] about what we're trying to do [after the Williams case]. We're trying to go into the neighborhoods and say look, we're going to be part of your neighborhood, but you gotta help us, because we can't do it by ourselves. It's the traditional, "Hey that's the cops, let them take care of it." It doesn't work that way anymore. They say it takes a whole community to raise a child, but also it takes a whole community to prevent crime. That's been our philosophy.... [W]e've been building partnerships with a lot of different groups.... [W]e're sending our second application to Weed and Seed, which is a national program through the Justice Department.... And a lot of what grew out of Nushawn has kind of opened. We have blossomed into so much. We were trying to do it. We were meeting resistance. And it was kind of ironic.[130]

In the late 1980s, shifts in the globalized economy brought major and often traumatic changes to places like Jamestown, New York. As a result, such places were susceptible to new interventions from the underground economy. Although crack arrived "late" in Jamestown, it had important impacts. The city had no infrastructure in place to deal with a large intrusion of the drug. The populace had little direct experience with crack's impacts on individuals and social institutions. The novelty of crack in Jamestown helped to inflate prices, and that in turn attracted more dealers.

Chief MacLaughlin and other public officials attempted to meet the challenges Jamestown faced by reasserting the value of the political over the economic. Public interventions went beyond simple enforcement. The police department couldn't "solve" the problem by itself. The city encouraged grassroots efforts as police worked with other city departments to restore the citizens' faith in the livability of Jamestown neighborhoods. Police and economic development leaders believed that restoring neighborhood vitality would be a first step in reigniting the above-ground economy.

The emergence of a crack culture does not represent a breakdown in the marketplace. Rather, it is an indication of a market that acts without social or political restraint: the pleasure principle unchecked and unregulated. Crack is, in this sense, the ultimate expression of and testament to Reaganism. Crackheads and crack dealers follow different lines along the track of capitalist development. Only when capitalism is restrained, however, by the forces of citizenship and public participation—that is, democratic forces—can the crack economy be subverted.

As noted earlier, JoAnn Wypijewski said in her *Harper's* article on the Williams case that she hoped every kid she met in Jamestown would "get out." Such a statement implies that there are places in America where these marginalized youth can avoid the kinds of problems and temptations they face in Jamestown. The idea that pulling up stakes and "moving on" is a solution to one's problems, and the first step to opportunity, is an old one in the United States. Bright, well-educated, conventionally ambitious kids from Jamestown have in fact left—they have had opportunities to do so. But the kids that Wypijewski spoke with did not have such opportunities, and that was one of the reasons they chose not to leave. Could they find better lives in other places? Perhaps, but would other American communities accept what Chief MacLaughlin calls the "couch kids" with open arms? Do they have the skills to participate in the new economy? Could they find better lives in the dot-com boomtowns of Palo Alto, Arlington, or Phoenix? Perhaps. But the collapse of the Internet bubble indicates once again that there really are no capitalist utopias.

Postscript

On September 15, 1999, Officer David Mitchell was working a shift as an undercover narcotics officer for Jamestown's Drug Task Force. He walked up to the car of one of his informants, James E. Lewis, an eighteen-year-old African American, at 9:00 P.M., the agreed-upon meeting time. Lewis knew full well that Mitchell was a policeman when he shot Mitchell in the face. Lewis was apparently angered that Mitchell wanted him to involve his friend Tray in a drug deal for which Tray would eventually be busted.[131] Mitchell was seriously injured, and there were indications that he might not live. Lewis was charged with five criminal counts for the shooting, two of attempted murder, one of aggravated assault on a police officer, one of attempted aggravated assault, and one of criminal use of a firearm. He eventually pled guilty to several of the counts and is now serving a twenty-five-year sentence. Officer Mitchell eventually recovered from many, although not all, of the injuries that he sustained on that evening.

The Mitchell shooting spurred the Jamestown Police Department to undertake a major crackdown on local drug dealers. The shooting was the "icing on the cake" that led to a decision to significantly increase pressure on local drug dealers.[132] In December 1999, a major drug bust in the city resulted in 54 indictments and 29 arrests, and Chief MacLaughlin stated, "The ability to sell drugs in our community will never be the same again."[133] The Jamestown police conducted the arrests in concert with the Community Stabilization Team, which brought state troopers into the city to help with arrests and follow-up. Over a period of four weeks, 155 arrests were made in connection with the program.[134]

3

Of Myths and Monsters

FRIEND OF NUSHAWN WILLLIAMS: He was just like a cool dude. I don't know.
He was just suave.

JOHN MILLER (REPORTER): Hard to believe, looking at this mug shot.

World News Tonight with Peter Jennings, *November 3, 1997*

If there was a consistent theme or impression regarding the persona of
Nushawn Williams generated in the media's attention to his case, it was
this: he was "a monster." More specifically, he was the "AIDS monster."[1]
That this particular designation seems to have stuck is significant. Why did
Williams attract the level of vilification that he attracted? What did he do
that was so horrible as to transform him into a nationally prominent symbol of infamy? Why a "monster" rather than, say, an "alien"? To attempt to
answer these questions—and I don't believe that there are easy answers—it
seems useful to explore the meaning of the term *monster* and to examine
the actions of others who have been marked by it. Against this exploration, I will present a human portrait of Nushawn Williams that is based
on my personal interactions with him. This "humanizing" is not the same
as "praising"; I am not inclined to justify, much less laud, Williams's many
troubling and often illegal activities. My intent here is to offer some perspective on who he is and what he did. Media accounts of the case sacrificed

such perspective in favor of demonization. As a result, even attentive and perceptive observers had little basis for making reasoned and reasonable judgments regarding the nature of what Williams may have done, much less for evaluating the implications of the case for public policy-making. Williams did many bad things, but he did not, I would argue, deserve to be labeled a monster and cast from the human community.

Monsters and Meanings

According to the *Oxford English Dictionary,* a "monster" is a "warning," a "marvel"; something "malformed" or "misshapen"; an animal "partly brute" and "partly human"; a "person of inhuman cruelty."[2] A monster is, in other words, a visitor, ugly and repulsive, from a domain outside of the ordinary, harboring bad intent, who is probably, in effect, "evil" and carries ominous prophecies.

Specific monsters, however, may not be pinpointed easily. Monsters don't wear labels. A monster is not, in other words, an unreconstructed fact. A monster is an artifact, as much cultural creation as autonomous entity. A monster can be hidden, existing as a set of semiconscious cultural meanings and tropes that announce themselves in a particularly troublesome fashion, a culture trying to tell itself something about itself. In his "seven theses" on "monster culture," Jeffrey Jerome Cohen contends that "the monster's body is a cultural body," it is "pure culture." It exists "only to be read."[3] As representation, or cultural signification, the monster enters from the margins to disrupt cultural boundaries. The monster is, in a word, "transgressive," and, as such, it "and all that it embodies must be exiled or destroyed."[4]

It is easiest to make sense of the idea that monsters are "purely cultural" when one is dealing with the imaginative creations of poetry and literature. Many of those who write about "monster theory" are literary critics.[5] The archetypal mythical and literary monsters of the West are familiar: Grendel, Gargantua, Beelzebub, Dracula, Mr. Hyde, Frankenstein's monster, to name only a few. The shapes and contours of the monsters of a particular epoch are a literary trace of the fears and expectations of the time. In nineteenth-century Europe and the United States, for example, a turn toward biologically articulated monsters reflected cultural anxieties regarding real and disruptive changes occurring in industry, science, and medicine. Darwin and Mendel contributed to the notion that the biological is unstable and historically indeterminate. The literary works of Mary Shelley, Edgar Allan Poe, and H. G. Wells reflect this, as does the fact that genetic freaks and mutations became the subject of cultural fascination, not only among the scientific elite, but within the popular culture as well, as they were presented as staples of the circus sideshow.[6]

Definitions, in other words, do change. What might be recognized as a monster in one historical period (or in one cultural arena) might not be in another. In fact, the very idea of a "monster" is a relatively modern invention (Montaigne and Bacon were among the first Europeans to write systematically about monsters).[7] Yet the imaginary of the monster points to something "real." Monsters seem at times to appear historically as literal entities, once human beings who have committed acts so heinous as to exile them effectively from the community of the human. The twentieth century was stocked with such characters, monstrous killers who altered the course of global history: Adolf Hitler, Pol Pot, Slobodan Milosevic. At the same time, and perhaps not coincidentally, mass murderers of the more mundane variety came to have an important place in twentieth-century popular consciousness: the "Boston strangler," Ted Bundy, Charles Manson, and Timothy McVeigh, among others.

The line between the literary—the metaphorical and the imaginative—and the "real" is not an easy one to fix. Literature, history, and myth overlap and intermix. "Literal" facts are elusive, and interpretations are the products of individual subjectivities cast in vast oceans of cultural material, only bits of which may be accessible at any particular moment. The monsters of literature and myth, in other words, help to signify and make sensible (so far as it is possible) the more literal monsters that populate history books and newspaper front pages. At the same time, cultural anthropologists, historians, and theologians scrutinize the facticity of mythic icons and narratives in search of actual "truths." (Is the Loch Ness Monster "real"? Was Vlad the Impaler "Dracula"?) Monsters are then literal and literary, real and metaphorical, historical and imaginative all at the same time.

What, if anything, does this tell us about Nushawn Williams? He was cast as a monster in the press. He became popularly known as one. But does that make him one? Not necessarily. I will admit the possibility that there are some human acts so heinous that those who commit them might deserve the label "monster." Williams, however, has not committed such acts. His misdeeds are not even in the same ballpark with those that might legitimately be described as monstrous. A careful reading of newspaper accounts confirms this. For myself, personal conversations with Williams have reconfirmed it. Nushawn Williams may be a flawed human being, but he is nothing like the monster that he has been depicted to be. Representations of him as such are, I would argue, indicative of the monstrous workings of a system of popular-culture productions that appears dangerously out of control. The institutions of the popular media seem to need monsters to feed on. In the Williams case, the media's representation of monstrosity was radically disconnected from the realities involved.

Examples from recent history help to set the boundaries of what might legitimately be held to be truly monstrous. In most cases, for acts to be considered monstrous, they need to involve something more than ordinary criminal conduct. They need to be "beyond the pale." Frank Cawson describes the case of Ian Brady and Myra Hindley, the "monsters of Manchester," who at six-month intervals randomly selected and then tortured and killed a child, making detailed records of their deeds that were eventually used to convict them of murder:

> They lived methodically, single-mindedly establishing their joint career as killers by rituals of recurrence and order. Every six months they first abused and then killed another child. Their preparations were carefully planned and as carefully recorded. On each occasion they produced a check list of actions to be taken and materials to be assembled. Each time before the actual killing they bought a supply of mild stimulant called Pro-Plus.
>
> Ian Brady and Myra Hindley recorded the last hours of Lesley Ann Downey as others might photograph a holiday, to commemorate or preserve for future reference an event that gave them deep satisfaction. That same night, it was the day after Christmas, they took a polythene-wrapped body in the back of the minivan to a lonely spot on Saddleworth Moor and buried it alongside their other trophies. Later Ian Brady would photograph Myra Hindley sitting on the grave with her dog. In Myra Hindley's ironic words: "Another little flower for God's Garden!" This was their family and they visited regularly, driving up to Saddleworth Moor and eating a picnic beside the graves. On at least one occasion the family visit took the form of a call to offer sympathy to the bereaved parents of one of "their" children.[8]

The motivations of these killers are baffling. Anger, jealousy, greed—the usual motives behind most criminal conduct—don't seem relevant here. The actions exist beyond the boundaries of emotional feeling or rational calculation. Yet these two kept careful records. They gave no indication of being entirely irrational or insane, so it is difficult to attribute their behavior to external causes, such as disease. Casting such people as monstrous rings true.

The Columbine shooters, Dylan Klebold and Eric Harris, have often been described as monsters. *Time* magazine labeled them the "monsters next door."[9] These two boys were particularly horrifying not only because of the viciousness and senselessness of the acts they initiated, but because their hatred and planning went undetected by friends, family members, and institutional authorities. After the Columbine incident, numerous articles were published about what had gone awry with "our" culture, the culture of white suburban America, that it had produced two such efficient and self-destructive "killing machines." Peter Applebome summed things up well in a *New York Times* piece: "At the heart of the analysis of the killings last month at Columbine High School in Colorado has been a deceptively simple question: Were the killers chillingly aberrant monsters or were they a part, however perverse, of something in the culture as a whole?"[10] To have to ask such questions was itself traumatic for U.S. society. In the postwar period, millions of affluent white Americans had left the cities behind to escape urban "problems," only to find a "monster in their midst."

Unlike the privileged Harris and Klebold, Kody Scott was the definitive outsider. In his autobiography, *Monster: The Autobiography of an L.A. Gang Member,* he willingly, sometimes even proudly, accepts the designation. Scott joined the Crips at age eleven. His initiation into the gang involved an unprovoked attack on several members of a rival Crip "set." He fired a pump-action twelve-gauge shotgun into a cluster of young men eight times. The scene was one of "heavy bodies hitting the ground, confusion, yells of dismay, running, and then the second wave of gunfire."[11] For the next twelve years, Scott's entire existence was focused on moving up through the gang hierarchy: First, to "build the reputation of your name"; second, to establish your name "in association with your particular set," so that individual and gang identity become fused; and third, to "establish yourself as a promoter" of your gang. The ultimate goal was to become an "O.G.," an "original gangster."[12]

In Scott's pursuit of his goal, he was single-minded and utterly ruthless. By the age of sixteen, he had wounded and/or killed dozens of other gang members, sometimes in acts of revenge and sometimes simply because his victims happened to be rivals unfortunate enough to be available on the street for shooting. The violence was his "work," and after he completed an attack, he returned to his mother's house to smoke pot, drink beer, and catch an episode of *Benny Hill.* His street name Monster resulted from his participation in a particularly nasty act of brutality:

> In 1977, when I was thirteen, while robbing a man, I turned my head and was hit in the face. The man tried to run, but was tripped by Tray Ball, who then held him for me. I stomped him for twenty minutes before leaving him unconscious in an alley. Later that night, I learned that the man had lapsed into a coma and was disfigured from my stomping. The police told bystanders that the person responsible for this was a "monster." The name stuck, and I took that as a moniker over my birth name.[13]

Monster Kody's memoir is replete with images of war and battle. In fact, he frequently describes the conflicts between Crips and Bloods and between Crips and Crips as part of a land war between different factions, a war that he recognizes makes no sense, because the territories incorporated into its possession have no value other than the graffiti on the sides of buildings indicating which gang claims the turf. As in many wars, "civilians" are generally considered to be out of bounds, and some acts of violence are considered so heinous as to be illegitimate (as when, in retaliation for the kidnapping and raping of a "civilian," one gang member cut his victim's arms off and took them with him as a badge of honor).

Scott's battle imagery provides the reader with a rhetorical apparatus for making some sense out of participant motivations. More significant, perhaps, is the background: South Los Angeles, with its history of neglect, economic despair, and violence. Expectations hold that this is "just the way it goes" in such places. In fact, according to Scott, officers from the LAPD would notify his "troops" regarding the location of rival gang members with the assumption that attacks would be forthcoming.

Scott's descent into nihilism seems almost comprehensible given the circumstances that he confronted. He states, "Life meant very little to me. I felt that my purpose on earth was to bang. My mind-set was narrowed by the conditions and circumstances prevailing around me. Certainly I had little respect for life when practically all my life I had seen people assaulted, maimed, and blown away at very young ages, and no one seemed to care. . . . I didn't care about living or dying—and I cared less than that about killing someone."[14]

Scott's recognition of the absurdity of his situation, his self-reflection and his criticism of his own violence, and his eventual attempts to reform himself by raising his political consciousness give his narrative an arc, a moral purpose that transforms Scott from monster into flawed and interesting human being. The book becomes, as a cover blurb puts it, "one of the most disturbingly authentic triumphs of the human spirit ever executed in print." Yet although his story is extraordinary, Scott did not become a media sensation. His acts of monstrous violence did not garner national attention because his activity remained confined within certain relatively narrow boundaries. Had Scott and his friends taken to the hills around Los Angeles, attacking media moguls and movie stars, things would, no doubt, have been different. But Scott's hatred was mostly focused on those with whom he had the most in common. A resident of a middle-class suburb can read Scott's book with interest and distance, safe in the knowledge that Scott and his cohorts pose little if any immediate or long-term threat to the reader's social peace and prosperity.

Nushawn Williams is different from any of the people described above. He was labeled a monster, but it is difficult to understand why. He was not ruthless—he was not even particularly violent by the standards of those he grew up around. He didn't join a gang, either before he went to prison or after he got there, although he knew many gang members. He never murdered anyone. He wasn't arrested for assault. What Nushawn was charged with was having sex with others while being HIV-positive, after having been notified of his status. But there is more to it than this, of course. Nushawn did something that all monsters do. He crossed boundaries. He transgressed limits. He wandered. He didn't stay put. He wound up in a place where he "didn't belong." The very fact that he did *not* use force made him dangerous. He offered adventure, freedom, and relief from the boredom of life in a small town that had lost its economic vitality. He was a "cool dude." It was this very attractiveness that made him such a threat and turned him into a monster.

Initial Contacts

I first wrote to Nushawn Williams in January 2000. At that time I was well into a research project that involved his activities. I had interviewed a number of people in Jamestown who were connected in various ways to the case, and talking to him seemed to be a good idea, if not an outright necessity. He wrote back to me very quickly and also began to call the number that I gave him (collect). It was the beginning of what turned into a fairly enduring relationship. I have tried to help him out in certain ways while he has been in prison. I have sent him occasional packages, and I've visited him more than a dozen times. I wrote a letter to his parole board recommending that they take his petition seriously. I contacted his aunt in Cleveland to try to arrange a place for him to live and work once he gets out of prison that will be removed from the temptations provided by his old neighborhood in Brooklyn. He hasn't had an easy time of it in prison. His notoriety has followed him there, and that has led to problems with other prisoners and perhaps some of the guards as well. Fair game in the media, he is fair game in the prison. If those who have condemned him want him to suffer, there seems little doubt that their wishes have been fulfilled.

My first contact with Nushawn occurred not long after he did a television news show interview for WPIX News in New York. The interview, which was conducted while he was housed at the Comstock Correctional Facility outside of Albany, did not go particularly well for him. The story in which it appeared shed little new light on the case, although the TV promos for the story made hyperbolic claims about "new revelations" regarding the number of women Nushawn had slept with. The news program introduced the interview with the usual hoopla; Nushawn was a "one-man plague" and a one-man "AIDS wave."[15] He was "about to shock everyone," claiming he had more sex partners than first believed all over the East Coast." Nushawn then proceeded to claim that he had "been with" "two hundred," maybe "three hundred" women. This led into the display of a graphic of a map of the Northeast in which various states were highlighted: Massachusetts, Pennsylvania, New York, Virginia, and North Carolina. Nushawn mentioned about a dozen towns, all but one of which were located either in Chautauqua County or in the metropolitan New York area. He also mentioned "Charlottesville" and "North Carolina" in passing. The implication was that women infected by Nushawn Williams were strewn all over the East Coast.

Newscaster Jonathan Dienst implied that WPIX had uncovered new revelations that were being taken seriously by health department officials, who would follow up on them, but nothing ever came of this. A *Buffalo News* story about the TV interview quoted Dr. Berke as saying that the figures Nushawn gave seemed "pretty close to what we thought." District Attorney Subjack's comments to the *Buffalo News* were circumspect: "I think prosecution-wise, we're done. I don't think anyone else is going to come forward."[16] In the end, no health department official visited Nushawn after the broadcast. He stated that he would not "name names" on national television, not wanting to invade the "privacy" of his former partners. From a purely legal standpoint, it would not have been wise for him to reveal individual names, given that he could still be pursued by the criminal justice system for his past sexual activities. Yet it wasn't particularly wise for him to boast about sleeping with hundreds of women either.

It was clear from the outset of the interview that modest standards of objective news reporting did not apply. At one point, Dienst described the numbers that Nushawn bragged about as "sick," but it is hard to know exactly why he felt that was the case. Since when had American male posturing about sexual conquests become a "sickness" in the popular consciousness? Was there not a kernel of truth in Nushawn's suggestion that some of his critics might "want to take my place"? We live now in a world where former Senator Bob Dole makes commercials for Viagra. As Nushawn's cousin Delores Alans stated to the *New York Daily News,* "He liked sex, that's all."[17] At about the same time Nushawn was bragging about his exploits, Donald Trump was, as usual, hawking his own, this time in a biography that was carefully scrutinized by the national media. Trump's male posturing has long been treated with a certain ironic disdain,[18] but no one refers to him as "sick" or accuses him of sexual perversion. Columnists, in fact, have postulated that his ambitions for financial success and power are linked to his hyperactive libido.[19]

During the WPIX interview, Nushawn also expressed regret for infecting women with HIV, for having as he said, "given a death sentence to" them. Yes, he regretted "having sex without a condom, not having safe sex, stuff like that." Jamestown's mayor at the time, Richard Kimball, given the opportunity to respond on the air to Nushawn's statements, said that he couldn't believe that Nushawn had not shown "more remorse" and accused him of being a "pathological liar." The determination of appropriate levels of remorse is probably best left to individual subjective judgments, but Kimball's liar accusation is simply difficult to square with the facts. There is very little evidence that Nushawn Williams is a liar. In fact, to the contrary, he was quite cooperative in terms of providing names of sexual partners and other information sought by authorities. The one important point that raised significant questions regarding his veracity concerned the matter of whether he had been informed by the Chautauqua County Health Department regarding his HIV status. Although he pled guilty to charges of reckless endangerment, he continued to deny that he had known that he was HIV-positive before he was tested at Rikers. Although he may not have been truthful about this, such denials of guilt are not, I would suggest, "pathological."

The interview itself led to a new round of media speculation and reactions. *New York Times* columnist John Tierney invoked Francis Fukuyama's book *The Great Disruption* in noting that Williams was, of all things, a "cad." The decline in family values had allowed "cad-ness"—that is, the pursuit of multiple female sexual partners—to move from its place as an activity of only the most privileged men, where it had remained for most of Western history, to become an activity of the common folk, the hoi polloi, the Nushawn Williamses of the world. This, according to Tierney, was one result of convenient birth control and women's entry into the workforce.[20] It was only a matter of time, it seemed, before Nushawn Williams's name would be invoked to criticize feminism.

For the most part, however, media reactions to the WPIX interview were somewhat more constrained than the first media responses to the case. *New York Times* reporting on the interview was relatively fair and rather perceptive. *Times* writer Michael Cooper noted that Williams "appeared to be in denial about his health status couching his comments by saying, 'If I am HIV positive,' and 'I still don't even know if I got it now.'" He described Williams's presentation as encompassing "a mixture of candor, regret, and braggadocio."[21] That interpretation appears to be more or less on target.

When I received my first letter from Nushawn Williams, he was still smarting from reactions to the interview. He began his letter by stating that he felt "grossly mis-represented" by the interview and that he had granted it "hoping to give voice to the person many call a monster." He then expressed the hope that I might print his "true feelings regarding this whole tragedy." He also said that he did indeed have "regrets"; he felt that "no one should have to endure such a disease. And I am very sorry for those infected." He said that he was the "first to admit that my irresponsibility has caused me to become HIV positive as well as others. I am very sorry for it." At the same time, however, he noted that he too was "a victim of this virus," and he became infected "very much the same way they say I infected others." He resented that no one ever seemed to mention his victim status, nor was any attempt made to find who infected him or to prosecute that person. This didn't mean, however, that he wanted the woman pursued. In fact, he told me that he knew who had infected him (a woman from Colorado) and that she eventually visited him in jail to express her regret. He did not, he said, harbor a grudge against her. As he put it, "I know who passed the HIV virus on to me, but I'm not angry at them nor do I wish them ill-will. Actually, I'm protecting and respecting their privacy."[22]

Whether Nushawn knew who had infected him and how sorry he may or may not have been or continues to be is not for me to judge, but some of the things that he stated in his letter seemed undeniably true: "If society believes that by imprisoning me it's going to stop or to slow down the spread of the HIV virus it's dangerously wrong! Just look at the statistics of people young and old who are becoming or have become infected since I have come to prison." In his commonsense view, if the penal model, with its simplified cause-and-effect presuppositions, were valid, it would have begun to work. The infection rate would have begun to stop or slow down if prosecution were an effective deterrent. That didn't seem to be the case. He also noted, quite accurately, that politicians "use people like me and others to pass New Laws. And New Bills, in the House. Saying it was a Black Man running around passing this virus all over the U.S.A. I feel it is wrong the way Politics has a way of deceiving the public, just to gain votes and to pass new bills." He closed the letter by saying, "Again, I apologize to all those involved in my situation. In fact, I apologize to all those infected in the world."

The next letter I received from Nushawn began with the introduction, "This is something that I thought you might like to read. It's my belief, something that played a big part in my life." And, "I hope these papers are as good to you as they are to me."[23] What followed were seventy-eight hand-printed pages copied out of Lao Tzu's *Tao Te Ching*. I had read this work with intense interest as an undergraduate, so I recognized it immediately. I was just a bit surprised to find it written out by hand by the "AIDS monster." Clearly, there was more going on here than was apparent in media stories on the case. I was convinced and remain so that Nushawn Williams is not simply a victim of the criminal justice system. He knowingly engaged in various illegal activities, most of which he was never tried or even arrested for. But his depiction as a monster seems increasingly strained.

Visiting Nushawn

Auburn, New York, is in many respects quite an attractive city. It has wide streets and beautiful, historic homes. It was an important stop on the

Underground Railroad. William Seward lived in Auburn, as did Harriet Tubman. Her house has been restored and now exists as one of the town's main tourist attractions. Auburn is also home to the oldest penitentiary in the United States.[24]

Given that Auburn is less than an hour from where I live in Ithaca, I had traveled through the town once or twice in the past, but I had not spent a good deal of time there, and when I set out to visit Nushawn, I did not know where the state penitentiary was located. It was raining, and I asked a young woman on the street with a rain slicker clutched up over her head how to get to the prison. For some reason I had imagined it would be sitting right in the middle of the town, a glowering and dominating presence over the city's architecture. That was not the case, however. And the woman I asked didn't seem to know where it was either, or at least that's what she told me. "All I know is that it's over there someplace," she said, pointing off to the right. "I can't tell you how to get there. But I know it's over there."

Did she live in Auburn? I wondered. Could you really live in a town this size and *not* know where its large prison is located? Not know "how to get there"? Perhaps when one lives in a prison town there's a certain shame connected to it, as though the town itself is somehow imprisoned by the penitentiary's walls, as though the townsfolk themselves are somehow responsible for the crimes of those restrained there, as though the economic life of the community is tarnished by association with a place that no one knows exactly how to find, an institution that is more than 150 years old, but the location of which is difficult to pinpoint. Then again, perhaps she didn't live in Auburn after all, but was just there on business or visiting a relative, and thus only vaguely familiar with the city's geographic layout.

Whatever the case, it turned out that the prison was only a few blocks away from both business and residential districts, on a fairly desolate road. The prison stood on one side of the road and on the other side was a large field that looked as if at one time it may have been a railroad yard. Sprinkled along the highway were a few convenience stores and run-down bars. The day I made the trip turned out to offer one of those all-day drenching rain storms that are inextricably and justly connected to upstate New York's climatological reputation, almost as closely as are the area's seemingly interminable winters. The weather was apropos, adding to the sense of gloom that marked the scene for me.

Auburn was actually the third prison in which Nushawn, who was now going by one of his aliases, Shyteek Johnson, had been confined. The first was Clinton Correctional Facility, way up north on the outskirts of the Adirondacks. Then he was moved to Comstock Correctional Facility at Great Meadows, a couple of dozen miles outside of Albany. I had made arrangements to visit him at both of these places, but each time the plans had fallen through. The first time I learned just before I was to leave home that I did not have the proper approval for the visit. It took me a couple of months to get it, and I eventually did, but the day I was supposed to do the interview, Nushawn was again moved, this time to Auburn. I found it somewhat frustrating that they kept moving him, and it also seemed odd to me. Was it a practice in the New York State prison system to move prisoners around every few months? If so, that seemed contrary to establishing some sense of stability in the inmates' lives, and also an unnecessary expense for the state's taxpayers.

But New York taxpayers, not unlike the taxpayers of many states, seem perfectly willing to bear the costs of prison maintenance and construction. New York doubled the amount of money it spent on prisons in the 1990s, often at the expense of school construction projects, teacher salary enhancements, and state university budgets. To be exact, funding for prisons increased 76 percent from 1988 to 1998, while public university operating budgets fell by 29 percent. In fact, there was an almost dollar-for-dollar trade-off: prison operating budgets increased $761 million in the ten-year period, and state universities lost $615 million. Moreover, these figures do not include money for new prisons, which in the 1997–98 fiscal year was $300 million to provide for 3,100 prison spaces. In New York, neither political party has a monopoly on support for prison spending. Democrat Mario Cuomo was governor for six of the ten years in which prison budgets increased dramatically; Republican George Pataki was governor for four of those years.[25]

Most of the increased spending can be attributed to prison populations that ballooned as a result of the Rockefeller drug laws, which are some of the most draconian in the nation. A person convicted of selling two ounces or possessing four ounces of any narcotic receives a mandatory fifteen-year sentence in New York. As a result, the proportion of violent offenders in the state's prisons has actually declined, from 35 percent to 27 percent, and more than 60 percent of those sent to prison now have been convicted of nonviolent offenses.[26]

These trends have had disparate impacts on various population segments. Whereas annual prison commitments for drug offenses have increased by 93 percent for whites, they have gone up a staggering 1,615 percent for Latinos and a whopping 1,311 percent for African Americans. In fact, 90 percent of those in prison for drug offenses in New York are either black or Latino. In New York there are now more black and Hispanic prisoners than there are minority students at the state universities.[27]

On my first visit to Auburn, the prison authorities were expecting me; everything had been arranged in advance. I arrived a few minutes early and was told to wait. I went to use the rest room and, while in there, I heard some guards vigorously debating the merits of the new union contract they were being offered. Two were very much against it; a third was leaning toward support. A prison counselor then came down to escort me to the hospital, where Nushawn was being housed. He had been there for several weeks, as he had informed me on the phone, complaining rather bitterly about his situation. He wasn't there because he was sick, but because there was no a place for him in PC (protective custody). While in the medical unit, he was allotted no time out in the yard, and he had no access to a television set. One apparently needed to be sick to be given a TV. At the same time, however, he was being made to wear a hospital gown, which he found to be somewhat humiliating.

The counselor, who had worked in the prison for many years, seemed like a very decent person. He gave me some of the prison's history on the walk to the hospital building. Auburn had been an invention of the nineteenth century, the total institution, a result of the belief that criminals could be, with the proper routines, reformed and placed back into the world to carry on productive lives. Auburn's contribution to this particular ethos was what came to be called the "Auburn system." At Auburn, prisoners were required to meditate silently on the misdeeds that had brought them there. This meant that the prisoners were not allowed to talk at all, except for one hour on Sunday. A severer form of discipline would be difficult to imagine.[28]

As my guide noted, the twentieth century's approach to penology was quite the opposite. Now prisoners were encouraged to speak about themselves as much as possible. "Withholding" has come to be seen as a sign that an individual is harboring proclivities toward violence and other antisocial behavior. One needs to talk, to confess, in order to heal and become well. This, of course, reflects the broad trends in American talk culture, where therapies of communication seem to dominate the popular consciousness, from Jerry Springer's and Larry King's television shows, to celebrity tell-alls, to dozens of "how I did it" success and management guides that fill the shelves of modern bookstore cafés. But recidivism rates at Auburn range around 48 percent, so one has to wonder whether all that therapy makes a difference in the face of the forces that shape the lives of the inmates before, during, and after their periods of incarceration.

Nushawn was brought down to a TV room at the end of a hospital hallway, where I sat waiting for him. He was left unattended with me. Although at this point we had talked on the telephone probably half a dozen times, this was the first time I had actually met him face-to-face. Several things struck me. First, the pictures that were used to demonize him so effectively, such as the one used on the poster that Commissioner Berke circulated throughout Chautauqua County, didn't, as one might expect, do a particularly good job of capturing his likeness. Nor even did the video footage of the WPIX interview. One of the more common reactions many people had had to the Williams case was to wonder how such an unattractive fellow could have seduced such a reportedly large number of women, but having met him, I no longer thought it implausible that women might have found him attractive. In person, he seemed a far cry from the disheveled, semi-catatonic freak depicted in numerous photographs and news clips.

What also struck me was how young he was. He had already served three years in prison when we met, but he seemed like just a kid. He was twenty-three years old. When he first arrived in Jamestown, he was seventeen. When his picture was posted around the county, he had not yet reached twenty. Here I was sitting across the table from a supposed "monster," but he just struck me as a big kid who hadn't had enough sleep the night before.

We talked for almost two hours. I explained to him that I had indeed bought the junk food that he wanted, but the prison officials wouldn't let me bring it in with me, so I would send it to him via mail sometime in the next couple of days. That seemed to cheer him up a bit, but I could see that he hadn't had enough sleep and he was slightly bored by our conversation—perhaps he was disappointed now that we had finally met. I wasn't quite sure what he had expected me to be. Part of the problem was that we were covering much of the same old ground we had covered before. How did he get to Jamestown? Where did he live? Who did he know there? What kinds of drugs did he traffic in? He had told me much of his life story at this point, or at least as much of it as he wanted to divulge, and we didn't seem to be making much progress in getting beyond that.

I tried to suggest to Nushawn that he should get his GED while incarcerated, but he didn't seem interested. "I'm only going to be around for another fifteen years," he said. "Why's that?" I asked him, even though I knew it was a reference to his infection. "Because of the HIV," he responded. I suggested that fifteen years is a pretty long time, and that during that time new treatments could be developed that would extend his life further than that. Still, he expressed no interest in continuing his education, even though I knew him to be an avid reader and writer. All he wanted to do was to get out, first off the hospital ward and then out of the prison. I couldn't blame him, but I also thought that unless he found something else to do other than sell drugs, it wouldn't be very long before he would be right back in another prison. With a third felony, he would be sentenced to fifteen or twenty years the next time. (I later learned, when he was in a more positive mood, that he had already made substantial progress toward his GED, and he had completed all of the vocational programs that the prison had to offer.)

He told me that he planned to move to Ohio when he got out. He would stay with his aunt there. She had "lots of money." I remained skeptical, but let it go at that. I later learned that he did have an aunt who lived outside of Cleveland who ran a successful business and support groups for Christian women. She had, he said, agreed to put him up and employ him after he was released from prison.

Discussions of "social background" and crime are mostly now discredited in the popular press and intellectually unfashionable, but when you sit and talk to someone like Nushawn Williams and you see the bravado and the walls and the hurt, you can also see exactly how he ended up in prison. His mother lived on the streets, a sometime prostitute apparently hooked on cocaine. The last time he saw his father was through a glass divider at Rikers Island. He and his uncle shared confinement for a period of time at the Clinton Correctional Facility, until the uncle was transferred to Elmira. Only his grandmother had a life that was reasonably together, and it was she who had been there for him. "She would love me no matter what I did," he told me, and, having talked with her on the phone several times, I got the impression that she was indeed a kind and remarkable woman. Unfortunately, she died in the summer of 2000, leaving Nushawn with little to fall back on in the way of emotional support.

I asked Nushawn how his father happened to be in prison. "Drugs," he replied. Just about everyone Nushawn had ever known either was in prison or had been in prison, mostly on drug charges. Most of the prisoners in Auburn and all the rest of New York's prisons are there because of drug charges. The impact of the notorious Rockefeller laws had reached the point that even Republican Governor Pataki had expressed reservations about them. His tentative moves toward changing them met with resistance from both Republicans and Democrats in the state legislature. As a result, he dropped his proposals for moderate reform.[29]

The prison counselor who had brought me to the hospital unit suggested that there might be a conspiracy in all this. He had worked with hundreds of young men who had been in prison for sale and possession of drugs. "They could stop it," he told me. "The government could stop it. They could cut off the money flows. It takes a huge amount of money to transfer the amount of drugs that make it into this country each year." The way to stop it, he believed—probably correctly—would be to choke off the sources of capital. But of course going after capital flows would mean attacking people of a different class from those confined to the Auburn Correctional Facility. "There's simply too much at stake," he concluded. I thought he had a point.

One of the things that my talks with Nushawn Williams revealed to me was that it would have been a near miracle for someone like him to make it into the respectable middle class or even to become a member of the class of the responsible working poor. Even apart from questions of racism, which of course cannot be dismissed, the circumstances within which he operated were overwhelming: poverty, a broken home, surrounded by the temptations of the street. He was a restless kid with a lot of energy and ambition, but his energy was not directed toward positive things. When he was eleven years old he hung out with two older guys in his neighborhood who were robbing people with fake weapons. Nushawn would hold a phony AK-47. "I'll never forget that," he said. One can no doubt imagine why. Inevitably the group was caught, and the two older guys went to jail for armed robbery. One received fifteen years in prison. But as a "juvey" Nushawn was released into his grandmother's custody. What puzzled me was not that he was in prison, but that he hadn't been imprisoned previously for a truly horrible act of violence. As it was, he had pled guilty to small-scale drug trafficking, statutory rape, and reckless endangerment—felonies, indeed, but not of the highest order.

At some points in our conversation there were uncomfortable silences as we both searched for something to say. It may sound like a cliché to say so, but it was undeniable that we inhabited entirely different worlds. Our one common connection was Jamestown, New York. "I knew that whole town in and out," he told me. I had once felt the same way, but we no doubt had different, although not perhaps entirely different, ideas about what that meant. Despite differences in times and circumstances, we both knew the same streets, and we even had very distant connections to some of the same people. Nushawn liked living in Jamestown—he made this clear many times and in innumerable ways.

I could see that two hours was long enough for our first meeting. Nushawn seemed to be glancing down the hall as the guard prepared the lunch cart, and I told him it was time for me to go. They took him back to his cell. As I waited for my escort to return, I chatted with the guard a bit. He gave me some more insights into the prison guards' union's politics. It seemed that the guards had been working without a contract for some time. They had elected new leadership in the hopes of strengthening their position, but many felt that they were being sold out. The contract to which the new leaders had agreed wasn't much better than the old.

I asked the guard how long Nushawn would be confined to the hospital. He said that they thought he was going to be transferred out that day or the next. I asked why he needed to be in protective custody, and the guard told me that the other inmates "don't like rapists." This struck me as odd, because Nushawn had been convicted of consensual rape with a minor (statutory rape) and not forcible rape. The distinction seemed to be lost on the guard, and my guess is that it was lost on the other prisoners as well.

It turned out that Nushawn's transfers had been for his own protection. In each prison where he had previously been housed, he faced threats and was apparently in physical danger. The prison system authorities had been trying to find a place where he could be held safely. Nushawn had several times expressed to me his hope that he would be moved to a "minimum," and, in fact, there was some question about whether the nature of his crimes merited maximum-security status. His notoriety, however, did. It seemed likely that he would not be paroled before he had served at least his entire minimum sentence, and he would probably serve it in a maximum-security institution.

Nushawn had become a symbol both outside the prison and in. His crimes, although not particularly heinous by the standards of New York State maximum-security prisons, were no longer merely literal or legal facts, but had grown into a kind of urban legend. He was the "monster," the "AIDS monster." It wasn't what he was so much as what he represented. He conjured a primal fear of the disease, the virus. He wasn't just a victim or a carrier, he was the transmitter, a "devil incarnate" in the words of Health Commissioner Berke. He would take his place along with Dahmer, Gacy, and Berkowitz. He had terrorized a town and frightened a nation, and for that he would pay a hefty price.

Follow-Ups

My second visit to the prison came on the heels of the publication of Nushawn's second public interview, which was conducted by Lisa Kennedy for *Poz*, a magazine aimed, as the name implies, at an HIV-positive audience. Kennedy had flown to New York from Arizona for the interview, picked up Nushawn's grandmother, Elenora, and then driven up with her to Dannemora, where Nushawn was then being housed. Kennedy was one of the first journalists to speculate in print that Williams might not be simply a dangerous, oversexed thug. Although she agreed with the Chautauqua County Health Department's finding that Williams had been told about his HIV-positive status on September 6, 1996, she was also the first reporter to propose that there might have been a certain amount of denial involved on Williams's part, and that his "knowing" transmission of HIV involved a very complicated sense of what "knowing" can mean. Kennedy was also perceptive enough to pick up on Williams's statements about his own contraction of HIV; he had contracted the virus through sexual contact with a woman, he said, and that woman had come to visit him in jail on the day he was sentenced. He had forgiven her. "The message of this reminiscence is apparent," Kennedy noted in her article on Williams. "I've forgiven, he seems to be saying, I've moved on. So forgive me and let's move on." Kennedy portrayed Williams as a complicated figure, one whose "through-the-looking-glass ethics . . . capture the morality of the streets." He had defined himself as one who hadn't made the same mistakes as his mother, a crack addict, or his fathers and uncles, who received long prison sentences for very violent acts. He had, Kennedy suggested, "figured out one side of the equation, how to do better than the people around you, but not the other side: how to do right, period."[30]

I talked to Kennedy about Williams while she was in the process of interviewing him and writing her article for *Poz*, and I found that she and I had many of the same reactions. We both saw Nushawn as smart, manipulative, and occasionally demanding, but also as vulnerable and even likable. Like me, Kennedy continued to keep in touch with Nushawn, extending a professional relationship into something else not entirely defined. Nushawn, however, was upset by some aspects of Kennedy's article. For example, Kennedy quoted one of the girls who eventually brought charges against Nushawn as saying that she "wanted him to die." Nushawn claims that his girlfriends still hold him in affectionate regard, although testimony against him stands as hard evidence that this is not the case for at least two of the girls with whom he had encounters. Kennedy also quoted Nushawn's grandmother as saying that she had kicked him out of the house for selling drugs on the street corner in their neighborhood, and Nushawn was angry with Kennedy for using the quote. His version is that he left the Crown Heights neighborhood of his own free will in pursuit of the adventurous life that eventually led him to Jamestown.

It was a beautiful upstate day the second time I went to Auburn, but I was a bit apprehensive about the visit. I had arrived in town early to buy two cartons of cigarettes, Newport 100s, at the local supermarket to take to the prison. I couldn't send Nushawn cigarettes while he was at Clinton, but the rules were different at Auburn. Lisa Kennedy had agreed to pay for one carton, and I sprang for the other. I hadn't realized how expensive cigarettes had become—forty dollars a carton with sales tax. The woman behind the counter commented on it. I had to agree that smoking had become an exceptionally expensive habit, and I was glad that I had given it up a very long time ago.

My trip this time was not institutionally sanctioned in the same way as the first. This time I had no tape recorder, no escort to the part of the prison where Nushawn was being held. I was just a visitor, and I wasn't exactly sure how the system worked. The guards, however, were friendly and accommodating. I felt a little odd laying down a plastic bag full of cigarettes after filling out the package form, but the guard didn't seem to take much notice. After I filled out a couple more forms, they brought me through the metal detector, searched me, stamped my hands to indicate that I wasn't an inmate, and led me into the visitors' room. I was one of the first folks there.

The guard indicated that I should take a table up front. "We like to keep a close watch on the PC prisoners," he told me. I felt a little conspicuous, but otherwise things seemed fine. The room was well lit, with numerous windows. It had an institutional feel, but apart from the guard uniforms, it was vaguely reminiscent of my high school cafeteria.

It took about half an hour for the guards to bring Nushawn over. He looked remarkably different than he had the first time I'd seen him. He was alert and cheerful. I told him that I'd brought the cigarettes and that he'd get them as soon as the package cleared. I thought that the cigarettes were his main concern, given that he had called me three times in the previous week to remind me about them. He did indeed seem pleased, and he filled me in on the workings of the prison's cigarette economy. He said that he was perfectly willing to smoke cheaper, nonbrand cigarettes, but he wanted Newports because that's what the "high rollers" liked. He could trade some of them for his own cigarettes and still have some left over to trade for other things that he wanted, such as stamps. Moreover, the commissary was open only every other week, and some inmates were impatient. He could "give" packs to the impatient ones and demand double on the return once the commissary opened. He was able to keep his supply of cigarettes stable or even growing because of his talent for trade. The entrepreneurial skills that served him as a drug dealer in Jamestown carried over into the more licit activities that were endemic to prison life.

Unlike the first time we met, Nushawn seemed eager to talk on that second visit. He told me he had been too tired to talk the first time. He was clearly much happier being in the PC unit than he had been in the hospital. His medical condition was good: there was no active evidence of the virus. He was stable, and the side effects of his medications were tolerable. He looked good. I noticed none of the puffiness that is often associated with the drugs used to treat HIV. He said that he was taking his meds "every day." It occurred to me that, in an odd way, he had been lucky to end up in jail. Before his arrest, he had obviously been in denial about his HIV status. It is unlikely that he would have sought medical treatment (even though it was available in Chautauqua County). Over time, his health would have deteriorated until the problem was no longer deniable, at which point treatment would have been less effective. The prison medical staff had found a treatment regime that worked for him, and he was required to follow it regularly. It probably saved his life.

We talked about a variety of topics. One of the most important to Nushawn was his autobiography, a book that he had been working on since he had been placed in prison in 1997. He told to me that his "whole life" was in it, and that he wanted to publish it. He was looking for me to help. (He also seemed to be looking for some avenue around New York State's

"Son of Sam" law, which forbids anyone convicted of a crime to profit from writing about that crime or otherwise selling the story. I was skeptical and told him that I wouldn't violate any laws for him.) I told him that I knew from personal experience how difficult it is to get a book published, and that I surely couldn't make any promises. I didn't want to dampen his enthusiasm or to snuff the spark that was pushing him to write, but at the same time, I thought that he needed a dose of realism, something he did not always respond to well.

It did seem that even over the relatively short time that I had been in contact with him, something had changed. He seemed much more positive about his situation than when we had previously talked in person or on the phone. He could perhaps begin to see the light at the end of the tunnel, as he was eligible for parole in less than a year from that point. He recognized the change in himself. He said that he was now meditating and "laying back." But most of the change he attributed to the reading and writing he was doing. When he was first incarcerated, he told me, he had received numerous tickets (disciplinary write-ups), mostly for stupid things, such as disobeying simple orders. He just did this out of spite. But he hadn't been written up in more than two years, and he understood what he had to do to keep himself on the up-and-up.

He talked quite a bit about books that he had read. He was very interested in the works of those who, like himself, had inhabited an underground world of drugs, sex, and crime. Iceberg Slim was a particular favorite. He could identify with these authors, not only as people who had lived the street life, but as people who had transformed themselves through writing. I encouraged him to keep reading and writing. He had definitely found something to respond to in the world, a potential path out of the self-destructiveness that had to that point marked his young life.

His autobiography was not the only thing that he was working on. He also wrote rhymes, something that challenged him but that he considered himself to be good at. He had won contests at other prisons. He said that the person who had sparked his interest was Tupac Shakur, whom he had met on Rikers Island in 1993, when Nushawn had been awaiting trial on a murder charge (of which he was eventually acquitted) and Tupac was in for rape. (During this prison stay someone suggested that Tupac contact Suge Knight. On his release, Tupac hooked up with Knight and began an association that further contributed to his image as the premier gangsta rapper of the twentieth century, but that also eventually may have cost him his life.)

Although hardly a rap critic myself, I was impressed by one particular rhyme that Nushawn gave me. In the rhyme, titled "If I Were a Gun," he takes the role of a gun used by "mad thugs" with the power to "move crowds making every ghetto foul." In the course of the rap, the gun moves from expressing feelings of power and rage to a sense of weariness and even remorse, tired of being used "for blacks to kill blacks." It refuses further participation. Finally, as one would-be killer pulls the trigger, "I didn't budge sick of the grudge sick of raften the next man's grudge." As the gun's owner is shot by a "newer me in better shape," the gun expresses relief, but short-lived: "Now I'm happy until someone else grabs me damn." The rhyme is clever, and well executed, and it includes a kind of moral. It doesn't romanticize violence, unlike some rap. If the test of rap authenticity is to have lived the life of the streets, then Nushawn Williams is certainly "real." Few of the many talented street kids who have such experiences, however, are able to parlay them into lucrative recording contracts.

Troubled Times

The first week in August 2000, I received a call from Lisa Kennedy. Nushawn had been put into keep lock (cell confinement) for forty-five days, and he had asked her to call me to let me know not to send any packages, such as books, because he wouldn't be able to receive them, although letters were still allowed. I asked her what had happened, and she said that he had "failed a urine test." Traces of marijuana had shown up in his urine. She didn't know much more about it than that. I couldn't help thinking that maybe he had traded the cigarettes that I'd given him for some pot, smoked it, and failed the drug test, but things may have been more complicated than that.

The confinement turned out to be only twenty-five days, and I spoke to Nushawn again at the end of August. He explained his version of what had transpired. He said that some fights had broken out between some black and Hispanic gang members, and the two groups had ended up positioned at either end of the cell block. Acting as a mediator, he had been moving back and forth between the two factions, trying to get them to work things out. While this had been happening, the Hispanic inmates had been smoking pot. HIV medicines, he contended, made his body especially absorbent. Once the ruckus was brought under control, the guards required everyone involved to take a urine test. He was tested along with the others, and his sample turned up positive for marijuana. Hence the keep lock.

I wondered if this incident would affect his "good time." Could it affect decisions about his parole or his conditional release (CR) date? He didn't seem to think so. He'd had a good record in the prison for a long time. He had a fairly good relationship with the guards—at least they weren't out to make his life any more difficult than it had to be. He told me of another inmate, however, who had hooked a water bag into his underwear and squirted it into a jar when he knew that he was going to be tested. When the guards discovered this, and that he tested positive for an illegal drug, they had the inmate charged not only with violations of the prison rules but also with drug possession. For this he was criminally prosecuted and sentenced to an additional fifteen to twenty years. But, Nushawn contended, this other guy was someone the guards did not like. When that was the case, they could find ways to help you extend your stay in the prison.

Nushawn's grandmother had died at the end of July, and when I visited Nushawn a few days later, he was keen to talk about her upcoming funeral. The members of his whole "crazy" family, he said, were now vying for the little wealth that his grandmother had, primarily a brownstone in Brooklyn and a large, recent-model Lincoln Continental. I wondered how his grandmother had acquired this stuff, given that she didn't seem to have a job. He told me that she had helped to run numbers in the neighborhood for years. Although I had talked with her on the phone a couple of times, I had never had the chance to meet her, and I regretted that. She had apparently lived a fairly wild life until the day she died of a massive heart attack at the age of eighty.

Nushawn was deeply affected by her death. She was the one member of the family with whom he had pretty constant contact through his life, even while he was in prison, and who had given him some means of both financial and emotional support over the years. Only a week before she died, she had told him that she'd taken a job and that she would be able to send him more packages of the junk food that he coveted.

In the end, Nushawn never made it to New York for his grandmother's funeral. He had been operating under the assumption that he would be escorted there by prison guards, which is apparently not an uncommon practice in such circumstances. In fact, I had spoken to prison officials myself who had told me that he was slated to be taken to New York for the funeral. His request was denied at the last minute, however. He was told that his high-profile status made escorting him potentially risky for the corrections officers involved. People were gunning for him, and the guards would be at risk of being caught in the crossfire. "Are there people out there who really want to kill you?" I asked him when we discussed this. It didn't seem likely to me, but it was not altogether implausible either, I supposed. Some of the girls with whom he had been involved had expressed deep-seated and understandable resentments toward him, but as far as I knew no direct threats had ever been made. "They just want to show me that I'm in prison," he surmised, "that they've got the power."

My own experiences with the guards at Auburn were generally not unpleasant, except for one occasion. During an October visit, one of the guards, someone with whom I had not interacted previously, was clearly in a foul mood. The guards' union had signed a contract, and the guards at the prison entrance were vigorously debating it. None seemed particularly happy with what they'd received, although some seemed more dissatisfied than others. This one particular guard had apparently decided to express his dissatisfaction by treating the visitors rudely. I had become comfortable enough with the routine by that time that his behavior didn't especially bother me. After all, there wasn't much he could do to me, and if he did become abusive, there were plenty of witnesses, and I had access to resources that most prisoners' families don't.

Stories from the Streets

In the many conversations that I had with Nushawn Williams, we often returned to his life in Jamestown. He was never the least bit shy about discussing his experiences there, even when what he told me amounted to admissions of crimes for which he could conceivably still be prosecuted. He knew that I was writing a book, and he was sharply aware of his status as a figure in the popular culture. Although he was displeased with some of the specifics of what had been said and written about him, he also seemed to enjoy the attention. Sometimes I think that he overestimated his own notoriety, but I found that to be understandable. New York's governor had, after all, gone out of his way to condemn Williams for his actions (before he was convicted of any crimes). Who could blame Nushawn if he had a somewhat inflated sense of his own infamy?

His belief that people were listening to him encouraged him to tell me about his adventures in the underground so that I could tell others. He also, I think, sometimes believed that he might cash in on his notoriety, if he could find a loophole in New York's "Son of Sam" law and get his story published as a book (or screenplay). The glamorization of "gangstas" and thugs in the popular culture no doubt contributed to his belief that he had important things to say. Moreover, he had a historian's impulse to create a record. He wanted the "truth," or at least his version of it, to be told. Perhaps others might learn from what he had to say, although the moral component (as in "others can learn from my mistakes") did not seem to be crucial to him. He simply felt compelled, as so many have, to report on the facts of his life. He would leave judgments about its meaning and value to others.

Over time, Nushawn left quite a record, not only in terms of our conversations but in terms of all of the writing that he did in prison, a large portion of which he gave to me. I was always impressed with his memory and the clarity of his recollections about his life before prison. It was difficult for me to gauge what he might do when released, but other than his being sorry for having transmitted HIV to some of his partners, he never expressed regrets about the life he had lived. It was simply his life, and he left little doubt that he had enjoyed much of it. Sometimes when I talked with him or read what he had written, I felt as though I was entering a kind of parallel universe, a place with a set of moral rules that were almost completely unfamiliar to me. He would talk with nonchalance about stealing, selling drugs, and violent acts. I would not, however, consider him to be a vicious person. Violence for him was sometimes a necessary means to an end, but it was not an end in itself. He was pragmatic. He also followed a loose code of conduct that helped him organize his moral universe when he had difficult decisions to make. The central principle in that code of conduct was loyalty. One's primary obligations were to family and friends; those outside of the immediate circle were less worthy of consideration. A couple of stories that Nushawn told me illuminate his hierarchy of values. The first involved another dealer named Bags. The other involved someone named Jason.

Bags

Bags was Nushawn's sister's boyfriend. Nushawn did not especially like Bags, but he treated him with a modicum of respect because of Bags's relationship with his sister. Bags was arrested for drug possession in Jamestown, and one of his cohorts, Disco, was supposed to bail him out. One of the practices of people in the drug trade, Nushawn told me, is to have a little "side dish" of money put aside for bailing people out of jail when they get arrested. But Disco, who was responsible for the bail money in this case, had not kept it. There was a reason: Disco had decided that he wanted to move in on Bags's franchise, and he was not unhappy that Bags was in jail. Nushawn rounded up the money from a bail bondsman and managed to get Bags released. In the meantime, Disco persuaded Nushawn's best friend, Maleek, to go with him to Bags's apartment to steal all of Bags's stuff. This included his car, his police scanners, an entertainment center, and a large stash of drugs, including several pounds of marijuana and about sixty thousand dollars' worth of crack. Once Bags was released and discovered what had occurred, he figured out who had done it, tracked Disco down, and shot him in the back. Disco lived, but he lost the use of both of his legs. Bags escaped to New York.

Nushawn had not been a central player in any of this, but when his "little brother" Maleek became involved, he had to choose sides. He had conflicting loyalties. Bags was his sister's boyfriend. But his best friend Maleek, who had brought him to Jamestown, had turned on Bags. Nushawn decided in favor of Maleek—Bags wasn't "blood." His sister could, he decided, "always find herself another boyfriend."

He went to New York to avenge Disco's shooting. He found Bags in his Brooklyn apartment and hung out with him for a bit, feigning continued friendship. Then, knowing that Bags would fall asleep after smoking pot, Nushawn offered him some. They smoked quite a bit, and, as predicted, Bags fell asleep. Nushawn then proceeded to steal everything from Bags's apartment, he told me with relish, including a number of guns, a large amount of crack, some marijuana, a considerable pile of cash, and a diamond-encrusted golden crucifix that was hanging from a chain around Bags's neck. Bags, apparently unwilling to take Nushawn on, never attempted to avenge the theft. Nushawn didn't bother him again. He had settled the score and satisfied Maleek that Bags had paid an appropriate price for what he had done to Disco.

When Nushawn finished telling me this story, I was curious about what happened to Disco. Had he remained in Jamestown? Yes, Nushawn told me. "He's got a little store. He's in retail." I found this to be fairly improbable. Very small retail stores were no longer viable in the area, especially clothing stores. The Wal-Marts of the world had driven them all out of business. "Retail?" I asked. "Yeah," he said. "He brings up stolen clothes from New York and sells them. . . . Retail."

Jason

Nushawn's story about Jason was more disturbing. It involved an act of violence that had become almost legendary in Jamestown. Nushawn's drug-dealing friend Bobo believed—wrongly, as it turned out—that another dealer in town, Deshawn, was fooling around with Bobo's girlfriend. Bobo talked Jason into going to Deshawn's apartment with several weapons, including a .347 Magnum, to "scare him." When Deshawn came to the door, Bobo immediately opened fire, hitting Deshawn in the chest. The impact was so great that Deshawn was knocked across the room and out a second-story window. He died almost immediately.

Nushawn had no knowledge of any of this until after it was over. Frightened and unsure about what to do, Bobo and Jason went to Nushawn for help. He told me that he didn't have much sympathy for either of them. For one thing, Nushawn had had no grudge against Deshawn. He also thought that what they had done was stupid. Nushawn never expressed the slightest bit of possessiveness to me regarding any of the women he knew. He slept with a lot of women, and he had no qualms about the women he slept with sleeping with other men (which was, of course, part of the problem). It was hard for him to understand how someone could shoot someone else out of jealousy. Still, Nushawn felt an obligation, especially to Jason, to help. After Bobo, Jason, and Nushawn met in Nushawn's apartment, Bobo tried to leave town and was caught by the police. He was eventually tried for murder and received a sentence of fifteen years to life. Nushawn and Maleek helped Jason get out of Jamestown by driving him out of the city in the trunk of a car. Having caught the trigger man, Bobo, the police were satisfied that they had solved the crime. Jason went to Virginia, and Nushawn later heard that he had been killed there by the Jamaican mafia. "All these guys were Jamaican," Nushawn told me. They were "vicious." "But he got what was coming."

In the hours of conversation Nushawn and I shared, he regaled me with many stories of the thug life in Jamestown. Seldom if ever did he express regrets about anything he'd done. Jamestown was a place where he made money, found women, and had fun. There was something of an inconsistency between the obvious enjoyment that these memories stirred and what seemed to be his sincere desire to straighten himself up once he gets back out in the world. He was firm about his determination to find a legitimate job and avoid the temptation to traffic cocaine when he is released. Lisa Kennedy and I sometimes wondered, however, whether he recognized how difficult it is to achieve a position of economic security in the U.S. economy. For someone with his skill level, lack of experience in the workplace, felony convictions, and health problems, the world of work offers few opportunities. Low pay and dismal working conditions are probably the best he can hope for. The well-paid, low-skilled assembly-line jobs of a previous era no longer exist. When he was angry or frustrated about prison life, Nushawn would sometimes express his frustrations by implying that when he is released he won't play it straight, that he'll get ahold of a pile of money and buy himself a new car, some clothes, and a nice apartment. I could sympathize with his frustration, but the way he talked made me realize how easy it might be for him to turn frustrations outside the prison into activities that will land him right back inside.

Nushawn has plenty of street smarts, and he impressed me, in general, as a very intelligent young man. But I was sometimes struck by his lack of knowledge about the world of discipline and work. His willingness and ability to repudiate a social and economic system that had forsaken Jamestown gave him a kind of freedom that was one of the things that made him attractive to the city's young people. In time-honored fashion, he played the role of the outlaw who takes what he wants from a corrupt and broken system. Whether he can survive in that system playing within its rules is a question without a clear answer.

Setbacks

By the fall of 2000, Nushawn was starting to see his eventual release as a real possibility. His parole hearing date was set, he said, for February 2001. He was somewhat optimistic about being released because he had observed a number of other inmates being released from Auburn prison. It seemed to be a place that people did leave. He wasn't counting on receiving parole, but he thought that with his "good time" he would be released on his CR date in 2003. Even being incarcerated for two or three years seemed tolerable. Although he was still, of course, HIV-positive, he was not experiencing any symptoms of AIDS. He looked quite healthy, in fact, and his infection was something that we talked about very little—not, it seemed to me, because he was in denial, but because it appeared to be under control. The potential for AIDS was clearly not in the forefront of his mind as it had been only a few months previously, when he expressed concerns that he might die in jail.

I had agreed to write a letter to Nushawn's parole board. I didn't have any reservations about this; given the crimes of which he had been convicted, I thought his sentence was unusually severe. Had he been convicted of any of the numerous crimes he told me about committing, he would have spent considerably more time behind bars, but that is no doubt true of many people in this world, from many walks of life. I thought that he deserved another chance. Release with parole oversight under the supervision of someone in his family, some time in a halfway house, and slow reintegration into civilian life seemed like his best chance to remain out of prison. If he were simply to be given a bus ticket back to New York and a few dollars, there would be no telling what might happen, but some of it would likely not be very good for him or others with whom he might come into contact.

In January 2001, Nushawn received word from prison authorities that he would have his parole hearing in July, rather than in February, as he had been anticipating. He told me that at one time he had had in his possession a sheet of paper showing April 1 as his earliest possible release date, but he had sent it out to have it verified by someone and it was never returned. He had no proof that he had been told he might be released by April 1. He thought the prison authorities were "playing with his time." I had no way to check this. A July hearing date would make it possible, although I thought highly unlikely, that he could be released on parole in September.

In the meantime, Lou Schipano had moved into the cell next door to Nushawn's. Lou was something of a jailhouse lawyer. He had looked into Nushawn's case and concluded that there had been an error in his original sentencing, that he had been given a year beyond what he had actually deserved. Lou sent me a copy of the brief he had composed, something he had obviously spent a good deal of time researching and writing. "Nushawn Williams' case was a 'miscarriage of justice' that is clearly on the face of the record and very sad," Lou stated. [31] He contended that Nushawn had entered into a plea bargain for his drug charge before authorities in New York had known about potential charges arising from Nushawn's activities in

Chautauqua County. The plea specified that he would be sentenced to one year in prison, with mandated drug treatment upon release. Prosecutors withdrew the agreement, however, once word came down from Chautauqua County that there might be other charges. With Nushawn's guilty pleas on counts of selling drugs, reckless endangerment, and statutory rape, the agreement was nullified. Nushawn had a right, Lou argued, to have "specific performance" of the plea agreement—that is, to have his original plea reinstated. If that were done, given the configurations of his present sentence, the sentence would be reduced by one year. It seemed like a reasonable argument to me, and Lou had included legal citations to support it. With the help of a very good lawyer, Nushawn might have a chance in court, but given his position as a high-profile indigent prisoner, my guess was that there was virtually no chance that anyone would take Lou's brief seriously.

Lou convinced Nushawn, however, not only that he could have his sentence reduced by a year, moving his conditional release date to July 2002, but that he could sue the state for a civil rights violation and, as a result, claim a sizable damage award. The latter seemed especially unlikely to me, but Nushawn was very enthusiastic about the possibility. This struck me as a not entirely bad thing, because it focused his attention on legal issues rather than his present circumstances. I was concerned, however, that he might get his hopes up and have them dashed when the lawsuit didn't move forward as he had anticipated. He was so convinced that he would receive a multimillion-dollar damage award that he granted me power of attorney, giving me the legal authority to look after his money while he was still in prison. I wasn't entirely keen on this idea and I told him so, but he insisted.

In March, Nushawn went back under keep lock. Apparently there had been a fight. One of the inmates had attacked a transvestite on the block and beat him up pretty badly. The injured prisoner was taken to the hospital, and the rest of the prisoners were confined to their cells. No guard had been present when the fight broke out. According to Nushawn, after all the inmates on the block were put back into their cells, a guard came and told him that Nushawn had been determined to be the responsible party. Two guards had signed the ticket, even though neither had seen what had happened.

Nushawn claimed that several other inmates vouched for him, that he was not involved, but if two guards signed a ticket, there was little that could be done to counter it. The inmate responsible for the fight, who inhabited a cell next to Nushawn's, asked if he should come forward and confess. Nushawn told me that he was ambivalent about this. According to Nushawn, the other inmate was crazy, and he would have a hard time taking the confinement of keep lock. Nushawn said that he didn't care about being locked up for twenty days, seven of which had already passed at the point when I visited him. He was concerned, however, about what impact the ticket might have on his "good time" and hence his conditional release date. He didn't want to have his stay extended because he'd taken the blame for something he hadn't done. He was supposed to have a hearing about the matter, but that had been postponed. If there was no hearing within fifteen days, the charge would have to be dropped and he would have to be released from the lockdown.

The hearing never came. When the fifteen days expired without one, Nushawn assumed that he would be released. Instead, one of the corrections officers came to his cell to tell him that he, Nushawn, had refused the hearing. This, according to Nushawn, wasn't true. Refusing the hearing meant a thirty-day confinement. According to Nushawn, when the officers came to his cell, they were calling him the "AIDs monster" and a "shit bag." They told him that they weren't going to feed him or give him any showers, and that they were going to watch him "die slowly." If that didn't work, they were going to "beat the shit out of [him] and take [him] up to the box" and "kill [him]." Nushawn said that he had "seen too much" at Auburn, seen too many prisoners beaten by guards. He believed the guards thought he posed a threat to them. He worried that if he wasn't moved to another facility, he might be killed. But by the time I got Nushawn's letter explaining this, he had been released from the lockup. He said that he never had his hearing.

Once this incident passed, life returned pretty much to normal for Nushawn. I hoped that would be the end of it. I had no independent means of verifying any part of his story. Clearly, however, real conflicts were occurring between Nushawn and at least some of the guards. Nushawn's version of events was not entirely unimaginable to me, but then neither was an entirely different one in which he had done the things of which he was accused. I was never able to talk to the guards, and I had no means of independently confirming or disputing any of the things Nushawn said.

In the meantime, the press continued to cover Nushawn's story. Nushawn told me that he was receiving letters from a television station in Rochester that wanted him to give an interview. I told him that I thought doing so would be a very bad idea. Clearly, he was not, to say the least, "mediagenic," and he did himself more harm than good when he exposed himself to media coverage. Moreover, I thought it very unlikely that a local news program would give him a fair shake. Such outfits are generally most interested in ratings and would have economic incentives to vilify him. He agreed with me and decided that he would not do any more television interviews.

When Nushawn came out of keep lock, Lou, the jailhouse lawyer, was

gone. He had been transferred to Attica. This made it much more difficult for Nushawn to communicate with Lou about Nushawn's potential
lawsuit, and as a result, Nushawn became increasingly frustrated with his
situation. One of his responses to his frustration was to make increasing
demands on me. He wanted me to call the prison warden to look into how
he was being treated. He wanted more junk food and more tobacco. He
wanted me to buy him fifty dollars' worth of reggae tapes. He was calling
me two or three times a week, each time asking for something else.

During a visit in April 2001, I began to ask him in more detail than previously about the visit the health department official had paid him when
he was living in Jamestown. He became upset by this, even though I wasn't
accusing him of anything, and we had a fairly animated argument. He
threatened to walk away. By the time I left, we had talked things through,
but I sensed that there was lingering acrimony on his part, and perhaps
there was some on my part as well. I had to admit that Nushawn was starting to get on my nerves. It seemed that I was getting on his nerves, too.

On my way out of the prison after I visited Nushawn in May 2001, I
picked up a copy of the hundred-plus-page manuscript he had written, the
first installment of "The Life and Times of Nushawn Williams," as he liked
to call it. There were two things in these pages that particularly caught my
attention. The first was Nushawn's description of what happened when
Chautauqua County Health Department employee Pat Johnson found him
in Jamestown and encouraged him to visit the department's Jamestown
office for some tests. According to Dr. Berke, in August 1996, more than a
year before the Williams story broke, Nushawn was tested as part of "some
other STD evaluations" that the health department was doing. HIV testing
was included as part of these evaluations. Nushawn's written recollections,
however, focus on his being asked to submit to an HIV test. According to
Nushawn, this is what happened:

> When I went back to the apartment, I opened the door, my people was up
> cooking and some of the girls was already eating, so one of my friends told
> me that some lady came by the house asking for me. I asked him who. He
> said he'd never seen her before. I said okay, if she comes here looking for
> me tell her I'm on 8th and Cherry. So I gave my little man Ace some money
> so he could go get some sneakers he wanted to get. Then me and Jason
> and Maleek went back out the door. As I was talking on the corner, I seen
> some lady walking to my apartment door. I never seen this lady before, so
> I waited to see if she was looking for me. Maleek and Jason sat in the jeep
> with the door open. I guess my friends told her I just walked outside. She
> came around the corner. I got out of the jeep. She walked up to me.
>
> She asked if my name was Face. I said yes, why? She said can I speak to

you? She said her name was Pat, and she just needed a couple of minutes of my time. I told her I had to take care of something. Besides, I don't even know you or why you are coming to my house asking for me. She said if you just come and give me an hour of your time, then you would know what it's about. It's very important. I said okay. Give me a minute. I told Jason and Maleek, I'm going to meet them by Misty's house. Take the jeep over there. Maleek said, what's up Face? I said I don't know yet. But I'll meet you by Misty's house, alright? So they drove the jeep to Misty's house. I got in the car with the lady they called Pat. She took me to the health center. I'm asking her, what am I doing here? She said it's only going to take a few minutes.

She took me to the health center, and right into her office. She started asking me questions about females that I dated that were coming to the health center with health problems. She said a lot of the ladies that have been coming here have said they had sex with me. She asked me if I had sex with a lot of females. I said yes, but what's your point? I don't see anything wrong with that. She said, do I always have sex with the same girls? I said no, I meet girls all the time, and a lot of them look for love and affection. She asked me how many ladies I thought I had sex with. I said a lot. She asked did I use condoms on all of the ladies that I been with. I said, some I did, some I didn't. She said, can I remember any of them girls' names I had sex with? I gave her a list of girls names. [According to Dr. Berke, Nushawn gave twenty names at this point, which Dr. Berke described to me as "very good partner notification."] She started asking me questions about some of the girls whose names I gave her. Then she asked if I used drugs. I said, I smoke weed and every girl that I had sex with smoked weed. What's the point? She said, did I ever think about HIV and getting HIV from one of these ladies I had sex with? I was like no. A lot of ladies I dated tell me not to use a condom. They want kids from me. So I must say that I never really thought about it, because me and a lot of the ladies I dated was real close. But what are you getting at? Are you trying to say I have HIV? She said she didn't know. That's what she was trying to figure out.

She asked, do I want to take an HIV test? She said she would be in contact with me. I said alright and left. At that time, I went back to doing what I was doing before I met her. I didn't feel like I had HIV. I felt good. So I went back to selling crack and making money and meeting different ladies.[32]

There's no defensiveness here, just a simple statement of fact. "I went back to what I was doing before," which just happened to be "selling crack," "making money," and "meeting ladies." And why not? Nushawn said that he "felt good," and he "didn't feel like" he had HIV; that was enough for him. HIV, to his thinking, was a sickness, something that would make him feel lousy. How could he have it? He was completely forthcoming to Pat about having sex with many women because he didn't see anything wrong with that. He gave a list of names because he had nothing to hide. That was the shape of his eighteen-year-old world.

Nushawn signed his birth name to the consent form to have the HIV test done and dated it August 15, 1996.[33] According to the health department's write-up of the test results (a copy of which Nushawn eventually secured from his lawyer and in turn gave to me), Nushawn's HIV-positive status was established on August 26, 1996, but no immediate follow-up was done. Coincidentally, however, Nushawn was arrested in Jamestown on September 3, 1996, for unauthorized use of a motor vehicle and was placed in the Chautauqua County Jail.

Dr. Berke and Nushawn disagree about what happened next. Dr. Berke says that when Nushawn was arrested on the automobile theft charge, he was "posttested." On September 6, 1996, according to Dr. Berke, Nushawn was given the entire "posttest story"—that is, he was told, as Dr. Berke stated in an affidavit filed as part of the health department's effort to release Nushawn's name to the public, that "engaging in sexual relations with others would put those individuals at risk of contracting the infection."[34] According to the affidavit, Nushawn said at the time of his notification that "I am going to fuck as many women as I want and there is nothing that you can do about it," but the person to whom he said this is not specified, and neither Dr. Berke nor anyone else from the county repeated this publicly as events unfolded. In his "request for particulars," Nushawn's lawyer, William Cember, asked for all of the county's written documents giving evidence that Nushawn had been notified of his condition. In response, the prosecutors provided the consent form for testing and the statement of results.[35] They provided no written documents showing that Nushawn was notified of his HIV-positive status.

When I spoke with Dr. Berke, he indicated that after Nushawn was notified, "he left. . . . I forget if he went to Rochester, somewhere in the system and then was released. We lost him. I mean there was nothing to do. But at that time he'd given us twenty names." Nushawn actually spent about a month in the Chautauqua County jail before he was sent to Rochester to face a previous charge of drug possession. Given the circumstances that had led the public health officials to him in the first place, and given the statements that Nushawn is said to have made when he was notified of his infection, it is a little surprising that health department staff didn't attempt more follow-up. As far as I can tell, Nushawn received no counseling beyond the initial "posttest story" alluded to by Dr. Berke.

At any rate, the Rochester charge was dismissed, and Nushawn was released after two days, at which point he went back to New York City. He spent the next ten months traveling back and forth between Jamestown and New York, doing what he had done previously, selling drugs and pursuing women. It was during this period that the Chautauqua County Health Department discovered the HIV "cluster" and eventually determined Nushawn to be the common denominator, resulting in the public release of his name and picture and the subsequent media panic.

Nushawn still denies that he was told that he was HIV-positive while he was in the Chautauqua County Jail, although his guilty plea on reckless endangerment charges serves as a legal admission that he knew about his status. A trial would presumably have revealed in more detail exactly what transpired on September 6, 1996, and how Nushawn reacted to the news. For a period of time while I was working on this book, I was not entirely sure what to believe about the events of this particular day, given the absence of a written record. The critic's role is, after all, to question the official story. Although the legal issues are moot, I remained curious about what happened. Among the papers that Nushawn gave me was a copy of his psychiatric evaluation conducted in February 1998. In it, Dr. Alexander Bardey states, "Mr. [Williams] related that he was told he was HIV positive approximately one year ago while serving time briefly. He added that he was unsure as to whether this was true or not, as he never actually felt sick."[36] This seems to refer to Nushawn's fall 1996 jail time. Nushawn's statement to Dr. Bardey constitutes an admission, but it also reveals a kind of denial not uncommon among HIV-positive individuals when they are first apprised of their status.

Denial has been a feature of the AIDS epidemic since its beginnings. As HIV infection rates have increased in various parts of the world—the former Soviet Union, parts of Africa, and Asia—communities and public officials in those areas have often denied the scope of the health problems they face. In the United States, denial of the possibility of infection has been especially acute among African Americans, many of whom associate AIDS with white gay culture and some of whom, for understandable reasons, are suspicious of the white medical establishment.[37] Even within the savviest elements of the gay community, such as in San Francisco and New York, denial is evident in a reemerging willingness to take risks with sexual behavior. According to a recent survey of gay men in San Francisco, the rate of condom use "every time" an individual has anal sex fell from 69.6 percent in 1994 to 49.7 percent in 2000. In addition, there is some debate in the gay community concerning how much responsibility HIV-positive individuals have to notify sexual partners of their status.[38]

Given the layers of denial that still attach to HIV infection, it is certainly not surprising that a young black man from New York City, held in an upstate county jail, might doubt the results of an HIV test reported to him by institutional authorities with whom he had no previous positive contact. I would not suggest that this constitutes an excuse for irresponsible behavior, but one has to wonder about the track that this case took: a promiscuous and HIV-positive young man was arrested, notified of his status, released, and then ultimately rearrested and prosecuted for his sexual behavior. One cannot help but wonder whether a more effective intervention on the part of public health authorities at a crucial point in this course of events might have resulted in a less tragic set of long-term outcomes.

Postscript

In the course of my discussions with Nushawn about the possibility that he might be paroled, he gave me the name of his aunt Unique, who lives in Cleveland and owns a business of some kind. He told me that she might be willing to take him in when he is released. Unique Kalia, it turns out, runs a church-related support group—"women helping women," as the message on the answering machine puts it. After I talked with her, I began to feel somewhat better about Nushawn's chances on the outside. She told me that she and her family are prepared to do everything in their power to help Nushawn once he is released. She seems to be the one solid support in Nushawn's otherwise dysfunctional family. She has already taken in other members of the family, including Nushawn's sister's baby. Things are difficult for Unique. Three of her immediate family members are in jail. Yet she is determined to hold together as much of the family as possible, and she has expressed a strong sense of obligation to Nushawn. I gave her the telephone number for the parole board, so that she could inform the board of her possible involvement in Nushawn's future. She told the board that when Nushawn is released, he will have a job and a place to stay.

Nushawn stopped calling me for a while in the summer of 2001. He'd found a new girlfriend. Earlier in the year, he had asked me to post his name on some Internet bulletin boards. He gave me a list of Web addresses that he'd found in *Poz* magazine and other places. Some were for people interested in corresponding with prisoners, and some were for people who are HIV-positive. As he requested, I put his name on three or four lists, and as a result, he started corresponding with several people. He told me about them during my prison visits. I was at that point very glad that he had found people to communicate with other than me and Lisa Kennedy. He became increasingly friendly with one of his correspondents, a woman named Jessica, and his phone calls to me became less frequent, at least for a while.

During the first week of July, I received a phone call from Jessica. Nushawn, she said, had been having trouble again with the guards, with one guard in particular. There had been some kind of a scuffle and Nushawn had had his phone privileges suspended. Jessica also said that she had received a letter from someone she thought might be a guard. It had been post-marked in Brooklyn; the return address was hers. The letter writer's stated purpose in contacting her was to warn her that the prisoner with whom she had been corresponding, Nushawn Williams, had AIDS. (Ironically, Jessica herself is HIV-positive.) I found this level of harassment, if truly the work of a prison guard, leveled against a person outside the prison to be rather appalling. I called Prisoners' Legal Services and the New York State Department of Corrections to find out how Nushawn could file a grievance against any guards who might have been involved. PLS promised to send a lawyer to the prison to talk to Nushawn once the agency received his complaint in writing. The woman I talked with at the Department of Corrections in Albany said that Nushawn should go through the prison grievance process, but if he found that to be inad-equate, he should write directly to the commissioner of corrections. I sent these instructions, along with the appropriate names and addresses, in a letter to Nushawn.

A few days later, in the evening, I received a phone call from Nushawn's aunt. She had heard from someone that Nushawn had been stabbed and was badly cut on his face and back. Another inmate had used the sharp edge of a tin can to do the job. After Nushawn was cut, the guards had re-fused to help him because he is HIV-positive and they were worried about possible transmission of the virus. He had lost a good deal of blood and was now in critical condition in the prison hospital.

The next morning I called the prison and spoke with a woman on the hospital floor. I asked her if Shyteek Johnson (Nushawn's prison name) was on the floor. She said that she couldn't divulge information about a prisoner on the phone. Inmates had phone privileges, she told me, so if they wanted to call friends or family members about their medical con-ditions, they could do so. I asked her, "What if an inmate was so badly injured that he couldn't use the phone?" She asked for the name again. When I repeated it, she said that it didn't "ring any bells." Was she saying that that particular inmate wasn't on the floor? No, she said, she wasn't saying *that,* but the name I gave her was unfamiliar. It suddenly became clear that there had been no stabbing; everything Unique had heard was wrong. I confirmed this a week later when I visited Nushawn. He was as perplexed as I was about the story. Still, I was concerned about all the bad things circulating around Nushawn two weeks before he was to have his parole hearing.

Over the relatively long period during which I had fairly constant con-tact with Nushawn, I often wondered what the nature of our relationship was. When I first requested an interview, he asked for one hundred dollars. It constituted a clear and open exchange. He knew that I wanted something, information. He, in turn, wanted money. We both were entirely aware of the nature of the relationship. I had no reservations about paying for the interview. It was a compact that we both entered into freely and equally. Over time, however, the relationship evolved.

The phone number of someone who will take your collect calls and show an interest in what you have to say is a scarce commodity in prison. In New York, most of the prisons are located upstate, and most of the prisoners are from the downstate metro area. Inmates would love to talk with family members and friends who can't make the long trip to visit, but the families of most prisoners are not affluent, and the inflated cost of collect calls is often too heavy a burden for them. It was a cost I was willing to bear, at least to a point. For one thing, Nushawn continued to be a valuable source of information, not only regarding specific events that had happened in Jamestown, but also about the life of a high-profile prisoner in a maximum-security prison. In spite of my occasional frustrations with him, I was intrigued by much of what Nushawn told me. I was particularly impressed by the contrast between his extensive knowledge of life in the underground, something about which I didn't have much of a clue, and his naïveté regarding some of the basics of life in the everyday world of business and work. He helped sharpen my understanding of the diversity and complexity of life across American race and class divides. I also began to appreciate the difficulty that inmates have in adjusting to life outside when they leave an institution. Nushawn, for example, is sure to find few legitimate pursuits that will give him the same income and control over his schedule that he had while selling crack cocaine. I am not sure he fully realizes this.

On July 31, 2001, Nushawn went before the parole board. Things did not go particularly well for him. He and I both understood that it was unlikely that he would be paroled his first time before the board, but his difficulties went beyond a simple denial. For one thing, although none of the girls presumed to be infected by him testified against him at the hearing, County Attorney James Subjack wrote a letter to the board "vehemently protesting an early release." Subjack's reasoning was that "the law made it very difficult to prosecute and he got away with a lot." Subjack stated that he'd had a difficult time prosecuting the case because "only five individuals were willing to come forward to even speak with law enforcement officials, including myself," and "of the remaining four, only one victim wished to pursue charges against the defendant."[39] One possible reason for the county's inability to bring more charges was that some of the women involved with Nushawn did not see his behavior as criminal and so did not

Of Myths and Monsters ▼

want to pursue criminal charges against him. Still, Subjack made it clear not only that he wanted parole denied on this particular attempt, but that he wanted to see Nushawn serve his entire twelve-year sentence.

Subjack also noted the difficulty he had in convicting Nushawn on any serious charges. Given the construction of New York State criminal statutes, reckless endangerment was the most serious offense he could hope to charge Nushawn with. Yet immediately after the case concluded, the county attorney brought his concerns before the state legislature, and that body refused to pass an HIV-specific criminal transmission statute. Given that the legislature, by its inaction, had seemingly endorsed the idea that conviction for HIV transmission should be very difficult, the fairness of using that difficulty as an argument for Nushawn's continued confinement was at least somewhat questionable.

More problematic for Nushawn than the county attorney's letter, however, were his own statements at the parole hearing. As the transcript of the hearing that was released to the press shows, he continued to deny that he knew he was HIV-positive when he'd had sexual contact with his many girlfriends, and he also stated that he did not know that the thirteen-year-old girl he'd had sex with was underage at the time. Neither of these statements qualified as an admission of guilt or a statement of remorse, the kinds of words that would indicate to parole officials that Nushawn was being rehabilitated. Instead, both showed the limitations of his understanding of what the system expected him to do and cast some serious doubts on his judgment. As the parole board put it, "During the interview you were devoid of virtually any appropriate insight into your behavior."[40]

The parole board also took Nushawn's behavior in prison into account, characterizing him as a "problem prisoner."[41] As a writer for the *Buffalo News* put it, "At Auburn, Williams, 24, has been charged 14 times with rule violations, including using drugs, fighting and disobeying orders from guards. The violations have forced officials to place him in special 'keep lock' facilities where he is confined 23 hours a day; of his days in prison, 291 have been spent locked in his special cell or in one of the special disciplinary units."[42] On the face of things, this was an accurate statement, but I couldn't help but think that there was more to the story than that.

At the end of August 2001, I received a letter from Nushawn informing me that he had been transferred from Auburn to Southport Correctional Facility in Pine City, New York. I was pleased to hear that he had been moved from Auburn, a place where he had encountered numerous problems. At the beginning of September, I received a letter from the state corrections commissioner himself that stated that Nushawn's complaints about his treatment had been investigated, and the investigation had found that there was no merit to any of the charges he had made against the guards at Auburn. Commissioner Goord also noted that Nushawn's transfer to Southport should make any issues that he may have had with guards at Auburn, as he put it, "moot." I would never have any firsthand insight into what happened at Auburn, but I was interested to see whether Nushawn would continue to be plagued by disciplinary problems at the new facility.

4

State Power, Law, and the Sequestration of Disease

The demonization of Nushawn Williams in the media may seem to be but a blip on the pop-cultural radar, but it has broad implications. It augurs historical transformations that may be changing the relationship between disease epidemics and the social and political forces organized to manage them. The formulation and application of a punitive model of disease containment through the media may mark an intensification of the processes by which media are used as mechanisms of social control. The Williams case, considered within a larger frame, encourages a reinterpretation of the state's role in controlling disease, a reinterpretation that casts doubt on the standard narrative of the progressive nature of historical change in the West.

The narrative of Western progress has multiple manifestations. Common to most versions, however, is the idea that the modern period, associated with the liberal political theories of Locke and Hobbes and with the scientific theories of Bacon, Galileo, and Newton, marks the advancement of rationality over the forces of superstition that dominated European society in the medieval period. The emergence of science, the discovery of natural rights, and the eventual organization of democratic governments vindicate the idea of the West as a civilizing force. Control over various diseases represents an important part of this narrative, as the discoveries and practices that evolved out of Western medicine, such as the use of anesthesia, antibiotics, and sophisticated surgical procedures, are evidence of the value of scientific progress.

Law has an important place in this narrative as well. In the liberal narrative of law, formalized legal rights and practices evolved from the common law practices of premodernity and were eventually transformed (sometimes through the use of revolutionary violence) into systems for the protection of individual rights and the control of state power. For example, in the United States the rights stated, but originally unrealized, in the Declaration of Independence were eventually turned into legal and social practices through a slow but steady process of interpretation and application.

Against this narrative, I propose a counternarrative that is both a specification and a revision of the one stated above. An investigation of the social control of disease reveals not so much a steady expansion of individual rights as it does the emergence of various systems of social control that exercise power in diverse ways. In the premodern period, the social control of disease was primarily *ritualistic*. The defining features of this period are attempts by European societies to control contagious diseases such as leprosy and bubonic plague. The period is marked by highly developed rituals sporadically practiced in social systems on the verge of collapse. These ritualistic practices represented attempts to provide explanations for and assert cultural control over events, such as disease outbreaks, that were otherwise entirely inexplicable. Although sometimes expressed as legal rules, the controls were not organized into highly formalized systems of law. The diseased were often confined because of their diseases and punished for them, but these practices cannot be considered a system of criminal prosecution of the type that seems to be evolving now.

Medieval practices eventually gave way to modern attempts to control disease through the implementation of formal legal rules and the application of medical discoveries attributed to positivist science. These *legalistic* attempts to control disease, although organized more systematically than premodern rituals, were often unsystematic in actual practice. In the modern period, a legal discourse emerged that was premised on a balancing of individual rights and community interests. The community would be protected from contagion, when possible, but the rights of the infected could not be entirely disregarded. Individual rights to "due process" promised comprehensive, rational, and fairly applied legal rules. In actual practice, however, legal determinations were often inconsistent, sometimes ignoring the rights and interests of the infected or potentially infected, and at other times taking their claims seriously.

According to narratives of Western progress, the passage of time yields increasingly satisfactory realization of legal and political rights. If that general premise is true, we should now be observing an increasingly rational connection between the threat of disease outbreaks and legal attempts to manage or control them. Legal rules should, over time, become more finely calibrated in their recognition of the relationship between disease threat and the necessity to assert social controls. But that, I would argue, has not occurred. Rather, the Nushawn Williams case suggests that legal repression has reasserted itself. Society now shows less willingness than in the past to find a balance between the rights of the infected and the interests of the community. A criminal model of disease control is evolving that may be without historical precedent.

The current situation could be characterized as both postlegal and hyperlegal: hyperlegal because formal law not only exists but at times seems utterly pervasive, and postlegal because law's meaning and legitimacy are subverted by institutional forces beyond legal control. Rights discourse, for example, is now ubiquitous. Everyone claims rights. Yet, in many respects, unequal treatment under law is apparent. The verdicts in the Rodney King beating case, errors in death penalty cases, O.J.'s acquittal, Clinton's impeachment—all suggest (in different ways to different people) a legal system driven as much by celebrity as by fairness. Legal rules may be pervasive and rights claims may be manifold, but legal outcomes in high-profile cases, those that epitomize the "rule of law" to much of the public, are driven by images. In fact, if the modern period can be characterized as dominated by the legalistic and bureaucratic, our postlegal period is dominated by the *imagistic*. Media images invade and transform legal rules. Various social forces attempt to marshal these images toward supporting their interests and the assertions of their rights, but the process by which this unfolds is chaotic, offering scant evidence of a steady march toward the expansion and fair implementation of rights. The state, as repository of legal authority, is delegitimated in the process.

Disease and the Emergence of State Power

Leprosy is the quintessential premodern disease, and its hold on the Western imagination is strong.[1] It has a prominent place in various biblical narratives. Moses is said to have separated the lepers from the unafflicted. The Book of Leviticus provides for their exclusion: "He shall live alone. His dwelling shall be outside the camp" (13:46). In the New Testament, Jesus' compassion is prominently signified in his willingness to minister to lepers, that most excluded of all groups. And, as Allen notes, "lepers haunted European memory long after the disease had died out in most parts of Europe."[2]

Contrary to the image that may exist within the popular imagination, lepers were not, with some notable exceptions, treated harshly in the Middle Ages.[3] Ritualized practices existed for their exclusion from the society of the healthy, but although these may have been widely invoked, systematic efforts to implement them were difficult to organize, and thus they were sporadically administered.

Lepers often underwent a symbolic "death" that preceded their removal from the rest of society. A leper would be required to stand in a grave in a cemetery while three spades of dirt were put on his or her head, symbolizing death and burial. The priest then said, "Be dead to the world, be reborn to God," as the leper asked to "be reborn on the final day." The infected person was then required to put on a costume that indicated his or her status as diseased and was given a bell, horn, or clapper to use to warn healthy people of his or her approach. The leper was then led to a hut, generally on the edge of town, and given utensils, alms, and a cross. The priest would ask those gathered not to injure the leper but to have "remembrance of the human condition and the formidable judgment of God" and "to provide liberally for [the leper's] needs."[4]

Later, as the treatment of the mentally and physically ill became more institutionalized, lepers were confined to asylums, where they were required to take monastic vows of poverty. Because there were no remedies for leprosy, lepers went to these hospitals less for treatment regimes than for the Christian "charity" they provided—shelter, food, clothing, and protection from vice (no drinking, gambling, chess, or sex with other inmates was allowed).[5] Under French law, lepers were denied the legal right to own property.[6] Lepers admitted or confined to hospitals were expected to stay there until they died.

Enforcement of the complex of laws regarding the treatment of lepers in medieval European society was, however, quite lax. As Brody notes, "Although lepers were the victims of constant persecution, abuse and vilification, in general their mobility was not hampered and they were not effectively isolated from society. A mass of evidence suggests that in practice the sequestration of lepers was not rigidly enforced."[7] Lepers were often allowed to leave the houses where they were confined, and the legal processes required to sequester them were complicated and difficult to implement.[8] As the disease peaked in the twelfth and thirteenth centuries, so did attempts to separate lepers from the rest of the population. But even these attempts had uneven impacts. Lepers were, for example, banned from Paris in 1321, 1371, 1388, 1394, 1402, and 1403, which suggests, as one observer has noted, that "the bans cannot have been very effective."[9]

The lax enforcement of the laws pertaining to lepers was due partly to the contradictory ways in which lepers were perceived, on the one hand as sinners deserving of punishment and on the other as having been "given special grace by God."[10] Moreover, premodern European legal systems were permeable and inconsistent in the application of legal rules generally. Medieval laws concerning leprosy were also not strongly enforced in part due to the nature of the disease. Leprosy acts slowly, and it was sometimes difficult to distinguish the infected from the healthy. And although it is an endemic disease that sometimes appeared in outbreaks, it did not ravage entire communities as plague would eventually do. The existence of ritual also no doubt eased people's fears regarding the potential spread of the disease and lessened the necessity for authorities to enforce rigid controls.

Plague was different. Its impact on European society cannot be overstated. It created economic and social catastrophes on a level that were previously unknown. Death was swift and horrible. When an outbreak occurred in a given locale, 70 to 80 percent of that area's population could die within four to seven days.[11] As the result of an outbreak that occurred in 1348, one-third to one-half of the population of Europe and the Middle East died.[12] Such massive population loss led to famine, as there were not enough people available to plant and harvest sufficient crops. Cannibalism was not unknown. Governments and court systems collapsed under the weight of the pandemic. When plague turned up in a town, those with means—that is, the administrative leadership—fled, so that "the administration of justice [became] impossible and no one [could] obtain his rights."[13] In Italy, there was "neither 'order nor justice and no one to administer justice.'"[14] Florence became a "vast oversized and empty urban shell."[15] The entire social order unraveled in numerous places. The feared *monatti*, or grave diggers, gained notoriety for violating female corpses.[16]

Plague had a tremendously disruptive impact on the worldview of medieval Christians. The ritualistic practices of sequestration organized around leprosy were insufficient to deal with it. Believers sometimes concluded that divinity had been overthrown by wickedness, that God had deserted the world and sovereignty had shifted from heaven to hell. The Luciferians, a sect of mendicants, taught that God had usurped heaven and that he would someday be replaced there by its rightful ruler, Lucifer, whom they worshipped.[17]

The breakdown of social order, religious beliefs, and ritualistic practices led to a search for scapegoats. According to Nohl, there was "an incapacity to believe that so uncanny a disease as the plague could be attributable to natural causes," and that led to "the fateful misconception" that it was artificially produced.[18] The belief that humans acted deliberately to spread plague was not without foundation. Some did intentionally infect others.

In some cases, those who were infected preferred not to suffer alone. Some held the mistaken belief that they could rid themselves of the infection by passing it along to others.[19] Sometimes infected individuals passed on the plague out of the desire for revenge or out of spite. Nohl reports the case of a man who fastened a piece of plaster covered with pus onto the peephole of his neighbor's door. "When he thrust his head out to see who was there it stuck to his beard without his noticing it," until his wife saw it and asked about it, at which point "both were seized with terror."[20] Then there was the case of the scholar Hemkengripper, who, upon learning that he had been infected by a contaminated manuscript sent to him by his great adversary Zahnebrecker, offered to meet with his enemy for a reconciliation. Upon meeting, they embraced and Hemkengripper kissed Zahnebrecker; both died within several hours.[21]

Many held to the belief that groups of malcontents were using secret and magical powders and poisons to infect whole villages or districts. Those unfortunate enough to be accused of such deeds were often tortured on the rack and with other devices until they confessed, at which point they were usually either hanged or burned, or both. Rumors abounded throughout Europe that bands of provocateurs were traveling about smearing windows, walls, doors, and church pews with pus and poisons in order to generate outbreaks. Although little evidence exists regarding any basis in fact for such beliefs, the deep paranoia these stories engendered turned neighbors against neighbors and family members against one another.[22]

After the Reformation, so-called artificial generation of plague was sometimes blamed on Lutherans, but more often it was attributed to Jews. Traditional Jewish sanitary practices encouraged the drawing of water from running streams rather than from the often contaminated public wells that were primary sources of various kinds of diseases. This generated the suspicion that Jews were avoiding wells because they had poisoned them.[23] The destruction of Jews thus became justifiable as a matter of theology and self-defense. In 1348, in Germany, a Jewish physician was tortured on the rack until he "confessed" that he had been spreading plague. This resulted in a wave of attacks against Jews that persisted for several years.[24] The entire Jewish population of Strasbourg was marched to the local cemetery and thrown into a massive flaming pit that became their common grave. The town's council then declared that no Jews would be allowed to live there for two hundred years.[25] Hudson relates that at Muehlhausen "all of the Jews were slaughtered, at Nordhausen at least part of them." At Basle, the town council demanded the burning of the town's Jews and forbid Jews to settle there for a period of two hundred years. "At Esslingen the whole Jewish congregation were burnt in their synagogue,"

Hudson notes. "At Nuremberg, all the Jews were murdered, as they were at Egar, Gotha, Eisenach, Dennerstaedt, Kreuzburg, Arnstadt, Ilmen, Nebra, Wiehe, and Frankenhausen." The list goes on. Similar treatments were meted out in Spain and Italy.[26]

Yet, although plague reinforced superstitious beliefs and practices, anti-Semitism, and general paranoia, it also undermined the authority of the Catholic Church and could be considered to be one of the primary forces that impelled Europeans into modernity. Egon Friedell has asserted that "the year of the conception of modern man was the year 1348, the year of the Black Death," and A. L. Maycock has suggested that "the year 1348 marks the nearest approach to a definite break in the continuity of history that has ever occurred."[27] The authority of the church was undermined because representatives of the church responded poorly to the needs of plague victims and provided them with little in the way of either reassurance or explanation. Not only were the clergy unable to help, but they too were infected in large numbers, indicating a mortal vulnerability that undermined ecclesiastical authority. Moreover, the deaths of many members of the church hierarchy left a void in leadership. For example, 94 of 450 officials of the Avignon pontifical court died in 1348 and 1349, and 207 of 375 bishops also fell victim to the epidemic. This depletion in the church's ranks resulted in higher proportions of young, inexperienced, and less authoritative priests, which affected the organizational structure of the church as a whole.[28] At the same time, the rough beginnings of modern medical science can be seen in attempts to control plague, as physicians and others tried desperately to find ways to combat the spread and effects of the disease. For example, intensive study of the plague led to a number of seemingly reasonable, but ultimately false, conclusions, such as that the disease was spread via eyesight. Other more sustainable ideas also arose, however, such as those regarding immunity and the concept that certain persons might be "carriers."[29]

Plague spreaders were not usually disciplined through the application of formal legal rules. In fact, the absence of rules and ritualistic practices may have encouraged the public to single out various individuals and groups arbitrarily. Yet, although the breakdown in social order created opportunities for violence, it also allowed resistance to medieval hierarchies. In England, for example, when so many had died that the fields were not being tilled, political authorities began to concede to peasants' demands for land redistribution. Various waves of plague over several centuries helped to undercut the stability of the feudal system. The peasant revolt of 1381 in England can be at least partially attributed to the plague that had arrived three decades earlier. Indirectly, plague had resulted in peasants' "tast[ing] a freedom never savored before."[30]

Plague also encouraged the introduction of public hygiene practices designed to protect communities from the recognized contagiousness of the disease. The first such measures to be enforced with some regularity were instituted in Italian cities in the 1340s. These required, among other things, that all meetings dealing with plague issues be open to the public, so as to prevent corruption; that rules be drawn up concerning the disposal of bodies; and that those infected be sequestered from the rest of society.[31] In Florence, eight of the city's most respected citizens were chosen to exercise control over matters related to plague; some scholars have deemed this office the first European department of public health.[32]

Embargoes were set up in various cities beginning in 1348. In 1377, the first actual quarantine measures were instituted in Ragusa, although, according to McNeil, the "idea of quarantine had been present as early as 1346," drawn from biblical stories regarding the separation of lepers. Plague sufferers were initially treated as "temporary lepers."[33] Quarantine rules required that persons seeking to enter a city from areas of known infection be sequestered outside the city walls for a period of a month. In 1383, Marseilles, perhaps the French city most ravaged by plague, established a forty-day detention period. The term *quarantine* is derived from this French practice. Violations of quarantine rules were punished by fines.[34]

That formal quarantine rules were promulgated does not mean that they were either followed or enforced with regularity. Enforcement was difficult and expensive, and as a result quarantines rules were often ignored or allowed to lapse as soon as the immediate threat of outbreak seemed to have subsided. Moreover, sanctions for violations of quarantines were relatively mild, generally restricted to fines and almost never including imprisonment. The laxity of enforcement is one reason the actual value of these quarantine measures is still the subject of intense debate among historians. If quarantines were ineffectively administered, how can we know their practical value? One cannot prove a negative. How can we know whether the absence of an outbreak indicates the effectiveness of quarantine measures or the intervention of an indefinite number of other social and medical circumstances?

It could be argued, then, that the late-medieval and early-modern periods were marked by the breakdown of ritualistic mechanisms for dealing with disease and their slow replacement with more formalistic and scientific measures. But the process was an uncertain one, with the emergence of formal, bureaucratic mechanisms of control open-ended enough that there was wide latitude for resistance against them.

The Search for Balance: Formal Assertion of State Power over Disease

The "contagion/anticontagion" controversy erupted early in the nineteenth century, not long before Louis Pasteur's discoveries led to the dominance of "germism" as the explanation for most disease transmission. Anti-contagionists sought environmental explanations for the presence and transference of diseases. Anticontagionist Charles MacClean, for example, contended that plague resulted from certain atmospheric conditions and an "inequapable" atmospheric state. According to this theory, people con-tracted plague or other diseases independent of one another; cases were connected only in the sense that the individuals involved were subjected to the same external elements. The contagion/anticontagion controversy is important because of the role it played in arguments regarding the value of quarantine.

By the eighteenth century, practices of quarantine were well established in both North America and Europe. In the American colonies, quarantines were first used in the seventeenth century. Massachusetts passed a compre-hensive quarantine law in 1699.[35] Some of the earliest regulations were de-veloped in response to yellow fever. A number of quarantine hospitals were built throughout the colonies in the middle of the seventeenth century.[36] In the eighteenth century, the scourge most feared was smallpox. During the smallpox epidemic of 1730–31, Massachusetts passed a law that required any household where someone was infected to display a red cloth. In 1742 this rule was extended to cover all contagious diseases, and eventually the state was given the power to quarantine the sick in specific hospitals.[37]

Sometimes quarantines were written into local ordinances and thus made more permanent. In Virginia, for example, the colonel of North-ampton County proclaimed that no person would be allowed to leave his or her home until thirty days after he or she had been infected by smallpox, "least the sd. disease should spread by infection like the plague of leprosy," and those who ignored the rule and "beast like" acted contrary to it "may expect to be severely punished according to the Statute of King James."[38] Shipping was a frequent quarantine target, and boats were routinely isolated for ten to twenty days prior to entry into the port towns of Massachusetts, Connecticut, and New Hampshire. Quarantines were mostly considered a local matter, but in 1796, the U.S. Congress passed the first national quar-antine law in response to a yellow fever epidemic. This law gave the presi-dent the power to aid localities in quarantine efforts. Thereafter, the federal government assumed a role in enforcing maritime quarantines.[39]

Quarantines were often unpopular because they were considered to be arbitrary and ineffective, and they caused inconvenient disruptions in people's lives. Although in some places, such as Boston, they were applied in a systematic enough fashion to have some effect on the spread of small-pox, in general "their application in the colonies was so irregular, tenta-tive, and inconsistent that the benefit to the public health must have been negligible."[40] Much of the resistance to quarantine measures came from commercial interests, which had much to lose from restrictions on commercial activity. Business interests not only resisted quarantines but often sought to deny the presence of disease or epidemic in their local communities. As Cassedy notes, "Since trade was easily discouraged by the presence of communicable disease, business interests tended to try to suppress all news about epidemics of smallpox, yellow fever, or cholera in their respective communities, and to resist the imposition of quarantines."[41] Public health departments were reluctant to challenge powerful local business interests, which were more often concerned with a favorable public image than with efforts to improve sanitation and control disease.

Anticontagionism provided scientific justification for the elimination of quarantines. Contagionism and quarantines were linked to superstition and the ecclesiastical authority of the Catholic Church. MacClean, for example, denounced the practice of quarantine as resting on "a purely imaginary foundation"; quarantine was a "popish strategem, bolstered by absolutism in church and state, it was everywhere an instrument of tyranny." "The whole issue of quarantine," in fact, "hinged on contagionism."[42]

Contagionists fought back, and some, such as London physician Augustus Granville, attempted to establish links between the movement of goods and people and the emergence of disease outbreaks, in an attempt to show that quarantines had been successful in excluding plague from certain areas in England.[43] But quarantines challenged social forces that extended beyond the scientific and medical academies. London business interests brought considerable pressure to bear to loosen quarantine regulations, which they saw as an impediment to trade. Although quarantines had "aroused resentment and even boycott" throughout European history, anticontagionism gave antiquarantine forces additional ammunition.[44] Resentments against quarantine came primarily, although not exclusively, from the commercial class. As the power and prestige of business owners grew in the nineteenth century, scientific analysis came to accommodate their very practical interests. The debate regarding contagionism, then, was never a strictly "scientific" debate; rather, it hinged on its connection to quarantine. As Hudson notes, "Anti-contagionist ranks were joined by a rapidly expanding group of merchants and industrialists for whom quarantine meant loss of money, coupled with what was perceived as stifling bureaucratic domination."[45] Thus it was a coalition of merchants, industrialists, and liberal (antistatist) physicians who pressured the French Academy of Medicine in 1828 to repeal the quarantine law of 1822.[46]

Under pressure from free-trade ideologists and anticontagionists, the British Parliament began to unravel its web of quarantine regulations in the first half of the nineteenth century.[47] Baltimore significantly weakened its quarantine laws in 1808. Benjamin Rush, a vocal and articulate defender of anticontagionism, helped to influence the president of the Philadelphia Board of Health to undercut enforcement of local quarantine regulations.[48] The city government of Boston abolished that city's board of health during the same period in order to do the same.[49]

The appearance of Pasteur and the advent of "germism" in the middle of the nineteenth century helped generate a shift to a more individualist and medicalized view of disease transmission.[50] Anticontagionism was almost entirely discredited. This shift had important consequences. For one thing, it removed the onus of responsibility for sickness from the soul or character of the infected. Such a construction of disease probably, as Rosenberg notes, "offered more comfort than the traditional option of seeing oneself as a reprehensible and culpable actor."[51] The shift to germs as the explanation for much sickness reinforced the growing secularism of the nineteenth century, emphasizing the individual nature of disease infection and narrowing causal explanations for it. Germism did not, however, remove the "environment" as an important factor in causing disease. The "vapors" and "effluvia" that were central to the explanations of anticontagionists were replaced with a discourse that incorporated elements of germism into environmental explanations. Thus the concepts of "cleanliness" and "sanitation" began to mark the language of the new environmentalists. We now associate this language with the emergence of a modern public movement. With it, the formal recognition of legal rights in law related to quarantine began to emerge in greater detail.

Medicine as Social and Political

The concept of germism helped to reinforce the idea that quarantines were useful, because if one could point to specific agents of transmission, one should be able to curtail disease by isolating those agents. When Italian city-states established administrative boards to oversee quarantine rules in the sixteenth century, the boards' jurisdictions extended beyond the cordoning or controlling of various spaces. The boards examined food and water supplies and regulated burials as well as the activities of beggars and prostitutes.[52] This recognition of the connections among medical, social, and political factors helped to provide the foundations of what would emerge first as "social medicine" and then as "public health" movements.[53]

The concept of "social medicine" can be traced to Germany and the writings of Rudolph Virchow. In a report to the French government on a typhus epidemic in Upper Silesia in 1848, Virchow associated the spread of the disease with the impoverished and miserable conditions under which the population had lived. He surmised that medical treatments alone would be of limited use in controlling such outbreaks. Political action was the mechanism he recommended for making medical progress. As he put it,

State Power, Law, and Sequestration

"My medical creed merges with my political and social creed." After participating in the March Days in Berlin, which had been inspired by the uprising and establishment of the commune in Paris earlier that same year, Virchow wrote, "Medicine is a social science, and politics nothing but medicine on a grand scale."[54]

Although Virchow was an early proponent of social medicine, he was not alone in his thinking. As Rosen notes, social medicine was a reaction to the social problems generated by the Industrial Revolution, which "led various investigators to study the influence of such factors as poverty and occupation on the state of health."[55] Advocates of social medicine collapsed distinctions between social and medical sciences and concluded that to improve the health of a community or a nation, one had to understand the nature of that locale's social problems. Thus advocates of social medicine developed an intense interest in statistics. According to Rosen, Virchow "conceived the scope of public health as broadly as possible, indicating that one of its major functions was to study the conditions under which various groups lived, and to determine the effects of these conditions on their health. On the basis of this knowledge it would then be possible to take appropriate action."[56]

Just as the scope of explanation and investigation of causes and conditions expanded, so did the potential boundaries of medical practice. For advocates of social medicine, the practice of medicine "must be social as well as medical."[57] Social medicine thus provided for an amplified role for government in two ways. First, government would have an obligation to intervene to attempt to change those conditions—poverty, poor hygiene, dangerous working conditions—that contributed to declines in the nation's health.[58] Physicians and other advocates of public health became involved with the movement to improve the labor conditions of industrial workers. This included regulation of hours worked as well as the prohibition of child labor, the establishment of standards for ventilation in the workplace, and restrictions on the use of toxic chemicals.[59] At the same time, however, the state would have the right and duty to intervene to curtail the liberty of individuals in cases of disease transmission and mental illness.[60] In other words, the evolving public health movement justified an expansion of the state's obligation to protect the diseased and infirm as well as to control them.

Havelock Ellis articulated these twin aspects of public health in his book *The Nationalization of Health,* published in 1892. He noted, optimistically, that "we possess to-day a closer grip of the conditions of health than has ever been possible before; we now realize that these conditions are of a complex character, and we are able, to a large extent, to unravel their complexity to show clearly what a man should do who would live a healthy life." He associated drugs with barbarism and "the medicine man's incantations." For Ellis, the "key word of our modern methods is not *cure* but *prevention*." The best shield against illness, according to Ellis, is "fresh air and reasonable garments, cleanliness in the full sense of the word, pleasant work and varied exercise, wholesome and abundant food, the healthful play of the secretions and excretions."[61]

To facilitate the advancement of such conditions, authorities needed information. Thus the Infectious Diseases Notification Act was a crucial aspect of the nationalization of health. This law permitted "notification and isolation of infectious disease," allowing officials to "to limit epidemics, to define the areas in which they are found, and to trace the insanitary conditions by which they are produced and favored."[62] It encouraged, in other words, a significant advancement of state power.

The failure of the revolutions of 1848 did not mean an end to public health movements. In England, C. Turner Thackrah's 1931 treatise *The Effects of Arts, Trades, and Professions on Health and Longevity* had an important impact on factory reform movements. Henry W. Rumsey outlined a public health program in which medical personnel would act as "sanitary advisers" to the poor, visiting them in their homes, describing the effects of alcohol, and discussing the importance of cleanliness, diet, and the education and raising of children.[63] The practice of public health became "a matter of nothing less than the suppression of prejudice, error and ignorance, the encouragement of salutary labor, the development of a sense of dignity on the one hand and the conquest of cupidity, and injustice on the other."[64]

The European social health movement had important impacts on the U.S. public health movement. In 1920, Yale professor Edward Amory Winslow defined public health as

> the science and art of preventing disease, prolonging life, and promoting physical health and efficiency through organized community efforts for the sanitation of the environment, the control of community infections, the education of the individual in principles of personal hygiene, the organization of medical and nursing service for the early diagnosis and preventative treatment of disease, and the development of the social machinery which will ensure to every individual in the community a standard of living adequate for the maintenance of health.[65]

A broader mandate for medical practice is difficult to imagine.

The progressive impulse to use the powers of the state to generate social health must be seen as a positive historical development. In both Europe and the United States, this impulse was closely connected to reform movements advocating better working conditions, improved housing, and the provision of medical services for the poor. The social medicine movement in Germany influenced Bismarck's decision to provide a system of social insurance. Yet this expansive vision of what constitutes public health must also be evaluated within the broader ideological currents of the late nineteenth and early twentieth centuries. Notions of sanitation, cleanliness, and purity were deeply embedded in emerging doctrines of public health. Public health officials and social reformers felt compelled to clean the detritus from the body politic. This meant going into the factories and slums to take care of the injured and diseased, but it also meant keeping the social body free of elements that undermined its purity. The late nineteenth century saw the rise of public health movements as well as the emergence of genetic science and evolutionary theory. The progressive impulse to improve social welfare was connected with the reactionary impulse to discipline or eliminate those elements seen as "infecting" the social organism. Thus the expansion of state power associated with public health movements overlapped with and often reinforced racism, anti-immigrationism, and eugenics movements.

Germism competed with and sometimes reinforced evolutionary theory, which was intimately connected to developing notions of "race." As the concept of public health was expanding, some people were making connections among disease transmission, genetic makeup, and racial classification.[66] For example, some asserted symbolic and "scientific" connections between notions of health and favored "body types." The strong or healthy body was indicated by a large chest, clear eyes, and an upright demeanor. This was the nineteenth century's representation of the Greek athlete; it also became the twentieth-century Nazi construction of the model Aryan. On the other hand, some diseases represented both ugliness and genetic weakness. Tuberculosis was often considered to be a manifestation of an anemic constitution, which was physically marked by a "weak" body type: long neck, slender body, and abnormally red cheeks (supposedly the paradigmatic Jewish body type). The "ugly" body type, which, as Gilman notes, was "always associated with racial types such as the Jews," could be introduced into groups with the strong body type through intermixing.[67] Intermarriage between Jews and gentiles, many early geneticists—English, American, and German—reasoned, led to a progressive degeneration of the gentile race and a greater predisposition to tuberculosis.

Disease marked a threat, not only to the health of individual but to the collective beauty, health, and happiness of the nation as a whole. The viewpoint, as Gilman explains it, was that the ill "belong to a separate world, a dangerous world that is always attempting to colonize the world of the healthy."[68] The reverse was also true: the healthy citizen, the genetically gifted, the white, the Aryan, the Northern European was the embodiment of good citizenship. "The beautiful citizen is the good citizen; the healthy citizen is the good citizen. And citizenship in this context is a reflection of the body. The good citizen cannot be ugly and therefore cannot be infected by, or infect, members of society with dangerous illnesses, illnesses that would be marked on their physiognomies."[69]

These diverse and sometimes contradictory attitudes toward the health of the body politic can be found, in various guises, in the U.S. Progressive movement. Much energy within the movement went toward the reform of labor laws to, among other things, shorten the workweek and end practices of child labor; the expansion of health services for the poor; the extension of the franchise to women; the legal prohibition of the use of alcohol; and the reform of the drug laws. At the same time, however, many Progressives were hostile toward immigrants, favored various kinds of eugenics practices, and developed programs for the internment of prostitutes.[70] Theodore Roosevelt, concerned about the rising numbers of immigrants with large families, exhorted middle-class Americans to have children so as not to commit "race suicide."[71] There was, in fact, much crossover between the activities of Progressive reformers and those of proponents of the eugenics movement. Alliances between Progressives and active racists were responsible for the passage of numerous anti-immigration and sterilization laws in the first two decades of the twentieth century. During the 1910s and 1920s, nine thousand individuals deemed to be "genetically unfit" were sterilized for eugenics purposes.[72] Beauchamp may be correct that "many of the *most* progressive reformers were critics of mass quarantines," but many others supported quarantines and eugenics measures that were designed to purge the body politic of its least desired elements.[73]

Police Powers, Quarantine, and Equal Protection

Legal debates about how to balance the public good and private rights in relation to quarantine were encompassed within the broader issue of the limits of the states' "police powers." In general, states have the authority to "promote order, safety, security, health, morals and general welfare within constitutional limits."[74] The quintessential nineteenth-century police powers case is *Mugler v. Kansas,* in which several defendants were charged with brewing beer in contravention of an 1880 Kansas statute. The owners of the brewery claimed that their property had been taken by the state without just compensation. Justice Harlan, however, wrote a majority decision in which he offered broad authority to the state to establish regulations regarding the health and safety of the citizenry. Where the public interest, as represented through the police powers, was determined to be present, the private interests of business owners would have to retreat.[75]

The question of how far police powers would reach was one of the great constitutional conflicts of the late nineteenth and early twentieth centuries. Progressives and other reformers worked to pass many health and safety laws only to have them tossed out as unconstitutional. Although *Mugler* seemed to give states a fairly broad mandate to pass legislation that could be justified as within the police powers, later Supreme Courts were not averse to striking down state laws that limited the powers of business interests to control the workplace (such as in *Lochner v. New York*, in which the Court repudiated New York's attempt to limit the workdays of bakers to ten hours).[76]

Quarantine cases, then, brought together a complex array of ideologies and interests. The regulation and control of contagious diseases represented the epitome of the states' authority to control private behavior under the police powers. The states' power to order quarantines was not questioned—Chief Justice John Marshall had given this power constitutional legitimacy in 1824, in *Gibbons v. Ogden*.[77] But how intrusive a state could be in accomplishing its ends was not entirely settled.

Quarantines have an odd legal status. On the one hand, they are civil commitments. The quarantining of a house, a neighborhood, or a ship is not the result of a finding of mens rea, or criminal intent. Rather, it can be compared to a finding of mental incompetence, where an individual is confined to a mental institution to protect the person confined as well as others with whom he or she may come into contact. Such a person is generally confined because of a condition for which he or she is not legally responsible. Yet the comparison goes only so far, because mental incompetence is not contagious, and although immediate action may sometimes be a necessity, there is often time for some kind of hearing to be conducted before the confinement actually occurs. In quarantine cases, immediate confinement can be viewed as an outright necessity.

In numerous early quarantine cases, states' police powers were interpreted broadly, and the declaration of a public health emergency was considered sufficient to give public health officers authority to confine those deemed infected. The 1876 Maine case of *Haverty v. Bass* is representative of an expansive reading of police powers. In this case a police officer and city physician took the child of a Bangor woman from her arms and brought the child to a city hospital against the mother's express wishes. The child was believed to be infected with smallpox.[78] The city officers seized the child after a brief examination and did not obtain a warrant to do so. The officers acted under the authority of a state public health statute that allowed for the sick to be quarantined against their wishes. However, it also provided that a warrant could be issued by two judges "if need be." Although the most commonsensical reading of this provision seems to be that a warrant would be issued if there was resistance (as the legal basis for involuntary confinement), the majority on the Maine appellate court read a warrant to be optional and its necessity wholly determined by the public health officers. Municipal officers, the court stated, "can remove a sick person without the aid of a warrant, or they can use that instrumentality to enforce obedience to their commands, if a resort to such means of assistance becomes necessary. We do not perceive how it could be of importance to the sick man, whether a warrant was obtained or not. It would be the merest form in the world, as far as he is concerned."[79] The court did not answer the question of why public health officers would seek a warrant if they did not need one to use force. Furthermore, the ruling implied that a "sick man" would know that he was sick and that he would be grateful for the confinement. As a result, local officers would have complete discretion as to whom they would quarantine and how, generally without oversight from a judge or other officer of the court.

The court operated under the principle that in the case of a disease outbreak, an individual's rights would virtually disappear in the face of community interests. As the court stated, "The maxim *salus populi suprema lex* is the law of all courts and countries. The individual right sinks in the necessity to provide for the public good." If anything, the court noted, "experience probably shows that communities and individuals are not promptly enough aroused to the dangers that beset them in such emergencies."[80] Moreover, if an official were to inflict an injury on an individual, that person would have recourse through a lawsuit against the official, or a habeas corpus proceeding. Formal rights of redress would, then, exist only after the fact, and would no doubt face tremendous obstacles to their success.

In the 1921 Alabama case of *Dowling v. Harden,* a state court attempted to distinguish between the notion of quarantine and the idea of criminality. Gladis Harden was arrested on a vagrancy charge. While she was in jail, it was determined that she was sick with an infectious disease covered by the state's quarantine law. Harden made her bond and was released from jail, but she was then quarantined to a health facility. She brought a habeas corpus suit against the public health officer who ordered her confinement, Dr. J. D. Dowling, for her release. In this case the court recognized the broad authority of public officials to issue quarantine orders against individuals reasonably suspected of being contagious, but it also stated that "persons affected with disease are not for that reason criminals, and jails and penitentiaries are not made or designated for their detention."[81] Harden could be confined, but she had to be confined to a hospital—she could not be kept in a jail.

The 1917 New York case of *Crayton v. Larabee* is another significant quarantine case. Mary Crayton lived next door to a house occupied by a person who had contracted smallpox, and as a result she was confined to her home for a period of about two weeks in the summer of 1911. When her quarantine ended, Crayton sued Syracuse's city health inspector on the

▼ State Power, Law, and Sequestration

grounds that she had been injured by a quarantine order that the city had no right to impose, because it was never demonstrated that she had actually been exposed to smallpox. A trial court found validity in Crayton's claim, but the state's highest court sided with the defendant. The court's decision gave broad authority to public officials to make determinations about what particular houses could be quarantined in cases of suspected infections. The only limit the court set on a health official's actions was that "conditions must exist which render, within reason and fair apprehension, his action essential for the preservation of the health of the public." In making the decision, the court employed a flexible interpretation of state police powers in general, saying that in this particular case, public health officials acted "lawfully" to protect the public "against the consequent damages to persons or property."[82]

One of the most significant legal cases concerning a state's power to implement quarantines and control over individuals is the 1922 Illinois case of *Barmore v. Robertson*. When a number of persons who had roomed at a boardinghouse owned by Jennie Barmore became infected with typhus, Barmore submitted to an examination that determined that she was a typhoid carrier. The Chicago Department of Health subsequently put both Barmore and her rooming house under quarantine, and the city placed a placard in front of the house warning that a typhoid carrier resided there. Under the quarantine order, Barmore was directed to remain at home, was forbidden to accept boarders, and was not allowed to cook food for any person other than her husband. Although Barmore had not herself apparently ever shown symptoms of the disease, an examination of her stool indicated the presence of typhoid bacteria.[83]

Drawing on the then "new science" of public health for justification, the city's officials argued that the mere presence of germs was enough to warrant their depriving Barmore of her individual human rights. The court noted, in fact, that "among all the objects sought to be secured by governmental laws none is more important than the preservation of public health." The rules established by the city's board of health authorized not only quarantine measures, but criminal sanctions against those who violated them. That criminal penalties could be applied is important to note, but the sanctions were relatively mild. Violation of the confinement order was a misdemeanor, with a maximum penalty of a fine of two hundred dollars and imprisonment for up to six months. The Illinois State Supreme Court allowed for the imposition of such measures, but also kept them within fairly strict bounds. Courts could intervene against health authorities' decisions if those decisions were "arbitrary" and "unreasonable." And although the decisions would not be deemed so if "an epidemic actually exists," health officials could not "promulgate and enforce rules which merely

State Power, Law, and Sequestration

have a tendency to prevent the spread of contagious and infectious diseases, which are not founded on the existing condition or upon a well-founded belief that a condition is threatened which will endanger the public health." In other words, "the health authorities cannot interfere with the liberties of a citizen until the emergency actually exists."[84] The violation of individual liberties would require a public emergency of some kind.

Precedent for *Barmore* had been set a decade earlier in the celebrated case involving Mary Mallon, more popularly know as "Typhoid Mary." Mallon, an Irish immigrant and a cook, was the "first healthy carrier of typhoid to be carefully traced in North America."[85] She was also the first such carrier to be confined by a quarantine order. Mallon was implicated in three deaths and forty-four nonfatal cases of typhoid. She eluded her first confinement order, returned to society, and again worked as a cook. When she was recaptured, she was not charged with a criminal violation. Rather, she was civilly committed under quarantine and spent a total of twenty-seven years in confinement. Mallon was one of what some estimated at the time to be ten thousand typhoid carriers. Although some jurisdictions made attempts to register them, very few were actually held for long periods of time. According to Leavitt, "The fact that Mary Mallon was a woman, a domestic servant, single, and Irish-born significantly influenced how health officials and the middle-class public thought about what should be done with her." Also important was the perception that she was a "masculine" woman.[86]

The decisions authorities have made concerning whether and how to implement quarantines have involved complicated sets of considerations that have extended beyond determinations of how best to protect the public's health. On March 1, 1899, the governor of Texas, Joseph D. Sayers, acting under authority of a provision of the state's quarantine laws, established a quarantine on the Gulf Coast and Rio Grande against any place that was infected with yellow fever. On August 31 of that same year, a case of yellow fever was officially declared to exist in the city of New Orleans. Subsequently, other cases were reported as well. As a result, Governor Sayers placed an embargo on any common goods, people, and even mail from New Orleans, preventing them from entering Texas by train. Armed guards were posted at various Texas ports and train stations. Persons were allowed to enter the state after ten days' detention, but an absolute and indefinite prohibition against interstate commerce was enforced. The effect (and perhaps the intent) of these regulations was to "take away the trade of the merchants and business men of the city of New Orleans, and to transfer that trade to rival business cities in the State of Texas."[87]

In the U.S. Supreme Court case that arose from these events, *Louisiana v. Texas,* issues of public health and state and local police powers were joined by issues of commerce and free trade. The state of Louisiana argued that Texas was simply using the appearance of yellow fever as a pretext to justify shutting down trade from its most significant state competitor. The merchants and business interests of Texas, in other words, welcomed the quarantine as a means of protecting and increasing their competitive trade advantage. As the representatives of New Orleans put it, the effects of the embargo were to "impoverish [the city's] citizens, reduce the value of her taxable property, diminish her revenues, retard immigration, reduce the value of her public lands, and deprive her citizens of their rights and privileges as citizens of the United States."[88]

The question was not whether Texas had the authority to pass quarantine laws, but whether an absolute prohibition was warranted under the circumstances that were apparently present. The Supreme Court paid little heed to Louisiana's argument. Justice Fuller dismissed the complaint on the grounds that no case or controversy was present between the two states, and thus no grounds for federal court intervention existed. For such a controversy to exist, "something more must be put forward than that the citizens of one State are injured by the maladministration of the laws of another."[89] Such, Fuller argued (somewhat inexplicably), was not the case in this instance.

Ethnic as well as economic considerations also often played a part in decisions to institute quarantines. States and localities had used quarantines in targeted fashion against immigrant groups since before the American Revolution. In eighteenth-century Connecticut, the spread of disease became associated with Scottish and German immigrants, and laws were passed specifically quarantining those groups.[90] Such practices became more commonplace, however, in the latter part of the nineteenth century, as new waves of immigrants entered the country. The imposition of such quarantines was not always entirely irrational, in that new immigrants sometimes did carry infections against which settled populations had little or no immunity. These practices were explicitly discriminatory however, ignoring the principle of equal protection under the law. The rulings of the federal courts in such cases were not very consistent.

In 1893, in the case of *Minneapolis v. Milner,* a federal circuit court found that Michigan's detention of Scandinavian immigrants across from the Sault Sainte Marie Canadian border entry point was a legitimate use of police powers. The plaintiffs argued that although the quarantine rules were not specifically aimed at Scandinavians, given the predominance of this group's presence, the rules had a discriminatory impact. The court rejected the argument.[91]

In the 1902 case of *Compagnie Francaise v. Louisiana State Board of Health,* the U.S. Supreme Court sided with a state board of health against a class of affected person. The Louisiana State Board of Health had passed a resolution on September 29, 1898, that allowed any city or parish in the state to declare a quarantine. As a result of this resolution, a steamship, the S.S. *Britannia,* which had sailed from Italy and France, was detained at the New Orleans quarantine site. On board the ship were 408 passengers, some of whom were U.S. citizens, but the majority of whom were immigrants, mostly from Italy, who were seeking to settle in the United States. Although the plaintiff in the case (the company that owned the steamship), and the board of health, agreed that none of the ship's passengers was sick, the board of health claimed that it took the measure to protect both the passengers and the residents of the city from possible contagion. "The object," the board argued, "was to keep down, as far as possible, the number of persons to be brought within danger of contagion or infection, and by means of this reduction to accomplish the subsidence and suppression of the disease and the spread of the same." The subtext, however, was that New Orleans had become an entry point for Italian immigrants, to the chagrin of some of the local authorities. Excluding healthy immigrants from a healthy population was, on the face of it, somewhat suspicious, but not enough so for the court to intervene on the side of the ship's passengers.[92]

Louisiana claimed broad authority to quarantine under its police powers, contending that the number of "cases of such [infectious disease] . . . essential to cause a place to be considered as infected with them is left to the determination of the Board of Health."[93] The board thus claimed total authority to make decisions about the necessity and scope of the quarantine. The ship's company, representing the passengers, argued violations of the commerce clause, the Fourteenth Amendment due process clause, and various treaty obligations. The Supreme Court rejected all of these arguments and held in favor of broad local and state authority to enforce quarantines.

Justices Brown and Harlan dissented in the case, questioning the breadth of the state's power authorized by the Court's decision. According to Brown, "The Board of Health is authorized and assumes to prohibit in all portions of the State which it chooses to declare in quarantine, the introduction or immigration of all persons from outside the quarantine district, whether infected or uninfected, sick or well, sound or unsound, feeble or healthy; and that, too, not for a few days necessary to establish the sanitary status of such persons, but for an indefinite and possibly permanent period." In Brown's view, the quarantine was simply an "excuse" for the "wholesale exclusion" of immigrants. The possibility of infection was too small to warrant such drastic measures, and the ordinance was in conflict with various treaty obligations.[94]

Given the Court's general attitude toward police powers and its hostility to even the slightest expansion of the Fourteenth amendment's equal protection clause, evidenced in cases such as *Plessy v. Ferguson,* the case of *Jew Ho v. Williamson* (and a related case, *Wong Wai v. Williamson*) stands out as particularly interesting.[95] In 1900, a local government, the city of San Francisco, attempted to use its quarantine powers in a patently discriminatory fashion, and the Supreme Court displayed its willingness to restrict those powers on some occasions. The city based its power of quarantine on a city board resolution adopted in the spring of 1900 that allowed the board of health to "quarantine persons, houses, places, and districts within th[e] city and county, when in its judgment it is deemed necessary to prevent the spreading of contagious or infectious diseases."[96] The resolution was passed after two public health officials reported cases of bubonic plague. The infections were all reported to have occurred within a section of the city populated by Chinese immigrants, nine of whom had apparently succumbed to the disease.[97] As a result, the city gave health officials the authority to establish a quarantine within the district of the city where plague had been discovered and enlisted the police department's assistance in enforcing it.

Jew Ho was the proprietor of a grocery store who had patrons both within and outside of the quarantine boundary. He claimed that his business was severely damaged by the quarantine measures, as his customers were no longer able to conduct business with those inside the quarantined district. Moreover, he argued that the measures were anti-Chinese in that they were "enforced against persons of the Chinese race and nationality only, and not against persons of other races." And in fact, businesses within the quarantined areas that were owned by persons who were not Chinese were not subject to the same kinds of restrictions as Chinese-owned businesses.[98] Jew Ho also claimed that there were no actual cases of plague within the quarantined areas, no plague bacillus found, and no deaths from the disease. Lastly, Jew Ho argued that the buildings that were said to have been affected by the plague were not segregated from the rest of the quarantined districts, and that a quarantine of such a large area tended to have an effect opposite to that stated. That is, it would allow and indeed encourage the disease to spread within the cordoned district, which would endanger not only the inhabitants of the district but the entire city as well. If the public health authorities were correct in their diagnosis, in other words, they were setting up a kind of laboratory for the spread of contagion, and this in turn would have potentially drastic consequences for the city as a whole.[99] Thus, the plaintiff in the case contended that the resolution constituted "purely arbitrary, unreasonable, unwarranted, wrongful, and oppressive interference with the personal liberty of the complainant and the said Chinese residents." As a result, it should be found to be "unauthorized, invalid, void, and contrary to the constitution and laws of the United States" as well as the laws of the state of California, and a violation of the equal protection clause of the Fourteenth Amendment to the U.S. Constitution.[100]

The defendants in the case claimed protection for their actions in the state's police powers. Although the court recognized the potentially wide sweep of the police powers, it also indicated its respect for the protection of individual rights. The court suggested that although it had an undeniable responsibility to strike down infringements of state power, it had to use "utmost caution" in taking such actions and could do so only when the state infringed on "rights secured by the fundamental law." Moreover, in the case of a "great calamity" such as the outbreak of plague, "the court will go to the greatest extent, and give the widest discretion, in construing the regulations that may be adopted by the board of health or the board of supervisors."[101]

The court found, however, that the quarantining of several thousand people in an area of ten or more city blocks was an unreasonable application of quarantine regulations. Such action did virtually nothing to prevent the spread of disease among the local inhabitants, in contrast to the purported object of quarantine, which was to "confine the disease to the smallest number possible." That is, if plague had indeed been found in a specific house, then the quarantine should have begun and ended at that particular house. Moreover, the court found that the measure did indeed discriminate against the city's Chinese population and thus violated the equal protection clause of the Fourteenth Amendment.[102] This was especially significant given that there was a real question as to whether the affected people had actually contracted plague.

A related San Francisco case involved a substance known as the Haffkine Prophylactic, which California health authorities claimed, on highly dubious grounds, to be a vaccine against bubonic plague. Asian immigrants were required to take this substance or risk being quarantined or jailed. In *Wong Wai v. Williamson,* a federal district court was asked to overturn a California state court's decision to allow the city's board of health to implement an order under which the state department of transportation was authorized to deny Asians, as well as anyone else deemed likely to have plague or to be at a high risk of becoming infected with it, access to trains in the state of California unless they had certificates showing that they had submitted to the inoculant. The only justification offered by the health board was that "this particular race is more liable to the plague than any other."[103] Somewhat surprisingly, given other Fourteenth Amendment jurisprudence, the district court followed *Jew Ho* and overturned the city's order as a violation of the equal protection clause.

As the above discussion illustrates, at the end of the nineteenth century U.S. courts were involved in an uneven struggle to balance individual and minority rights and community health. On the one hand, local and state authorities were often given wide latitude to assert state power when it came to matters involving the spread of infectious diseases. These powers were reinforced by the assumption that quarantines were effective in containing potential disease outbreaks or epidemics. Yet the courts did not rule uniformly on the side of the states. The courts seemed, at times, to be searching for standards of fairness grounded in science and constitutional law. Moreover, that quarantines were legally sanctioned did not always mean that their enforcement was uniform or seamless. For instance, as noted above, when Mary Mallon was quarantined there were an estimated ten thousand typhoid carriers in the United States, only a few hundred of whom had even been identified.[104] Quarantines were, moreover, virtually always a civil matter, and criminal charges were seldom, if ever, brought against disease carriers.

Images and Discipline

As I noted at the outset of this chapter, in a standard liberal legalist narrative, Western history represents a progressive recognition of the need to protect various rights. In the American version, the U.S constitutional system embodies the most complete outcome of this process. This is the track that U.S. constitutional law textbooks often take when dealing with everything from free expression to civil rights.[105] This interpretation of American legal history is not entirely without merit. Particularly in the years of the Warren Court and immediately afterward, when Roosevelt, Kennedy, and Johnson nominees tended to dominate the Court's decisions, the Supreme Court carved out increased legal protections for the disenfranchised, the dissident, the nonreligious, and the arrested.[106] However, postwar liberal faith in the Supreme Court as an institution whose primary purpose is to offer support to those previously deprived of constitutional protections has become over time more difficult to sustain as first Richard Nixon's and then Ronald Reagan's and George H. Bush's Court appointees have had increasingly significant impacts on the Court's decisions. The equal protection rights promised in *Brown v. Board of Education* and the privacy rights promised in *Roe v. Wade,* for example, have been significantly eroded over time.[107]

In a law review article on law and tuberculosis published in 1994, Min incorporates a very specific representation of liberal rights narrative, arguing that a "new due process" emerged from the Supreme Court in the 1970s and that this legal paradigm has made it more difficult for courts now to use legal tools, such as quarantine, to compromise individual rights in favor of presumed community health interests as they did in the past. According to Min, "The due process clauses of the fifth and fourteenth amendments to the Constitution came to be interpreted as placing substantive limits on state legislation that deprives individuals of fundamental rights. The era of complete judicial deference to the use of the police power to protect public health and safety ended and was replaced by a new willingness to closely scrutinize legislation whenever fundamental liberty rights are involved."[108] Min argues that the Supreme Court now recognizes the "massive curtailment of liberty" that results from civil commitments of various kinds and has expanded privacy rights, rights of cohabitation, and rights to travel. This expansion of due process and privacy rights thus makes it unlikely that the Court would today find quarantine laws related to tuberculosis, HIV, and other infections to be constitutional.[109]

Min draws support for his position from the Court's decision in *School Board of Nassau County v. Arline,* in which the majority ruled that specific evidence of contagiousness is necessary for a person, in particular a schoolteacher with TB, to be removed from a public space (in this case, a classroom).[110] Given that involuntary quarantine is an even greater deprivation of liberty than the loss of a job, Min argues an even higher standard of "dangerousness" would be necessary to withstand judicial "strict scrutiny."[111] The increased willingness of courts to scrutinize state actions in a variety of areas has had an impact on the rights of the infected as well. This should (and implicitly will) carry over to those infected not only with TB, but with HIV and other transmissible diseases.

When AIDS first appeared in the late 1980s, calls for quarantine were not unheard of. Many of these came from the usual suspects on the radical right: Patrick Buchanan, Jerry Falwell, Pat Robertson, William F. Buckley. Scholars and activists expended a great deal of intellectual and political energy in combating this new politics of quarantine.[112] To a large extent they were successful. No systematic or large-scale quarantine of HIV-positive persons or even those with AIDS was ever carried out, not because the courts prevented such actions, but because Congress, state legislatures, and local city councils never attempted to impose them.[113] Although this must be considered something of a victory for individual rights, it may be increasingly beside the point. The threat of mass quarantines no longer looms large in policy discussions about HIV. That threat has been replaced, in a way that is almost without historical precedent, by a slow and steady criminalization of the infected. How this has occurred tells us something important about the role of the law in the current global media system.

In the minds of the public, the face of criminal HIV transmission is still probably most clearly the face of Nushawn Williams. Williams became the poster child for HIV criminality in a literal sense when his name was released to the public in October 1997. Not only was his name released, but his picture was placed on a poster that was displayed throughout the county. This image of a young, somewhat thuggish looking African American man was picked up by the media and became embedded in the popular-culture consciousness.

The image resonated deeply. Drawing on a long history of associating crime, drug use, and promiscuous sexuality with young black men, the national and international media turned Nushawn Williams into a monster, the "AIDS monster," or the "bogeyman incarnate," as one commentator put it.[114] The message: Nushawn Williams is the new face of AIDS and he's invading *your little town*. Thousands of images fade in and out of global media markets over any given period of time; their ephemerality is sometimes offered as an excuse for their superficiality. But this particular image had an impact. The Nushawn Williams case served to reinforce the trend in many states toward turning HIV transmission into a criminal offense. This trend represents a reemergence of the premodern. The optimistic attempts to balance individual and community rights that marked modern legal approaches to disease are being superseded by demands for punishment and retribution. Every infected person is now a potential criminal, and large numbers have no doubt engaged in what is now defined in many places as felonious activity.

Before the Williams case, there had been about a dozen HIV criminal transmission cases, most involving rather odd circumstances. One case, for example, involved an HIV-positive prison inmate who threw his own feces at guards in a vain attempt to infect them. Another involved a physician who injected his mistress with HIV-contaminated blood in order to infect her. (I present a more complete discussion of all these cases in chapter 5.) Since the Williams case, numerous states have passed statutes aimed at making it easier to convict those who knowingly expose sexual partners to HIV without informing them. Even in those states, such as New York, where there are (still) no HIV-specific criminal transmission laws, prosecutors have made attempts to use other statutes (such as those concerning reckless endangerment) to bring criminal charges against HIV-positive persons.[115] In 2000, *Poz* magazine featured a story on 101 "AIDS criminals"— that is, people who had been brought up on a variety of charges related to HIV transmission—around the United States.[116] Most of these people were charged after the Williams case received the attention that it did. There can be little doubt at this point that the images launched by the Williams case have helped to advance and sustain legislative and prosecutorial activities related to HIV transmission. This is not to say that the Williams case, by itself, "caused" these other developments to transpire. Williams's image interacted with other images already present, images related to race, crime, HIV, and drug use. A context exists, reinforced by media images, in which criminalization is viewed as a solution to many social problems, including public health issues, from psychiatric disorders to homelessness, to drug use, to the potential spread of infectious diseases.

The use of the criminal justice system as a mechanism for treating HIV transmission cannot be viewed in isolation. Largely because of the determined efforts of state and federal governments to stop Americans from using addictive and psychotropic drugs, prison populations have exploded over the past decade. There are now almost half a million people serving time in prison in the United States for violations of drug laws. Some 80 percent of these cases involve possession of illegal substances; 44 percent involve possession of marijuana alone.[117] Most of those imprisoned on drug charges are black or Hispanic, although there is virtually no evidence that minority populations use drugs at higher rates than whites or Anglos.[118] Although it seems unlikely at this point that states will marshal such massive resources for the purpose of prosecuting potential disease carriers, media constructions of cases like Williams's clearly prepare the ground for potentially greater future interventions.

The "rights revolution" of the 1970s, which was supposed to vindicate the liberal dream of equal treatment under law, has been badly undermined by numerous social forces in the past two decades. The "strict scrutiny" doctrine of the Fourteenth Amendment's equal protection clause, which embodied it, remains hypothetically intact (just as does the "right to privacy"), but in the case of the social control of disease, especially in terms of HIV, images launched into and by global media markets have overwhelmed the careful consideration of constitutional rights and good public policy. In certain respects, this is not new. The notion that media images interact with conservative political forces to discipline the unruly elements of liberal society by generating moral panics and crime controls can be traced back at least to the analysis of "mugging" in pre-Thatcherite Britain presented by Stuart Hall and his colleagues.[119] Now, however, the global media system is more centralized and pervasive.[120] Its images move faster and farther than in the past, just as the nation-state and the constitutional controls once associated with it continue to wither.[121] In any event, it now seems that quarantining of the infected has been transformed from a civil matter that was subject to much political debate into a criminal one that is the subject of very little such debate. Although Nushawn Williams received more media attention than other individuals in HIV-related cases, he is not alone in having been subjected to criminal prosecution due to his HIV-positive status. In chapter 5, I review and critique some other criminal cases involving HIV transmission.

5

HIV Culpability and the Politics of Crime

The criminalization of social problems has been a theme of American political and legal life for more than two decades. The nearly two million people currently in prison in the United States represent an important sector of the economy, sometimes labeled the "prison-industrial complex."[1] Although much of the rhetoric regarding crime policies has focused on high-profile instances of violence, the majority of those who constitute the prison population are incarcerated for drug offenses. Many have serious psychiatric problems. Prisons have increasingly become profit centers in the global economy and dumping grounds for the system of "public health." The criminalization of disease seems to be part of a set of social trends seen across the political spectrum for a period of three decades. The Williams case occurred within this context and contributed to it by spurring additional calls for the criminalization of HIV transmission.

Although I believe that the criminalization of HIV transmission represents a disturbing trend, I would not argue that individuals who deliberately transmit the virus should never be prosecuted. There are instances, some of which I outline below, in which the callous and wanton nature of transmission demands punishment. Such cases are relatively rare, however. In general, prosecutors should pursue HIV transmission cases only with great reluctance. When such cases occur, the suspects should be charged under general criminal statutes, such as those concerning reckless endangerment or even second-degree or attempted murder. That HIV transmission is difficult to prosecute successfully under these general statutes is a good thing, because it deters authorities from using criminal law as a substitute for public health strategies that focus on education and care. HIV-specific statutes are designed to ease the prosecution of such cases and to lengthen the possible sentences of those convicted. They represent a legal and political expression of the "punitive model" carried to extreme. Such statutes subvert reasonable standards of fairness and proof and undermine the integrity of the criminal law.

As of fall 2001, the following states had passed laws making it a crime for someone with HIV knowingly to expose someone else to the infection through sexual or other kinds of contact: Arkansas, California, Colorado, Florida, Georgia, Idaho, Illinois, Indiana, Kansas, Kentucky, Louisiana, Maryland, Michigan, Minnesota, Missouri, Nevada, New Jersey, North Dakota, Ohio, Oklahoma, Pennsylvania, South Carolina, South Dakota, Tennessee, Utah, Virginia, Washington.[2] Some of these states, such as Illinois and Missouri, have had criminal transmission laws on the books for more than ten years.[3] In 1997, however, several states enacted tougher penalties for those found guilty of knowingly infecting or exposing others to the virus. Florida, New Jersey, and Missouri raised the penalties the courts can apply when HIV-positive persons fail to notify sexual partners properly about their HIV status (up to thirty years in Florida). Washington State also raised the stakes on intentional exposure or transmission.[4] In April 1998, the Iowa State Legislature for the first time approved a bill making it a felony for a person who tests positive for HIV to engage in "intimate contact" with other persons without first informing them of his or her HIV status. A person convicted of such activity can receive a prison sentence of up to twenty-five years.[5] As the journal *AIDS Policy and Law* noted at the end of 1999, "a good deal of legislative activity has taken place since the Nushawn Williams case hit the front pages."[6]

Changes in state laws have not, however, been confined to statutes concerning partner notification and intentional transmission. New and troubling legislation has begun to appear that authorizes detention or quarantining of those merely suspected of having transmitted HIV infection. North Dakota has passed a statute under which a person can be confined for up to five days for HIV testing if he or she has exposed a police officer, firefighter, paramedic, or health care worker to blood or body fluids.[7] Washington's governor, Gary Locke, vetoed a similar provision passed by his state's legislature when he signed a 1997 bill to increase criminal penalties for deliberate exposure.[8] At times, it has appeared as though waves of new laws might make criminal quarantining a more active and acceptable public policy.

By 2001, more than one hundred cases of criminal HIV transmission had been documented, and the trend was clearly for states to use the criminal law more pervasively to punish those who transmit HIV. Of these cases, only five involved forcible rape. Fourteen involved sex with a minor, and forty-five involved consensual sex. Twenty-two cases involved spitting or biting. Only in eleven of the cases was it documented that the defendants' actions resulted in HIV transmission. In one case, an HIV-positive man was convicted of biting a Wal-Mart security guard (a charge he denied) in a scuffle over the theft of an eighty-six-dollar coat (which he admitted). The guard never tested positive, but the defendant received a twenty-seven-year sentence.[9]

Nushawn Williams and the Criminalization of HIV

Perhaps the best place to begin a discussion of some of the legal issues related to HIV criminalization is with New York State and Williams. Williams pled guilty to a charge of "reckless endangerment" in New York after he was offered a plea bargain that called for him to serve four to twelve years in prison and that included two other criminal charges: statutory rape and drug possession. As of this writing, he has served more than five years of his sentence, and it seems very likely that he will serve at least five more.

The case against Williams was prosecuted by Chautauqua County District Attorney James Subjack, who sat down with me for an interview about the case in July 1999.[10] I found him to be bright, open, and engaging, and I got the strong impression that he loves his job. I wasn't entirely sure what to expect from him, given the news accounts I'd read about the case, but I found myself, perhaps against my expectations, enjoying our conversation. He was extremely generous with his time and seemed eager not only to answer my questions but to debate the issues as well. He did not express the slightest doubt about the course Chautauqua County had taken with regard to the Williams case. In fact, the main impact the case seems to have had on him was to convince him that New York State needs to go further in criminalizing the knowing transmission of HIV. He told me he had made a decision to pursue reform of the state's criminal laws to simplify the prosecution of such cases, but he has been only partly successful in that effort.

Subjack explained to me that he favored three changes in New York

State's laws with regard to HIV transmission. First, he wanted to make what he called "HIV victimization as a part of criminal transaction" confidential. That is, he wanted to give HIV "victims" the same status as victims of sex crimes, so that their identities would be concealed if they came forward with charges that someone had knowingly infected them. In the Williams case, the identity of only one of the girls involved could be withheld from the public, because she was a minor. According to Subjack, the others were unwilling to have their names made public (and their status made known) simply for the opportunity to bring additional charges against Williams. Subjack argued that a kind of shield law equivalent to the one that protects rape victims would encourage the victimized to bring charges against those who infected them. He also expressed satisfaction that New York State had passed such a statute at his urging. (The passage of that law did not, however, result in more charges being filed against Nushawn Williams.)

Next, Subjack told me, he wanted to "lower the bar" to releasing the name of any individual deemed an "imminent health threat." He told me that county officials were "lucky" in the Williams case that they had gone before a sympathetic judge who believed that their reasons for requesting to be allowed to release Williams's name were valid. He wondered, however, whether such support would be forthcoming in a less "extreme" case. Suppose, Subjack suggested, someone who is HIV-positive is having casual sex with only half a dozen people. Getting permission to release that person's name as an "imminent threat to the community" might be difficult, but he or she could pose a substantial risk to others and could be the target of criminal prosecution as well. Subjack wanted to give the health department more discretion to release names to the public, but also to give the department the legal authority to give the names of some individuals to law enforcement *without* making those names public. In the latter such cases, only if these persons were arrested would their HIV status be made known, as part of the arrest record.

Finally, and perhaps most important, Subjack wanted New York State to pass a criminal transmission statute specific to HIV. Although some members of the legislature publicly backed the idea of passing such a law during the "crisis" raised by the Williams case, the concept died from lack of serious political support. I found Subjack's reasoning concerning the state's need for such a statute to be flawed and somewhat unsettling.

To prove "reckless endangerment" in a case such as Nushawn Williams's, the state must show that the defendant knew he or she was HIV-positive, or at least show that the defendant had been told that he or she was HIV-positive in such a way that he or she could understand the meaning and consequences of that status. If the person was HIV-positive but unaware of his or her status, then, even though that person might be transmitting the virus through unsafe sex practices, he or she would not have the requisite mens reas (criminal intent) to be charged with criminal conduct. (Williams, of course, pled guilty, although he continued to deny, to me and to others, that he had been told about his status. However, the evidence that he had been informed of his status is very compelling.) Also, to prove reckless endangerment the state must show that the defendant had sex with the person on whose behalf the state is bringing the charges. This might not always be a simple matter to prove if the contact was in the distant past, although, as in rape cases, presumably a man or woman's claim of sexual contact would itself carry considerable weight. Subjack did not envision that he would have had much difficulty proving that Williams had sex with various women.

Reckless endangerment is a serious criminal charge. It can, as in the Williams case, constitute a felony. Yet an offender is unlikely to receive more than a few years in prison if convicted on one or two reckless endangerment charges. Primarily for this reason, Subjack was dissatisfied with the use of reckless endangerment statutes as the general mechanism for bringing charges in HIV-transmission cases. He believed that more serious criminal charges should be available. In the Williams case, Subjack told me, he would have been more satisfied with a charge of "assault, with depraved indifference to human life, consciously disregarding substantial risk which is going to lead to grave risk of death," a class I felony. This charge is very close to attempted murder, and a conviction on assault with depraved indifference can result in a very long prison term. Unfortunately (from Subjack's perspective), bringing an HIV-transmission case under this charge is a more complicated and demanding process than bringing such a case as reckless endangerment. When a defendant is charged with assault with depraved indifference in an HIV case, the prosecutor has to prove that the transmitter had knowledge of his or her status, that he or she knew the consequences of infecting someone else, and that the defendant infected the complainant. In other words, the state must prove both the defendant's state of mind and the presence of actual physical harm. The complainant must be shown to be infected, and the defendant must be demonstrated to be the source of that infection.

Generating such proof is neither easy nor cheap. Subjack explained to me that there are only two medical laboratories in the United States that do the phylogenetic testing needed to show that a particular victim was infected by a specific defendant, and that the test costs twenty-five thousand dollars. Moreover, even if a state or county could afford to pay for the test, questions regarding the validity of the results exist even within the scientific community. The prosecution would need to hire experts to appear in court to vouch for the test results, at further costs of up to one hundred thousand dollars. Even that, as Subjack said, "may not show that the test is reliable. It's up to the judge." Subjack is no doubt correct that proving that "the virus transmitted from the donor is the same virus which is now inside the victim, the donee," is not a simple proposition and that many people sitting on a jury might consider attempts to prove it to be a form of "witch-doctory," especially if the persons involved had multiple sex partners. Thus charging assault with depraved indifference in an HIV case is a "six-figure crapshoot," and relatively small counties like Chautauqua, with limited prosecutorial resources, can rarely afford to take that chance.

The other problem with charging assault with depraved indifference, Subjack noted, is that the prosecution has to show a "substantial risk of death." With HIV, especially given the treatments available today, this is not a simple proposition to prove either. As Subjack put it, "For every expert that I bring in that says HIV infection leads to AIDS, leads to death, you're going to have two experts that are going to say, because of the state of medical technology, you can prove the HIV, but you can't prove the substantial risk of death." It could also be argued that new treatments not now foreseen could reduce the chances of death from HIV even further in the future. What, after all, constitutes "risk of death" under such circumstances? If it could be shown that a person will likely die in ten years, would that be sufficient? What about fifteen years? Twenty?

Subjack's suggestion for dealing with these evidentiary problems was that the state should attempt to eliminate them. "Let's not," he said, "make it a prerequisite to have to prove a substantial risk of death. The statute ought to by itself say, 'You have unprotected sex, know of your HIV-positive status, with an unknowing victim,' that's it, crime over." The problem of corroborating that the sex occurred and that the donor knew of his or her status would still be there, but prosecutors would no longer be burdened by the difficult and contorted standards of proof demanded by an "assault with depraved indifference" statute.

That there are substantial evidentiary barriers to demonstrating that sex between two consenting partners, one of whom is HIV-positive, constitutes "depraved indifference to human life" seems undeniable. But whereas Subjack sees these barriers mostly as hindrances to conviction, another interpretation is possible. It may be that there is a certain wisdom within the criminal law in its establishment of such high evidentiary hurdles. These barriers are not just prosecutorial inconveniences; rather, they represent mechanisms that keep the criminal justice system from reaching into spheres of activity—in this case the sphere of public health—where it should go only with the greatest caution. Although lowering the barriers to conviction in HIV-transmission cases would make prosecution easier, it would do so by ignoring valid concerns regarding the wisdom and fairness of prosecuting many such cases. The potential impact would be the imposition of determinations of guilt by what amounts to evidentiary fiat.

To expose the serious conceptual problems raised by Subjack's proposal (and, by implication, similar HIV-transmission statutes) I must address three separate issues: (1) the demonstration of intent, (2) specific proof of transmission, and (3) proof of the risk of death. First, the prosecution must demonstrate intent in most criminal cases. *Black's Law Dictionary* defines intent, as "design, resolve, or determination with which [a] person acts."[11] This seems straightforward enough, but intent is a very complex and slippery notion in many cases. For example, "accidental" is not "intentional," but risky behavior that results in accidents can be. A driver's accidentally running over a child who has unexpectedly run into the street does not constitute criminal conduct, but criminal conduct may be present if a driver hits a child who has run into the street after the driver has driven at high speed through an intersection to beat a red light. In the latter instance, the driver's actions may be interpreted as "reckless endangerment." HIV-transmission cases are difficult to prosecute because they often traverse the boundary between the accidental and the intentional.

In most cases of HIV transmission, intent is likely to be indefinite. This is especially the case because many persons who are HIV-positive have "knowledge" of their status but only vaguely recognize or understand what that means. Denial is a documented aspect of being infected with HIV. As *Poz* columnist River Huston has put it, "When I was handed a death sentence nine years ago, I went through all the described stages—denial, shock, anger, sadness, acceptance. But it didn't stop there, it kept going— denial, acceptance, shock, anger, acceptance, denial denial, denial, shock, anger."[12] One may suspect that one is HIV-positive but avoid a medical test in order to avoid confirming one's fears. One may even choose to deny the truth of test results in order to secure the stability of one's ordinary existence. The tendency to deny may be especially intense when one is told "against one's will" that one is HIV-positive. When a person who is entirely asymptomatic is found to be HIV-positive when tested as part of some medical or legal routine, he or she may be caught entirely off guard. When the information comes out of the blue in this way, the person may be expecially resistant to accepting its implications. Deep-seated suspicion of official authorities, such as that found often among the poor and individuals engaged in a variety of ongoing criminal activities, can also encourage denial.[13]

In Nushawn Williams's case, the charge of "reckless endangerment" removed the question of intent from the equation. That Williams "deliberately" infected others was never proven, and in fact was never part of an indictment. It didn't have to be. By pleading guilty, Williams admitted to having been informed of his status and to engaging in unprotected sex in spite of his having that information. But that is the sum total of what his plea implied, which is why a charge of reckless endangerment, although serious, doesn't generally result in a fifteen- to twenty-year sentence. The "monster" label that the media attached to Nushawn Williams seems to have come from some commentators' mistaken conclusion that Williams had "hard" intent to infect those with whom he had sex. This mistake is entirely understandable, given that this was the impression that was fostered, whether deliberately or not, by media reports. People thought that Williams was a "monster" because they believed that he wanted his "victims" to become infected and die. There is little if any evidence that this was the case, however. In my own interview with Andrea Caruso, she suggested that Williams knew that he was HIV-positive (although he never told her that he was), and that he had raped her.[14] But no legal charges were ever brought against him that matched the gravity of these charges. No written legal record exists, as far as I know, in which Williams expressed any desire to harm his partners by transmitting the virus. District Attorney Subjack, aware of this, chose to go forward with the charge of reckless endangerment. It seemed to fit. It made legal and, perhaps, "moral" sense.

There is a certain logic, then, to the use of reckless endangerment as a criminal charge in such cases, because it avoids the question of intent beyond simply having to demonstrate that the donor of the virus knew that he or she was HIV-positive. If prosecutors want to up the ante and bring charges that include malice and malicious disregard for human life, they should have to prove that these elements are evident. Using an HIV-specific statute as a substitute for demonstrating actual depraved indifference, which is what Subjack would like to do, elides the question of intent in such a way that, although it may be convenient for prosecutors, undermines gradations of intent that are an important part of the conceptual integrity of the criminal law.

Another problem with prosecuting HIV-transmission cases under more serious criminal statutes, such as assault with depraved indifference, is the difficulty of showing that transmission occurred in a particular case. Prosecutors must show not only recklessness, but actual caused harm. To draw an analogy: the prosecution must show not only that the defendant shot the gun recklessly, but that he shot it deliberately with a desire to injure or kill, and that someone was hit with the bullet and thereby injured. In some cases these elements may be relatively easy to demonstrate, but in others proving them may be difficult—for example, an accuser may have had multiple partners or may be an intravenous drug user. As Subjack noted, it is very expensive and difficult to demonstrate HIV transmission using scientific methods for matching viral strains. Furthermore, juries and even judges may perceive the science involved as "witch-doctory." Juries' ambivalence about convicting based on such evidence, however, reflects problems with the actual state of science in the field. Juries are skeptical of such findings because they should be.[15] District Attorney Subjack favored an HIV-specific statute as a way around these problems of proof. In a case where a defendant was HIV-positive and his partner originally was not and then the partner became infected, it would simply be assumed that the defendant caused the infection. This would certainly make for simpler prosecutions, but one has to wonder about the wisdom and fairness of allowing the state to make such assumptions rather than having to prove important "elements of the crime" at trial.

The last issue to be considered at this point is whether, given the medical treatments currently available, transmission of HIV means that there is a high probability that an infected party's life will be extinguished. Again, the ambiguities that Subjack noted reflect ongoing transformations that are occurring in the meaning of HIV to those living with the virus. HIV infection is no longer the "death sentence" that it once was, or at least it is no longer the same kind of death sentence. Drug regimens to treat HIV are expensive and demanding, with troublesome short-term side effects and perhaps unknown long-term effects.[16] Yet, partly because of new drug interventions, HIV/AIDS mortality rates in the United States have dropped substantially since 1996, to the point that HIV/AIDS is no longer considered a "leading cause of death" in the U.S. population as a whole.[17] An HIV-specific statute, as conceived by Subjack, would attempt to finesse the matter of HIV's evolution under treatment by simply assuming that transmission, whether intentional or not, constitutes not only a malicious *desire* to end someone's life, but an action that will result in that person's actually dying from the infection. Subjack's statute would assume progression toward AIDS and death within a specified period of time even though that may no longer accurately reflect the progress of the infection's impact and may reflect it even less so in the future.

One could argue that those who have knowingly transmitted HIV to others did not know what the state of medical science would be when their victims became infected, and therefore we should assume that they assumed the worst. This would be a rather large assumption to make regarding particular persons' state of mind and their knowledge of a specific disease. In most cases, it would likely have little connection to what a given person was thinking while pursuing or engaging in unprotected sex. Moreover, most of the criminal HIV-transmission cases that have been brought have been relatively recent, and if Subjack and others with a prosecutorial bent have their way, the numbers will grow. Should statutes assume graduated states of intent that take into account ongoing developments in treatment? Trying to do so would be close to impossible, if not entirely ludicrous. Not doing so, however, would be more than slightly unfair to those engaging in unprotected sex. Should a person really be subject to a twenty-year prison sentence for infecting someone with a treatable disease? If so, why stop with HIV? Should the risky behavior that results in the transmission of any serious disease be subject to criminal prosecution? How serious must the disease be? Ironically, rates of HIV transmission may grow in the coming years in the United States, as many people come to believe HIV to be easily treatable and so take fewer precautions. Although this constitutes an important public health challenge, it is probably not one that is most appropriately addressed through increased criminal prosecutions.

Subjack was never able to influence lawmakers enough to move an HIV-specific statute through the New York State Legislature, but prosecutors continue to bring charges under the state's reckless endangerment laws. In May 2000, for example, Miguel M. Marrero was charged with reckless endangerment for having sex twice with a woman he had met the week previous to their becoming intimate. Marrero told the woman that he was HIV-positive when he saw her on the street several days after they had had sex.[18]

The above examination of the kind of HIV-specific statute favored by Subjack only scratches the surface of the conceptual and policy problems associated with the criminalization of HIV transmission. A host of other issues become apparent when we look more closely at specific criminal HIV cases. In the following section I present a survey of a number of such cases, along with an analysis of the wisdom of pursuing criminal charges in such cases.

Applications of General Criminal Statutes to HIV Cases

A good place to start a survey of criminal HIV cases is with those that, like the Williams case, involved the application of general criminal statutes to HIV transmission. Although some states have passed statutes explicitly singling out HIV transmission for criminal prosecution, in a number of cases prosecutors have attempted to apply existing statutes concerning assault and attempted murder.[19] As noted above, when the state brings such charges, it often has to prove intent to harm. Because of the nature of HIV transmission, in most cases this is difficult to prove, and as one might expect, the record of convictions upheld on appeal is mixed.

Oregon is a state that has never had an HIV-transmission statute on the books. Although the state has laws that prohibit the intentional transmission of communicable diseases, they have not been applied to HIV. Rather, in HIV-related cases the state's prosecutors have relied on invoking attempted murder charges. As a result, very few cases have been prosecuted in the state (only three in the 1990s), but those that have gone to trial have tended to be cases involving particularly egregious conduct.

State of Oregon v. Hinkhouse was the first of such cases. It involved multiple counts of attempted murder and first-degree assault. The defendant, Timothy Hinkhouse, learned that he was HIV-positive in 1989. At that time, he began an on-again, off-again sexual relationship with a fifteen-year-old girl. During the relationship, the defendant refused to wear condoms. In November 1990, Hinkhouse told his probation officer, Bill Caroll, that he was HIV-positive, and Caroll warned Hinkhouse not to have unprotected sex. Caroll reportedly told Hinkhouse that if he infected anyone it would be considered "murder."[20] There was no question at all in this case about Hinkhouse's having knowledge of his infection. Not only did he know about it, he was clearly warned that he should stop having unprotected sex. But that wasn't the end of the story.

In 1992, Hinkhouse was taken into custody on a parole violation. He and Caroll continued to have conversations about HIV. Hinkhouse not only continued to have sex with a number of women, he apparently bragged about it. Taken in on another parole violation, Hinkhouse signed an agreement not to have unsupervised sexual contact with anyone without his parole officer's permission as a condition of his release. Even this was not enough to deter him, however. He continued to have sexual relations with a number of women, in some cases refusing to wear a condom and in each case failing to disclose his HIV status. There was strong evidence that he specifically denied his positive status on at least one occasion. As if that were not enough, one witness testified that Hinkhouse stated that he planned to "go out and spread" the virus.[21]

The Oregon appeals court was unsympathetic to Hinkhouse's claims that he did not intend to harm or kill anyone, finding that he engaged in a "persistent pattern of recruiting sexual partners," "consistently concealed or lied about his HIV status," "refused to wear condoms," engaged in "rough and violent intercourse," and "told at least one person that he intended to spread the disease to others by such conducts."[22] Moreover, it turned out that Hinkhouse was not entirely opposed to wearing condoms and consistently wore one when he engaged in sex with his fiancée. This suggested that Hinkhouse distinguished between women he cared about and those he didn't, offering further evidence that he intended to harm those with whom he didn't have caring relationships. Although none of the women with whom Hinkhouse was involved contracted HIV, the appeals court upheld the trial court's determination that the defendant had acted "deliberately to cause his victims serious bodily injury and death."[23]

The criminal law of assault and attempted murder, as noted, sets the bar high for demonstrating intent to harm. That does not mean, however, that this bar cannot be hurdled. Hinkhouse is about as unattractive a character as one can imagine. His actions appear to be horribly malicious, and the Oregon appeals court's affirmation of his conviction confirms this. It also fits an intuitive sense that, in some cases involving HIV transmission, the perpetrators should be treated severely by the criminal justice system. This case also clarifies, however, that not all cases of knowing HIV transmission are as egregious as Hinkhouse's, and that is precisely why general criminal statutes are best for dealing with them.

Another Oregon case could be included in the same category as Hinkhouse's. "Andrew B" was charged with attempted murder for forcing an eighteen-year-old mentally handicapped person to have sex with him when he knew that he was HIV-positive.[24] Rape is a terrible crime. Few would disagree, moreover, that raping someone while knowing one is HIV-positive is a particularly nasty thing to do. Add to that a victim who is particularly vulnerable, and a very serious criminal charge and a long prison term seem to be in order.

The Washington State case of *State v. Stark* is another that involved a defendant who was warned to change his behavior but didn't. Calvin Stark learned that he was HIV-positive in 1988 and subsequently was advised to practice safe sex and to alert any sexual partners that he was HIV-positive. Upon learning that Stark was disregarding this advice, Dr. Locke, a county health officer, issued a cease and desist order. When Stark still did not stop his activities, Locke went to the county prosecutor to gain support for enforcing the order. The state HIV statute permitted taking Stark into custody to do so.[25] The prosecutor responded by charging Stark with three counts of second-degree assault, one for each of the women with whom he had sexual relations while knowing that he was HIV-positive. (In each case he apprised the woman of his status after the two of them had sexual intercourse.) The prosecutor pursued assault charges even though Washington has an HIV-specific statute because second-degree assault convictions permitted longer sentences.

Both the *Stark* and *Hinkhouse* cases make for interesting contrast with Nushawn Williams's case. In both of the former, the defendants were given repeated legal warnings to stop having sex, and explicit court orders document these warnings. Public health officials apparently approached Williams only once, while he was in jail, alerting him of his status and giving him a verbal warning about the implications of future sexual activity. He was not served with any written notice of potential legal consequences if he engaged in unprotected sexual activities without disclosing his HIV-status (at least I have been unable to uncover any legal documents along these lines). The clarity of the warnings Stark received, and his explicit and repeated refusal to take them seriously, undermines any sympathy one might have for him. His actions indicate his intent, if not to infect someone, at least to disregard clear legal directives. At the same time, however, the fifteen-year prison sentence he received seems rather severe, given that none of the women he endangered became infected with HIV. In Washington, the usual sentence for second-degree assault is from thirteen to seventeen months.

The judge in Stark's case justified the strict sentence by finding Stark to be a "future danger to the community." This was drawn from a statute designed to protect community members, especially children, from "sexual predators."[26] Such a finding stretches the notion of what constitutes a "sexual predator" beyond what was probably intended by the statute. Being moderately promiscuous and being a "predator" are not, one would hope, legally equivalent in Washington State, or in any jurisdiction, for that matter. Sexual predator statutes are generally intended to protect the very young from "child molesters." Each of the women with whom Stark was involved was an adult, and all the sexual contacts were consensual. Moreover, most Americans today are or at least should be aware of HIV's existence and modes of transmission. Any person having unsafe sex with another takes a calculated risk. It is wrong and sometimes illegal for a person who is HIV-positive not to tell sexual partners about that HIV status, but it seems an overstatement to label such a person a predator. (This term was, of course, applied to Williams on numerous occasions.)

The Washington State Supreme Court upheld Stark's conviction but wisely overturned his sentence on the grounds that Stark was not a "sexual predator" as covered by the sentencing statute. The court also nullified "future dangerousness" as a criterion for sentencing in non–sexual offense cases. The legislature had intended, the court ruled, to treat HIV-transmission cases with relatively light sentences, and the trial judge had overstepped his authority by attempting to expand Stark's sentence by labeling him a predator.[27]

One factor that makes criminal prosecution in HIV-transmission cases problematic is that it is relatively difficult for one person to pass HIV to another through sexual contact. Vaginal intercourse, for example, has relatively low transmission rates from male to female and even lower from female to male. The likelihood of transmission of course increases with the number of sexual contacts between two people. District Attorney Subjack told me that even he might have difficulty bringing criminal charges against someone who is HIV-positive who had only one sexual encounter with one other person. Obviously, if an infected person has frequent intercourse with one other person, the chances of that person's becoming infected increase proportionately. If an infected person has one or two encounters with each of a large number of partners, the chances of any one individual being infected might be quite low, but the chances of one of those multiple partners being infected might be relatively high. Williams was represented as someone who did both—he had numerous sexual encounters with each of his partners, and he had sex with a very large number of women. But he was charged with and pled guilty to only two cases of reckless endangerment. A trial court never looked at the actual numbers and the risks his actions posed in a serious way. Given that fact, it remains difficult to sort out the actual harms and risks from the media hyperbole in Williams's case.

The California Supreme Court took a serious look at the issue of the risk of HIV-transmission in the case of *Guevara v. Superior Court,* in which it dismissed assault charges against an HIV-positive defendant who had unprotected sex with several female minors. The defendant had intercourse with each girl only once, and the court ruled that a single instance of uncoerced sex did not amount, under the law, to "force likely to produce great bodily injury," a necessary condition for proving "aggravated assault" under the state's penal code. In the words of the court: "There is no evidence before the magistrate that a single incident of unprotected sex between an HIV-positive male and an uninfected female was likely to result in transmission of HIV antibodies *[sic]* to the female, and medical journal articles based on extensive studies reflect that the risk of transmission from male to female through unprotected vaginal intercourse is fairly low. Consequently, we do not believe that the magistrate had a 'rational basis' for 'assuming the possibility' that petitioner's act was 'likely to produce great bodily injury.'"[28] The California courts, then, unlike those in most other states, have been unwilling to assume that sexual contact with an HIV-positive person automatically means endangerment, assault, or attempted murder. Moving against the trends, the California Supreme Court in *Guevera* required some evidence of a demonstrable threat to health and safety before it would uphold a criminal conviction.

The *Guevara* case did cause something of a sensation, however, because, although Guevara himself was acquitted, the court opened the door to a person's possible conviction on aggravated assault charges "*if* his or her act is likely to cause great bodily injury to his partner."[29] This could include cases involving more than one instance of sexual intercourse or high-risk sexual practices. At the time, some legal analysts and AIDS activists worried that the court's decision could lead to thousands of HIV-positive individuals being subject to long prison terms for not notifying their partners of their status. Widespread prosecution of such cases in California has not, however, materialized.

One might think that sexual assault cases are among those HIV-transmission cases that would be most justly prosecuted under assault or attempted murder statutes, because it seems so clear that the intent of the assailants in such cases is to harm. In another respect, however, such cases reveal the great difficulty prosecutors face in trying to show a connection between sexual contact and the ultimate consequences of HIV infection. Does an HIV-positive rapist by definition intend to transmit the virus to a victim? Courts in Maryland have held that this is not necessarily the case. In *Smallwood v. State,* for example, the court overturned a conviction related to HIV transmission in such an instance. Dwight Smallwood was apprised of his HIV-positive status in 1991, and, at that time, a social worker directed him to engage only in "safe sex." He tested positive for HIV twice again in 1992. In September 1993, Smallwood, with an accomplice, participated in three armed robberies during which he raped three different women. He did not wear a condom during any of the rapes.[30]

Smallwood was charged with a variety of crimes, including attempted first-degree rape, robbery with a deadly weapon, assault with intent to murder, and reckless endangerment. He was also charged with second-degree attempted murder of each victim for having knowingly risked transmission of HIV.[31] Although he pled guilty to the rape and robbery charges, he pled innocent to attempted murder. He was ultimately, however, convicted of that charge as well.[32]

The Maryland Court of Appeals overturned Smallwood's second-degree murder convictions on the grounds that there was insufficient evidence of intent on Smallwood's part. The prosecutors had compared Smallwood's body to a loaded weapon that he fired into the bodies of the three women he had robbed and raped, a comparison that convinced the trial jury, but not the appeals court. According to the court, "The risk to which Smallwood exposed his victims when he forced them to engage in unprotected sexual activity must not be minimized, [but] the State has presented no evidence from which it can reasonably be concluded that death by AIDS is a probable result of Smallwood's actions to the same extent that death is the probable result of firing a deadly weapon at a vital part of someone's body."[33] In other words, the court deemed an individual's knowledge of his or her HIV-positive status and that person's sexual contact with another (even, as in this case, forced sexual contact) to be insufficient *in and of itself* to establish intent. Other evidence of intent would be necessary. In this case, the court found that there was no additional evidence of any intent, and thus it overturned the convictions.

A similar result occurred in Colorado, where Jesus Perez was convicted of "attempted extreme indifference murder." Perez was shown to have had sex with his ten-year-old daughter while he had knowledge that he was HIV-positive. Although his conviction on charges of sexual assault on a minor was upheld, his conviction for attempted murder was overturned on the grounds that the element of "universal malice" necessary to sustain such a charge was not shown, given that Perez's conduct was not intended to kill.[34]

Smallwood and Perez are both characters for whom most of us can have little sympathy, and their actions were completely reprehensible. Yet their partial acquittals reveal the difficulty of showing that an HIV-positive person's mere act of intercourse should be considered as equivalent to an intentional attempt to kill someone. The Maryland and Colorado court opinions discussed above support the idea that murder charges should be considered only very rarely in cases of knowing HIV transmission. The difficulties demonstrated by these cases have led state legislatures to turn to HIV-specific statutes as a way around them. Court decisions regarding such statutes have shown this to be a relatively successful strategy.

HIV Criminalization Statutes

If a state's main motivation for instituting HIV-specific criminal statutes is to remove the messiness and difficulty associated with proving intent, probability of transmission, and risk of death, then that goal seems largely to be reached once such statutes are in place. In the first Iowa criminal HIV-transmission case, for example, Aaron Dahlberg was accused of having unprotected sex with three men while being HIV-positive. Dahlberg's attorney argued that prosecutors needed to show a "significant, documented, or merely theoretical risk of transmission." None of Dahlberg's partners tested positive, and Dahlberg contended that he had engaged only in low-risk practices with each. The judge rejected the argument, ruling that prosecutors needed only to show evidence of sexual contact. The Iowa statute had effectively silenced arguments regarding the degree of risk involved.[35]

Constitutional challenges to such statutes are difficult to sustain, as the case of *State of Louisiana v. Salvadore Andrew Gamberella* illustrates. This case involved a defendant who was notified that he was HIV-positive after he donated plasma in June 1989. At some time after he had been apprised of his status, Gamberella started having a sexual relationship with an eighteen-year-old woman he had been dating for several months. Unaware that Gamberella was HIV-positive, but concerned about avoiding pregnancy, the woman demanded that Gamberella wear a condom. She became pregnant anyway, as the result of a condom's failing, and she then stopped requiring Gamberella to wear one. The couple lived together from before their baby's birth until several months afterward. Eventually, a routine blood test revealed that the woman was HIV-positive. As her then current boyfriend was HIV-negative, she reasoned that the defendant had infected her. She testified that Gamberella had never told her that he was HIV-positive, and that he had specifically told her that he was a blood donor and had never been rejected for giving blood. Gamberella, however, maintained that he had told the victim that he was HIV-positive soon after they started dating.[36]

Gamberella was tried and convicted under a Louisiana statute that stated, "No person shall intentionally expose another to any acquired immunity deficiency syndrome (AIDS) virus through sexual contact without the knowing and lawful consent of the victim."[37] He was sentenced to ten years at hard labor, without the possibility of parole. Gamberella challenged his conviction on several grounds. First, his attorney contended that the state had illegally obtained Gamberella's medical test results in the case, because it had not secured a court's permission to examine the records until after it had both requested and received them. This was a potentially significant claim, because allowing the state access to such records without a court's permission could lead to violations of privacy and abuses of prosecutorial authority. Questions of confidentiality have been important to HIV discourse from the beginning of the epidemic, because the public release of information about individuals' HIV status can have devastating consequences. The Louisiana court, however, gave the claim little weight, simply asserting that the "state's interest in prosecuting [the] defendant for his violation of [the criminal statute] outweighed defendant's interest in maintaining the confidentiality of his test results."[38]

The court also gave short shrift to the defendant's claim that his Fourth Amendment rights had been violated, reasoning that the material would "inevitably have been seized by law enforcement personnel in a constitutional manner."[39] The generalized application of such a rule could have truly frightening consequences. If any evidence that would "inevitably" be obtained in a constitutional manner were considered to be subject to search or expropriation by the police, then many of the protections offered by the Fourth Amendment would be undermined. Police could enter a house without a warrant, gather material, and later claim that the material would inevitably have been obtained in a constitutional manner, and thus no Fourth Amendment violation had occurred.

Gamberella also challenged the wording of the statute. His attorney argued that the terms "sexual contact" and "knowing consent" were vague. More significantly, he argued that the statute was improperly constructed and confused HIV infection with actual AIDS and thus did not accurately define the nature of the sanctioned behavior. (One cannot "transmit" AIDS, as the statute implied, because it is not a virus but a clinical syndrome.)[40] Gamberella would have had a good chance of conviction under a reckless endangerment statute. A written record existed to show that he had been informed of his HIV status, and he never denied that he had knowledge of it. The presence of an HIV-specific statute had the likely ef-

HIV Culpability

fect of increasing the severity of the sentence he could receive. The statute was poorly written, but in its zeal to uphold a conviction under the statute, the Louisiana Supreme Court refused to entertain legitimate questions about serious mistakes in its construction, such as the confusion of HIV with AIDS. This case offers evidence of the potentially damaging impact of such statutes to the overall integrity and fairness of the legal system.

Similar claims of poor statutory construction were leveled against a 1988 Missouri law that made it a class D felony for someone to "deliberately create a grave and unjustifiable risk" of spreading HIV through sexual contact. The statute made no distinction between HIV-positive persons who informed their partners of their status and those who did not.[41] The law was amended in 1995 to mark that distinction, but two defendants who had been convicted under the original law challenged its constitutionality. Sean L. Sykes had had sex with one woman and one girl without telling either that he was HIV-positive, and Charles Mahan had had sex with a man without informing him that he was HIV-positive. Sykes and Mahan had been sentenced to ten and five years in prison, respectively. They challenged the law on both vagueness and privacy grounds, but the Missouri Supreme Court rejected their arguments.[42]

Sykes and Mahan claimed that the statute was vague because common sense alone could not determine what constituted a "grave and unjustifiable risk." The prosecutor argued that, given that both defendants had been counseled several times about the nature of HIV infection, they were fully aware of the risks.[43] The court summarily dismissed the defendants' claims, stating that the heterosexual and homosexual intercourse in which they engaged created risks that fell under the meaning of the statute. Through this ruling, the court essentially gave the legislature license to make sexual contact, even with full disclosure of infection, constitutionally legitimate grounds for criminal prosecution.

In 1997, Missouri again revised its criminal HIV-transmission statute so that any HIV-positive person who subsequently tested positive for syphilis or gonorrhea would be considered, prima facie, to have violated the state's criminal transmission law. That is, the presence of a subsequent infection would be construed as clear evidence of the individual's having had unprotected sex. The legislature justified the law by asserting that prosecutors' previous reliance on the testimony of affected sex partners made it difficult to obtain convictions, because few people wanted to come forward to testify against those who may have infected them.[44]

In criminal HIV-transmission cases, the courts have upheld broad authority on the part of prosecutors to have access to HIV test results. Like many states, Missouri has confidentiality laws that prevent disclosure of HIV test results to anyone other than certain public health employees.

But although prosecutors are not given explicit access to these test results under the law, there is an exception in the law that allows non–public health employees outside of the health department access to test results if they have a "need to know" in the performance of their public duties.[45] The court simply ruled that this anticipated the release of HIV test results to prosecutors, judges, and juries.

Gender differences associated with risk of HIV infection are also erased by such statutes. In the companion cases of State v. Russell and State v. Lunsford, the Illinois Supreme Court ruled on the constitutionality of a state law that made it a class 2 felony, punishable by up to seven years in prison, for an individual to knowingly transmit HIV to another person through intimate contact. The court rejected challenges to the statute's vagueness. These cases are interesting because Caretha Russell and Miles Lunsford were treated as equivalent under the law, even though infection rates differ significantly between women and men. Caretha Russell knew that she was HIV-positive when she engaged in consensual sex with Daren Smith without telling him of her infection. Lunsford was charged with raping a woman when he knew that he was HIV-positive. Yet the two were treated the same under the Illinois statute with regard to the transmission of HIV.[46]

Overall, the cases discussed above suggest that HIV-specific statutes are more or less immune to constitutional challenges on grounds of vagueness or on grounds that they treat differently situated defendants equally. Legislatures' aim in passing such statutes is to make convictions easier, and they have succeeded in doing so, with very little restriction from state appeals courts.

Sentence Enhancement

One reason many states have implemented HIV-specific statutes is to make lengthier sentences available for those convicted of transmitting HIV. Reckless endangerment and assault charges are sometimes limited in terms of the potential sentences that can be imposed, and prosecutors and legislators want those convicted of HIV-related crimes to spend long periods of time behind bars. If specific criminal statutes do not exist to allow that, however, prosecutors may seek to "enhance" the sentences in cases involving HIV transmission. In other words, prosecutors and judges have pushed to strengthen the severity of penalizing HIV transmission in both conviction and sentencing phases. State judges often have a good deal of discretion when it comes to imposing sentences, and factors that might not be brought forward legitimately during a trial (such as the defendant's past criminal record) are fair game during a sentencing hearing. In Maryland, a trial judge took Jose Morales's HIV-positive status into account to "enhance" his twenty-five-year sentence for sexual assaults on a fourteen-year-old girl. Morales was, at the time of the assaults, unaware of his infection. On appeal, the state's highest court found that a judge has "virtually boundless discretion" in determining what to take into account in sentencing a defendant, and thus upheld the sentence.[47]

The case of *Tennessee v. Pipkin* had a similar result. Winford Lee Pipkin was sentenced to 105 years in prison upon being convicted of "especially aggravated kidnapping" and five counts of child rape. Pipkin's attorney objected that the sentence on the rape charges was enhanced because of Pipkin's HIV-positive status, even though Pipkin did not know about that status until the day before he was sentenced. As in Maryland, the Tennessee Court of Criminal Appeals ruled that it was appropriate for the judge to consider the defendant's HIV status as a factor in sentence enhancement whether or not the defendant had knowledge of his status.[48]

Texas courts have ruled that defendants' HIV-positive status is a legitimate consideration in sentencing in sexual assault cases. In *Najera v. State of Texas,* the defendant was found guilty of sexually assaulting a fifteen-year-old boy, and the jury took the fact that Najera knew that he was HIV-positive into account as an aggravating factor in giving him a ten-year prison sentence. The jury concluded, and the ruling was upheld, that Najera's "use of his sexual organ and bodily fluid in his penis constituted an 'intentional and knowing use and exhibit of a deadly weapon' toward his victims."[49] Najera's case became a cause célèbre in Texas. Najera had a successful lawn-care business, but during his trial it came out that many of his employees were illegal Mexican workers whom he had transported across the border and kept as virtual slaves at his Travis County home. His wife won the largest divorce settlement in Texas history after recounting two years of extremely serious abuse. Najera was also convicted of raping a sixteen-year-old girl, whom he locked out on his roof on a January night, where she subsequently died of exposure. He was sentenced to ninety-nine years for causing her death.[50] Still, the HIV charge was, at the time, a groundbreaking prosecution strategy in the state of Texas.[51] Given Najera's profile, jurors no doubt had little trouble accepting its validity.

Nushawn Williams's sentence also seems to have been enhanced due to his HIV status. If Williams's "reckless endangerment" had involved, say, the use of an automobile or a weapon, there is little likelihood that he would have received as stiff a sentence as he did. The expectation that he should be imprisoned for a very long time crept into considerations concerning his parole as well. On the occasion of his first parole hearing (held on July 31, 2001), at which point Williams had served the minimum four years of his sentence, the media brought a fair amount of attention back to the case. In District Attorney Subjack's comments to local newspapers, he repeated many of the things he had told me in our interview. Subjack said that he believed that Williams had not been convicted of all the crimes of which he was guilty, and the County Attorney's Office had been unable to obtain the lengthier sentences that he thought were warranted, because his hands were tied by the state's criminal laws. Because of this, Subjack believed that Williams should serve out his maximum sentence. One could question the legal fairness of a general principle that states that defendants should serve lengthier sentences when they have been accused of particular crimes, but not convicted.

In January 2001, the Washington State Supreme Court overturned the sentence of Randall Louis Ferguson, who had been convicted of assault in 1996. The assault conviction stemmed from Ferguson's having had unprotected sex with a partner in 1994 while knowing he was HIV-positive. Prosecutors presented testimony during the trial from six women who said Ferguson had had unprotected sex with them, and two of these witnesses stated that Ferguson had specifically denied that he was HIV-positive when they asked about his status.[52] The court ruled that Ferguson's ten-year sentence exceeded sentencing guidelines and that the prosecution had cited "deliberate cruelty" as an element of the crime and thus could not also use that to justify the lengthy sentence.[53]

Nonsexual Transmission Cases: Intent and Impossibility

The quintessential "easy" nonsexual HIV-transmission case is *Louisiana v. Schmidt*. Dr. Richard Schmidt had a clear desire to injure his mistress, Janice Trahan, with HIV, and he had the means to do so. Schmidt and Trahan had had a long-running extramarital affair that was serious enough that Trahan divorced her first husband. Schmidt in turn agreed to divorce his wife, but did not follow through with this promise. Convinced that he would never do so, Trahan broke off the relationship. Subsequently, Schmidt separated from his wife and reconciled with Trahan, but eventually he returned to his wife. Trahan broke things off a second time, but continued to communicate with Schmidt, from whom she was receiving an ongoing series of vitamin B_{12} injections. At trial, she testified that one of the injections Schmidt gave her was "more painful" than the others, and it was after this injection that her health seemed to deteriorate. Five months afterward, she tested positive for HIV infection and learned that she had contracted hepatitis C.[54]

Schmidt was eventually charged with intentionally injecting Trahan with HIV (although not the hepatitis C virus). During the course of the trial, it became evident that Schmidt, one of Louisiana's leading gastroenterologists, had drawn two blood samples from each of two patients—LL and DM—without following the usual procedures. Both samples from both patients were taken in Schmidt's office, and entries were made in both patients' files showing that two samples were drawn, but there were no corresponding receipts for any test results from the second samples. LL suffered from hepatitis C, and DM was HIV-positive.[55] This circumstantial evidence was also supported during the trial by DNA evidence, which became the focal point of the appeal.

During the trial, the state employed the services of a physician at the Baylor College of Medicine who testified that a "phylogenetic" analysis showed that the HIV discovered in Trahan was "closely related" to that found in DM. On appeal, Schmidt challenged the admissibility of this conclusion that the samples were "closely related." Although the use of DNA evidence was well established in Louisiana, the use of DNA to establish similarities in viral infections was without precedent. The Louisiana Appeals Court ultimately upheld Schmidt's conviction on charges of attempted second-degree murder.[56] The U.S. Supreme Court subsequently refused to hear the case.[57]

HIV cases such as *Schmidt* are distinguishable from sexual transmission cases in that the rate of transmission through sexual intercourse is much lower than that achieved through the direct injection of blood containing HIV. The former is a relatively inefficient mechanism for transmission and does not, in itself, indicate intent. The latter is a very efficient mechanism for transmission and does, on the face of it, indicate malice. A case like Schmidt's comes closest to the "loaded gun" analogy, although the analogy is by no means perfect even here, because it is impossible to inflict the same amount of immediate damage on another with an HIV injection as one can by firing a gun. Still, it is likely that few would object to the state's treating physicians such as Schmidt harshly under the criminal law.

A somewhat similar case occurred in Long Island, New York, in 2001, when a woman hired a man (who turned out to be a police informant) to inject her husband with HIV-tainted blood. Budhwantie Ferri's plan was for the man to find an HIV-positive man and bring him to the Ferri home. Once there, the hired man and his HIV-positive partner would assault both Mr. and Mrs. Ferri. Mrs. Ferri would feign an injury, and the two attackers would knock Mr. Ferri unconscious. Then they would inject Mr. Ferri with blood from the HIV-positive man. Needless to say, the scheme failed.[58]

The case of *State v. Caine* involved a defendant, Donald Caine, who was convicted of robbing a convenience store, taking a carton of cigarettes, and then stabbing one of the employees, Wanda Fitzgerald, with a syringe filled with clear fluid while shouting, "I'll give you AIDS."[59] The syringe itself was never actually found or entered into evidence at the trial, so it was never determined whether there was an actual threat of transmission, although it was determined that Caine was indeed HIV-positive. Three months after the incident, Fitzgerald still tested negative for the virus, making it seem unlikely that the contents of the syringe posed a threat to her life or health. Still, Caine was convicted of attempted second-degree murder, presumably based on his intent at the time. He was sentenced to fifty years in prison as a habitual offender. On appeal, Caine's attorney argued that intent to kill, a requirement for a conviction on a second-degree murder charge, had not been demonstrated. The appellate court showed little sympathy for this position and allowed intent to rest on the facts that Caine was HIV-positive and addicted to drugs and that the probability was high that Fitzgerald would have been infected if the needle that pierced her skin had been laced with the virus.

Caine is problematic, because one has to wonder whether the threat of stabbing someone with a syringe and claiming that it contains HIV is equivalent to demonstrating that the syringe actually contained a substance (i.e., blood) that could sustain the virus over a long enough period of time to infect someone if injected into him or her. The distance between *Schmidt* and *Caine* seems to be relatively great. Still it is at least conceivable that Caine could have infected another person with the syringe.[60]

Even more problematic are "saliva" cases, in which the perpetrators intend to do the impossible—that is, infect others with bodily fluids that do not contain the virus. The Texas case of *Weeks v. State* is such a case. Curtis Weeks who was HIV-positive, was being transferred from one prison unit in the state to another. Weeks was extremely violent during the transfer, to the point that he significantly damaged the inside of the van in which he was being transported. He threatened the guards in a variety of ways, including, at one point, saying that he would "cut one of [their] heads off." He also stated that he was "HIV-4." He then spit twice at the face of one of the guards. One guard stated that Weeks had said that "he had AIDS and that he was going to take as many with him as he could." The guard testified that he believed that Weeks had intended to kill him. Weeks was convicted of attempted murder, which in the state of Texas requires that "a person, with specific intent to commit an offense, does an act amounting to more than mere preparation and that tends, but fails, to affect the commission of the offense intended."[61]

The question raised on appeal was whether there was "sufficient evidence, when viewed in the light more favorable to the verdict . . . showing that appellant could have transmitted HIV by spitting on the officer." The court upheld the conviction on the grounds that it had "not been conclusively established and is not free from reasonable dispute" that it was impossible to transmit HIV through saliva. The prosecution relied on a number of medical experts, each of whom argued that it had never been proven that "HIV could not be transmitted through saliva."[62] The experts drew on some highly questionable cases in which it was alleged that HIV had been transmitted via such means. The defendant, given his two prior felony convictions, was sentenced to life in prison.

Another saliva case involved an HIV-positive Ohio man, Jimmy Lee Bird, who pled "no contest" to intentionally spitting in the face of a police officer. Bird was sentenced to a prison term of three to fifteen years. He then contended that he had made the plea because he had ineffective counsel, a claim that was rejected by the Ohio Supreme Court. The court ruled that Bird's plea indicated an admission of the validity of the allegations, and thus it was unnecessary for the court to decide whether spitting could actually result in the transmission of HIV.[63] One of the seven judges on the court did dissent, however. Justice Paul Pfeiffer ruled that Bird's "no contest" plea did not make the saliva a deadly weapon under the state's law. In Pfeiffer's words, "What if the indictment had said Bird assaulted office Shirk with a powder puff, a water balloon, or a jelly doughnut, and Bird had pleaded no contest. The fact that the indictment calls something a deadly weapon does not make it so. . . . A person who makes a plea of no contest does not become his own judge."[64]

In *Scroggins v. State,* Greg Scroggins, an HIV-positive Georgia man, was convicted of "aggravated assault with attempt to murder" after he bit a police officer in the arm when the officer attempted to break up a fight in which Scroggins was involved. The "bite was strong enough to tear through the officer's long-sleeved shirt, and left distinct, full-mouth bite wounds which took ten months to heal." The court ruled that whether the bite was actually a "deadly weapon" was immaterial to the disposition of the case. All that was required, the court determined, in an extremely confused opinion, was the necessary intent. In the words of the court, "The State indicted appellant Greg Scroggins for assault with intent to murder; this was all it needed to allege. There was no requirement to prove the method of assault was deadly or likely to inflict serious bodily injury." The appellant apparently "laughed" when asked if he was HIV-positive, and this was considered to be proof that he intended to "murder" officer D. P. Crook. Moreover, a "'wanton and reckless' state of mind is sometimes the equivalent of a specific intent to kill." The court analogized that if someone did not know that a toy gun was indeed a toy and intended to kill someone with it, that person would be guilty of the same offense. The court also ruled that a "theoretical possibility" of transmitting the virus was still a possibility, and that "as long as medical science concedes it," it could be considered as real by a jury.[65]

Prosecutors have not always been successful in these cases, however. In Idaho, a case was thrown out when the judge ruled that a person's biting a police officer's leg did not in and of itself indicate that saliva had touched the officer. The case involved the question of whether a person could be required to be tested for HIV if he was engaged in "certain crimes in which body fluid 'has likely been transmitted to another.'"[66] The prosecution's own expert had raised doubts about the likelihood of the transmission of HIV through saliva. Skepticism about the likelihood of transmission in cases where HIV is impossible to transmit, seems, however, to be the exception and not the rule.

Criminal Convictions Abroad

Panics involving HIV have not been confined to the United States, and sometimes other nations have used criminal laws to deal with HIV issues. In Sweden in 1998, in a case that received very little international attention, an HIV-positive Iranian immigrant was wanted in connection with his having had sex with what was reported to be more than one hundred women. Police had raided the man's apartment in connection with a rape charge and discovered a notebook containing the names of two hundred Swedish women along with notations on their sexual performance. Police published the man's name and photograph in violation of laws protecting privacy. Swedish law provides for a sentence of one to ten years in prison for knowingly infecting others with HIV.[67]

A Finnish court sentenced an American to fourteen years in prison for seventeen counts of attempted manslaughter when he was determined to have had unprotected sex even though he knew that he had HIV. Prosecutors charged that he had sex with more than one hundred women. Five of them turned out to be HIV-positive. The sentence was one of the harshest, short of life, that could have been imposed under Finnish law.[68]

Civil Liability

Issues of liability in relation to the transmission of HIV have not been confined to criminal proceedings. In what has been described as a "rare case," a gay San Francisco man, Alan Louie, was held civilly liable for "sexual battery" when he did not warn his partner, Mychael Robinson, that he was HIV-positive before they had unprotected sex. A federal court judge ordered Louie to pay Robinson twenty-five thousand dollars for "emotional pain and suffering," even though it turned out that Robinson was HIV-negative. The judge had reduced Robinson's original claim of half a million dollars in damages. The only previous claim in California on similar grounds involved a lawsuit by Rock Hudson's former lover, Marc Christian, against Hudson's estate after Hudson died of AIDS. Christian received an initial judgment of more than twenty-one million dollars, which was later reduced.[69]

The judge in the San Francisco case ruled that Louie had a "duty to tell Robinson that he was HIV positive prior to engaging in sexual activity with him." Objections to the opinion were, however, raised by Jon Davidson of the Lambda Legal Defense and Education Fund. Davidson contended that the ruling was contrary to the previous decision in *Kerins v. Hartley* (1994), in which a California appellate court overturned damages awarded to a woman who claimed emotional distress when she learned that a surgeon who had operated on her was HIV-positive. Davidson contended that you have to "prove that it's more likely than not that you're going to be infected."[70]

Conclusion

It is tempting to conclude that the complexities of the issues surrounding HIV transmission make it difficult if not impossible to draw general conclusions. Several observations are, however, worth making. First, the most crucial issues in cases involving HIV transmission are "intent," "consent," and "risk." A case that would presumably be least likely to generate criminal charges (or at least one in which I would be least likely to support criminal charges) would be one in which intent is absent (that is, the person involved did not know he or she was HIV-positive, did not fully understand the consequences of his or her conduct, or took measures to lessen the possibility of transmission). Moreover, in a case in which a partner would have consented, either implicitly or explicitly, to engage in risky activities (such as unprotected sex with a prostitute or a known IV drug user), this should at the very least be considered as a mitigating factor. And finally, certain kinds of conduct, sexual (e.g., oral) or not (e.g., spitting), in which the risks of transmission are small should not be prosecuted.

The kinds of cases that presumably would be most deserving of the application of criminal charges would be those that involve deliberate and stated attempts to transmit the virus, sexual assault, and high risk of transmission (sexual contact in which blood is exchanged). Some of the cases discussed above include all or many of these facts, but some do not.

The thorniest problems are raised by those cases in which there is consent to sexual contact and knowledge of HIV-positive status on the part of only one of the partners, with no additional known or controllable risk factors. Should cases like these be prosecuted? Presumably, a great many of the HIV-positive persons in the United States contracted the virus as the result of such activities. Obviously, except in a very small number of cases, HIV transmitters have not been prosecuted. Even the most ardent supporters of the criminalization of HIV transmission would probably not argue that they should have been. The problem is in distinguishing the irresponsible or insensitive from the criminal. Decisions to prosecute, I would argue, should be made only in the most clear-cut or obvious cases. HIV-specific transmission statutes, insofar as they encourage more prosecutions and severe sentences for those who put others at risk without demonstrable intent and effect, undermine the ethical foundations of criminal law and are of questionable practical value. They treat matters that can be more effectively handled by the public health system as criminal acts deserving of punishment and jail. No evidence exists that such laws lower transmission rates. Not only are they unwise and ineffective, they represent an approach to disease control that is virtually without historical precedent.

Conclusion

The problems that Nushawn Williams had been having at Auburn continued and seemed to grow worse toward the end of the summer of 2001.
He had been in prison for almost four years by that time. Primarily,
he claimed he was being harassed by inmates and that the harassment
was sanctioned by guards. I had no way of finding out whether or not this
was the case. I was concerned enough, however, to contact Prisoners' Legal
Services in Tompkins County and to send a letter to the state corrections
commissioner, attaching a letter Nushawn had written to me expressing
fear for his life. I received a response from the commissioner stating that
the matter had been investigated and that there was no merit to Nushawn's
claims. In August, after his parole hearing, I heard nothing from Nushawn
for almost a month. When I eventually received a letter from him, he told
me that he had been given 110 days in keep lock for allegedly throwing
feces at another inmate. Nushawn vehemently denied that he had done
this and claimed that another inmate had thrown urine on himself in front

of Nushawn's cell to make it appear as though Nushawn had done it. The guards immediately moved Nushawn to solitary confinement. He said that during his hearing on the matter, no evidence of feces had been offered. That was his story, anyway. He would, he told me, attempt to appeal the decision, using forms that had been provided by Prisoners' Legal Services.

As a result of this latest disciplinary sanction, Nushawn was moved to Southport Correctional Facility, which is about an hour south of Ithaca. When he eventually phoned me from there, I asked how he had been doing. His life, he said, "was a living hell." Southport is a place for the state's worst prisoners, and all are confined to their cells for twenty-three hours a day. I told Nushawn that I'd be interested in visiting, but he asked me to wait until he was transferred. He didn't want me to see him in his current condition. In October, he was transferred to Elmira Correctional Facility, about a half hour south of Ithaca.

Most central New York and western New York prisons, such as Auburn, Attica, and Elmira, are relatively old facilities. The most recent spate of prison building in New York State has taken place in the northern part of the state. The reasons for this are relatively straightforward. Prisons are built according to a formula derived from pork-barrel politics, and sites are chosen so as to provide jobs in areas of the state historically neglected by Albany. Thus many of the newer prisons are on the fringes of the Adirondacks (and far from the metropolitan areas where the prisoners' families tend to reside).

Elmira Correctional Facility, like Auburn, was built in the nineteenth century. Opened in 1876, it was the vision of Zebulon Reed Brockway, who rejected the Auburn strategy of "silence, obedience, and labor." Instead, Brockway proposed the concept of "reform." At Elmira, individualized treatments would be developed for each prisoner, and indeterminate sentences, with possibility of parole, would give inmates incentives to improve themselves. Under Brockway's administration, Elmira became known as the country's first "reformatory."[1] The prison is an imposing edifice, sitting at the top of a hill several blocks from the city center. The city of Elmira is the burial place of Mark Twain, and more of the city's signage points a visitor in the direction of that spot than toward the prison. Still, the prison is an important part of the community's economy, providing dozens of reasonably well-paying jobs to Elmira residents.

I went to visit Nushawn at Elmira a week before Christmas. Large letters on the front lawn leading up to the prison entrance spelled out "Merry Christmas" and "Happy New Year." From the outside Elmira isn't as grim looking as Auburn, but in spite of the decorations, it didn't have a welcoming feel. The brick structure is darkly Victorian, and, in spite of valiant attempts to spruce it up a bit for the holidays, *foreboding* is the adjective that came to my mind.

When I met with Nushawn, he was mostly concerned with attempts on the part of prison officials to move him into the general population. He was worried that he would be targeted there. (After the move, however, things seemed to be fine, leading me to think that his notoriety had dimmed to some extent, a fact with which he might not entirely have come to terms.) He was also understandably focused on being released. In spite of his problems at Auburn, he had not lost any of his "good time," so he would be released on his conditional release date, after six years in prison, in October 2003.

He also gave me a raft of legal documents, most of which dealt with the potential appeal of his sentence. It turned out that the issue Lou Schipano had discovered regarding the plea agreement Nushawn had reached with New York City prosecutors had some merit. Nushawn had agreed to a one-year sentence for cocaine possession and sale of a controlled substance for an arrest that took place on September 22, 1997, in the Bronx. Nushawn and his codefendants, Eric Cox and Marvin Jones, pled guilty to the charges.[2] Each received a one-year sentence, reduced to rehabilitation, as part of a plea agreement. But when Nushawn's name was released by Chautauqua County health officials, the prosecutors withdrew the offer.

The court's withdrawal of the plea was challenged at the time by Nushawn's New York attorney, William Cember. The prosecutors contended that the information coming out of Chautauqua County made the original plea inappropriate. The judge agreed with them, stating, "Based upon the information of the nature and extent of the possible new crimes committed and this defendant's criminal history obtained after the plea was entered, I cannot in good conscious [sic] impose the agreed upon sentence; and, therefore, I am offering to vacate the guilty plea at this time."[3] Although it is established law, that courts can withdraw plea agreements if new information about defendants' past criminal records comes forward, in this case, the new information was only at that point a set of accusations, accusations that had been widely circulated by national media outlets. Cember submitted an application for a writ of mandamus, a legal writ that would require action on the part of a public official—in this case, Justice John T. Byrne of the New York State Supreme Court—to honor the original plea agreement.

Cember claimed that Nushawn's case needed to be distinguished from a precedent (specifically, *People v. Selikoff*)[4] in which a previous conviction record, discovered during presentencing, was grounds for nullifying the plea. Here, Cember argued, the information that came forward had not been proven. In his words, "It's not as if the Court learned information that made my client either more culpable or committed acts pursuant to this particular case."[5] Moreover, Cember cited *People v. McConnell,* in which the New York Court of Appeals ruled that in those cases where the "defendant cannot be put back to the original position; in other words, he can't be put back whole," the original plea agreement must be honored, even if additional information makes the sentence inappropriate.[6] In Nushawn's case, because of the tremendous publicity, Cember argued, Nushawn could not, in effect, be "made whole." The case had become so contaminated by publicity that Nushawn could not receive a fair trial on the cocaine conviction.

Judge Byrne rejected the claim, but the memo that Nushawn had written in prison, with Lou's help, had raised the claim in a way that was convincing enough that the state had now appointed Nushawn a lawyer to appeal that part of his sentence. Nushawn was understandably pleased by the possibility that his conditional release date would be moved up by a year.

The other documents that Nushawn sent me seemed almost surrealistic. He included several letters from news organizations asking for interviews. The producer for the *CBS Evening News* wrote, "We're interested in getting your side of the story out there. Much has been said about you on television . . . but I feel you should have the opportunity to tell us about what happened. We are eager to speak with you and would be happy to accommodate your schedule."[7] This last part was particularly ironic, given that it was sent to Nushawn while he was at the Rikers Island Correctional Facility. A reporter for Fox News had also written asking for an interview, stating, "I would very much like to know the entire story from your mouth. . . . Sadly, who you are, what you are and what your intentions might have been are all being determined for your [sic] by the police and the prosecutors office and in order for you to get your side of the story out, you much [sic] find the courage and strength to speak out and defend yourself."[8] A producer for NBC's *Dateline* also wrote, stating, "At this point the press in New York is having a virtual feeding frenzy in this story, and I am sure there is a great deal of wrong information being printed about you and your case. We would like to give you the opportunity to speak for yourself to tell YOUR side of this story." The producer went on to "promise" that the program "would develop this story more sensitively and fairly than other news outlets that may have been in touch with you. 'Dateline' would like to be the first news organization to interview you and tell your side of the story—the real story as only you can tell it."[9] Even the *New York Daily News* and *The Jerry Springer Show* indicated that they were interested in Nushawn's side of things.[10] I couldn't help wondering why, with all of this purported concern about reporting the "two sides" of this story, the "other side," so to speak, had been absent from the media coverage of the case.

Another document that drew my attention was a memo that included reports on two psychiatric evaluations of Nushawn that were conducted at Bellevue Hospital.[11] Nushawn was referred to Bellevue for evaluation while he was confined to Rikers Island, before he had entered his final guilty plea, in February 1998. The New York State Supreme Court wanted a determination as to whether he was mentally competent to stand trial. Although news reports about the evaluations led to statements that Nushawn was "schizophrenic," in fact, both psychiatrists who evaluated him determined him to be mentally "fit."[12]

On the surface, he seemed to be a young man with serious psychological problems. One psychiatrist, Dr. Trachtenberg, reported that Nushawn had heard voices, that he stated that he had attempted suicide several times, and that he had engaged in cocaine and marijuana binges. Still, Trachtenberg described Nushawn's thought processes as "logical, coherent, and goal directed." Moreover, he said that Nushawn showed no "evidence of any delusions . . . during the interview." Nushawn also "regularly ate meals, attended closely to his personal hygiene, and took an interest in watching TV despite his complaints of depression." And, in fact, although Nushawn reported hearing voices, "there was no objective evidence of him talking to himself or responding to internal stimulation in any way." Nushawn scored high on "five of the eight primary scales in the 'definite' feigning range." Trachtenberg concluded that "while the defendant reports intermittently hearing voices and having suicidal thoughts, Mr. Johnson does not present the signs and symptoms of a severe mental disorder. In fact, at times he appears to be exaggerating or feigning psychiatric symptoms."[13]

Dr. Bardey's evaluation was even more positive. He found that "during [Williams's] stay in our service, there was no evidence of disorganization in his thinking, no evidence of behavioral dyscontrol, and no evidence of any psychotic symptomology." And although when Nushawn was interviewed "his demeanor became withdrawn, stone faced, and sedated," Bardey observed that "when in the company of his peers or nurses' aides, he manifested a full range of affect and was engaging and forthcoming." Although Nushawn denied that he could read or write, "he was seen frequently reading in his room, in which magazines, letters, legal correspondence and cards were neatly arranged."[14]

When I later asked Nushawn about these reports, he told me that he had been trying to fake schizophrenia and drug addiction, the first so that he could be moved into the psychiatric unit, which was apparently a more pleasant place than the prison, and the second so that he could be placed in a rehabilitation program, with the hope of having his sentence reduced. Although it is probably good policy for the state to offer inducements for drug offenders to seek entry into treatment programs, in Nushawn's case this seemed to have the somewhat perverse effect of encouraging him to feign an addiction he did not have.

For most of 2002, Nushawn's stay at Elmira was uneventful. He was not placed in protective custody again, and he seemed to settle into prison life reasonably well. He voiced few complaints about how he was treated by the guards. His routine seemed to revolve around working on his legal case, reading Jackie Collins novels, and corresponding with a number of people who had written to him after seeing his name on the electronic bulletin boards where I had posted it.

In April 2002, Nushawn called to tell me that he might be getting married. I was a bit surprised by this, and at first I didn't entirely believe him. Then, when I went to Elmira to visit him in May, he insisted that he might soon be calling me to invite me to his wedding. Ruth was the name of his potential marriage partner. She had found his name on a list of HIV-positive prison inmates who were seeking correspondence. They had apparently been writing to each other for some time, and Ruth had driven down from Vermont to visit Nushawn on several occasions. In July, I went down to the prison to meet Ruth and to serve as a witness at their wedding.

I was surprised to learn that weddings take place on a rather regular basis in the Elmira Correctional Facility. There were two the day that Nushawn and Ruth were married. A good-natured local judge was responsible for conducting the ceremonies, which took place in a small room next to the main visitors' space. As we crowded in for the short ceremony, Nushawn seemed slightly nervous. He later told me that he was finally happy, now that he had found someone with whom to spend his life. Ruth, by the same token, seemed quite devoted to him. She had been spending most of her time in Elmira and most of her days in the visitors' area with Nushawn. I spent the rest of the afternoon with the two of them. We all played gin rummy, and Nushawn won every game.

As the manuscript for this book was making its way through the final review process, I thought that Nushawn's story might have a reasonably upbeat ending. In spite of all his various failings and problems, Nushawn seemed to be achieving some stability in his life, and I hoped that once he was released from prison he might have a chance to end the destructive cycle that had led him there in the first place. Perhaps he even had a chance at parole at his next hearing. It at least looked likely that he would be released sometime before he had served out his maximum sentence.

Unfortunately, things took a turn for the worse. In January 2003, I received a telephone call from Ruth, this time from the Chemung County Jail in Elmira. She had been arrested in early December for smuggling contraband into the prison. Nushawn had convinced her to bring some marijuana into the jail for him. After at first resisting his entreaties, she had finally agreed. Unfortunately for her, the person from whom she bought the marijuana was working for the police. The prison authorities were aware that she was bringing the substance in when she arrived for her visit with Nushawn. Guards searched her and found the pot, and she was arrested. Two grams of marijuana is hardly enough for a slim joint, but bringing even that amount into a maximum-security prison is considered a serious crime. Ruth spent many weeks in the Chemung County Jail before she was even offered a lawyer, because the local public defender was working for the informant on another matter. Nushawn was immediately shipped to Southport Correctional Facility to spend fourteen months in "the box." He was also punished by having 180 days subtracted from his "good time." The likelihood of his receiving parole was reduced to near zero. For the first time since I'd met this young man, I was really very angry with him. Just when it seemed as though he was actually making some progress, he had totally blown it.

On January 20, I stopped to see Ruth in the Chemung County Jail on my way to visit Nushawn at Southport. I liked Ruth. She struck me as indomitable. She'd been in jail for about six weeks and had still not been arraigned. The county could hold her for forty-five days, not counting weekends and holidays, without arraigning her, and she would apparently be held for all of it. In spite of everything that had happened, Ruth still expressed her devotion to Nushawn and told me that she would wait for him even if he had to serve his maximum sentence, which he would not complete until 2010. She took full responsibility for what had happened, although she claimed that the woman who sold her the pot had, unsolicited, made the offer to her in the Elmira Correctional Facility visitors' room and had helped her to pack the drugs in such a way that she could avoid detection. Ruth would probably be arraigned, plead guilty, and be offered probation. There was little likelihood that she would be allowed to visit Nushawn again for the remainder of the time he spent in prison.

I left the jail to travel over to Southport for what I figured would be my last visit to a prison for a long time. Southport, a relatively new facility, is entirely turned over to solitary confinement. Prisoners make no movements within the prison without being handcuffed and shackled. These are the state's problem prisoners. Unlike at Auburn and Elmira, visitors talk to prisoners only through an iron cage. Visits are allowed only on weekends and holidays. The day I was there, I saw only a handful of other visitors.

I talked with Nushawn for about an hour. He was angry with Ruth for getting caught. He was angry with me for telling him that Ruth's arrest was his responsibility. Mostly, I think, he was angry with himself. He had been on the verge of a parole hearing. He had been so close to his conditional release date. He had been eligible to be moved to a minimum-security prison. All of that was now gone. He talked vaguely about an appeal. After all, he'd never actually possessed the drugs. But his arguments struck me as mere legalisms. He is resilient, and still quite young. He might yet turn his life around, get himself together in such a way that he might learn from his awful mistakes. The odds of this happening, however, seem to be increasingly remote. On my way out of the prison, I dropped off some Jackie Collins and John Grisham novels for Nushawn. Then I made my way home. I wouldn't return to that most depressing place.

I have kept in touch with Nushawn through letters. Not long after our last visit, he moved to the "tertiary level" at Southport, which gained him some small privileges, such as occasional access to a telephone. Given his good behavior, it looks as though his confinement there may be shortened, and he could soon move back to a general-population prison. Ruth has remained in Elmira, working as a painter and waiting for the disposition of her case. Her lawyer has informed her that the charges against her will probably be dropped. Still, she would not be able to visit Nushawn for at least a year.

I continue to believe that the treatment the Williams case received from the national press was terrible. Inaccuracy, incompleteness, distortion, and sensationalism dominated most of the coverage. Nushawn Williams's demonization served the economic ends of media outlets by selling advertising while reinforcing caricatures of race, sex, and HIV. The story helped to reinforce the trend toward criminalizing public health issues, which I believe is, in the long run, destructive. Moreover, turning Nushawn Williams into a monster has done nothing to help the millions of people around the world who are infected with HIV.

I visited Nushawn just before Christmas 2004. He'd been released from Southport and had been sent to the Wende Correctional Facility near Buffalo. There he'd experienced quite a bit of harassment. As a result, he was soon sent to Attica, also in Western, New York. He told me that both guards and inmates were making his life miserable there as well. In this part of the state his notoriety had apparently remained undiminished.

Still, he was in good spirits when we met. He looked good, with his hair grown out a bit, sporting a well-trimmed goatee. Ruth was also in town, and she would spend time with him over the next few days. Ruth would bring packages of food and books. She was also reporting instances of harassment to the Inspector General's Office. Most important, she had made an emotional commitment to him, the significance of which I think he understood.

In spite of various setbacks, Nushawn was back on the right track. He would probably not, however, be released for two or three more years. Yet I left Attica with the impression—more than just a hope—that, upon his release, he and Ruth had a reasonable chance to make a successful go of things.

Notes

Introduction

1. This study is not autobiographical per se, although I introduce some auto-biographical elements at various points along the way. Although positivists might view an observer's biographical connections to the social phenomena he or she is studying as a liability, I would argue that such connections can often be a strength, as in this case, when they are openly acknowledged as a component of the investi-gative and interpretive processes. All theory is to a certain extent autobiography, because the theorist can never entirely remove him- or herself from the process of theorizing. The researcher's best strategy for dealing with potential charges of "bias," then, is to be as self-conscious as possible about his or her personal histori-cal relationships to the subjects of study and to be honest about all methodologies and findings. The research process should be viewed as a process of discovery and self-discovery, or, as Steier puts it, "self-reflexivity." Frederick Steier, "Research as Self-Reflexivity, Self-Reflexivity as Social Process," in *Research and Reflexivity*, ed. Frederick Steier (London: Sage, 1991), 1–11.

2. I am not putting myself forward as an "objective observer" here. A volumi-nous literature exists in both the natural and the social sciences on the meanings of and potential for "objectivity." Challenges to the possibility of objectivity have been particularly fierce in political science, sociology, and anthropology, where claims of objectivity have been criticized (rightly, I believe) as assertions of power. Any researcher claiming objective understanding is, after all, positing a vantage point that exists outside and above influences of class, race, gender, and culture. (See Michel Foucault's assessment of knowledge as power in *Power/Knowledge: Selected Interviews and Other Writings, 1972–1977* [New York: Pantheon, 1980].) I make no such claims. Moreover, I fully embrace the position of advocate at various points in this volume. I am, for example, much troubled by the uses to which Nushawn Williams has been put by those who support and seek to reinforce poli-cies that criminalize HIV transmission.

In his book on the methodologies of field research, the great social scientist William Foote Whyte confesses that as he developed as a researcher he "gradually abandon[ed] the idea that there must be a strict separation between scientific re-search and action projects." He considered his obligations as a researcher to be to "advance science and enhance human progress," objectives that he considered to be entirely consistent with each other. William Foote Whyte, *Learning from the*

Field: A Guide from Experience (Beverly Hills, Calif.: Sage, 1984), 20. More recently, Robert Stake has defended the stance of researcher as "advocate": "Qualitative research can and does. It champions the interaction of researcher and phenomena. Phenomena need accurate description, but even the observational interpretation of those phenomena will be shaped by the mood, the experience, the intention of the researcher. Some of those wrappings can be shucked, but some cannot. Research is not helped by making it appear value free. It is better to give the reader a good look at the researcher. Often it is better to leave on the wrappings of advocacy that remind the reader: Beware. Qualitative research does not dismiss invalidity of description and encourage advocacy. It recognizes that invalidities and advocacies are ever present and turns away from the goal as well as the presumption of sanitization." Robert E. Stake, *The Art of Case Study Research* (Thousand Oaks, Calif.: Sage, 1995), 95.

3. The bar, for the most part, is not high. The bulk of published material on the Williams case comes from short newspaper articles and television programs. Most had little depth. An exception is an article by JoAnn Wypijewski that appeared in *Harper's*. Wypijewski spent time in Jamestown, and she admirably went significantly beyond the surface of most news accounts. Still, partly no doubt because of format constraints, she did not undertake detailed historical and legal research or media criticism. She was also unable to speak to Nushawn Williams, who at the time she wrote was under indictment. See JoAnn Wypijewski, "The Secret Sharer: Sex, Race, and Denial in an American Small Town," *Harper's*, July 1998, 35–54. In spite of some criticisms I have of her approach, I believe that her article is the standard by which this and subsequent studies of the case must be measured. Here, I have attempted to contextualize the Williams case historically, legally, and politically.

4. The interview techniques that I employed are standard practice in many qualitative research protocols. For a discussion of the interview as a form of conversation, see Sharan B. Merriam, *Case Study Research in Education: A Qualitative Approach* (San Francisco: Jossey-Bass, 1988), 71–86. See also Patrick Dilley, "Conducting Successful Interviews: Tips for Intrepid Research," *Theory and Practice* 39 (summer 2000): 131–37.

5. The interview method that I followed is sometimes referred to as "semistructured." This format "allows the researcher to respond to the situation at hand, to the emerging worldview of the respondent, and to new ideas on the topic." Merriam, *Case Study Research*, 74.

6. Legal analyses of various kinds are necessarily woven into the fabric of this study, but they tend to dominate chapters 4 and 5. My conceptualizations of law have been heavily influenced by a number of critical approaches. Although there are significant divergences among the critical legal studies movement (see, for example, "Critical Legal Studies Symposium," *Stanford Law Review* 36 [January 1984]: 1–673), critical race theory (see Richard Delgado, *Critical Race Theory: An Introduction* [New York: New York University Press, 2001]), and feminist legal analysis (see, for example, Zillah Eisenstein, *The Female Body and the Law* [Berkeley: University of California Press, 1989]), all three tend to be united around the notion

that law and legal analysis constitute systems of political power. They challenge the conservative view, that law is an accretion of cultural wisdom over time, and the liberal one, that law's primary function in the modern era has been to maintain order and to protect and expand the domain of individual rights. Although critical approaches often recognize the progressive potential of law, they also acknowledge law's capacity to oppress. In David Kairys's succinct phrasing, "Law is simply politics by other means." David Kairys, *The Politics of Law: A Progressive Critique* (New York: Pantheon, 1982), 17. For more complete explications of my views on law, see Thomas Shevory, *John Marshall's Law: Interpretation, Ideology, and Interest* (Westport, Conn.: Greenwood, 1989); Thomas Shevory, *Body/Politics: Studies in Reproduction, Production, and (Re)construction* (Westport, Conn.: Praeger, 2000).

7. Robert K. Yin, *Case Study Research: Design and Methods*, 2d ed. (Thousand Oaks, Calif.: Sage, 1994), 91.

8. Stake defines "triangulation" as "working to substantiate an interpretation or to clarify its different meanings." *Art of Case Study Research*, 173.

9. John W. Creswell, "Determining Validity in Qualitative Inquiry," *Theory into Practice* 39 (summer 2000): 127.

10. For a succinct explanation of how the desire for objectivity can impede the processes of inquiry in qualitative research, see Douglas J. Toma, "How Getting Close to Your Subjects Makes Qualitative Data Better," *Theory into Practice* 39 (summer 2000): 177–84.

11. See, for example, Stanley Cohen, *Folk Devils and Moral Panics: The Creation of the Mods and Rockers* (London: MacGibbon & Kee, 1972); Stuart Hall, Chas Critcher, Tony Jefferson, John Clarke, and Brian Roberts, *Policing the Crisis: Mugging, the State, and Law and Order* (New York: Holmes & Meier, 1978).

12. Mark Thomas Connelly, *The Response to Prostitution in the Progressive Era* (Chapel Hill: University of North Carolina Press, 1980).

13. See Richard K. Matthews, *The Radical Politics of Thomas Jefferson: A Revisionist View* (Lawrence: University Press of Kansas, 1984).

14. See, for example, James Fallows, *Breaking the News: How the Press Undermines American Democracy* (New York: Pantheon, 1996).

15. Cornel West, *Race Matters* (Boston: Beacon, 2001).

16. *State v. Schmidt*, 699 So. 2d 448 (La. Ct. App. 1997).

17. For example, *Smallwood v. State*, 680 A.2d 512 (Md. 1996).

18. See Daniel Beauchamp, *The Health of the Republic* (Philadelphia: Temple University Press, 1987).

1. Moral Panics and Media Politics

1. There are three conditions under which a court in New York can disclose confidential HIV information: "(a) a compelling need for the adjudication of a criminal or civil proceeding; (b) a clear and imminent danger to an individual whose life or health may unknowingly be at significant risk as a result of contact with the individual to whom the information pertains; (c) upon application of a state, county or local health officer, a clear and imminent danger to the public health." N.Y. CLS Pub. Health sec. 2785(2) (2001). See Andrew Z. Galaraneau,

"The Doctor Who Dared," *Buffalo News,* November 11, 1997, C1–C2. The first release order was signed on October 16, 1997. According to that order, the court found "that there is a clear and imminent danger to an individual whose life or health may unknowingly be at significant risk as a result of contact with the respondent" (Order Authorizing Release of Information, Index No. K11997016984, State of New York Supreme Court, County of Chautauqua, October 16, 1997, 1). An important justification for this order was that it would "encourage persons to testify against the respondent so that he can be removed from the community, where he may continue to spread the disease, to jail." Before Nushawn Williams's name was made public, however, officials learned that he was in jail in New York, and that eliminated the necessity of removing him from the community. Thus a second order was issued that stated, "The purpose of such release is to inform the public, and in particular those who have had relevant contact with the respondent, about the activities of the respondent which are exposing unprotected, uninformed sexual partners to the HIV virus" (Supplement Order Authorizing Release of Information, Index No. K11997016984, State of New York Supreme Court: County of Chautauqua, October 27, 1997). The shift in emphasis is important and somewhat disturbing. The first order was intended to help public officials find Nushawn Williams and prevent him from infecting more people. The second was a very public form of partner notification that, in the process of notifying potential partners, turned Williams into a figure of national prominence. Given Williams's established willingness to provide his partners' names, there exists a real question as to whether the release of his name was justifiable once it was discovered that he was already in custody.

2. The exact charges were "criminal sale of a controlled substance in the third degree" and "criminal possession of a controlled substance in the third degree" (Grand Jury Report, Grand Jury Number 46329/97, County, Bronx, October 7, 1997).

3. Senate, State of New York, *An Act to Amend the Public Health Law, in Relation to Human Immunodeficiency Virus Infection and Reporting Cases of Such Infection to Spouses and Known Sexual Partners,* April 11, 1999. See Richard Pérez-Peña, "Albany Passes Bill Requiring H.I.V. Tracking," *New York Times,* June 19, 1998, A1.

4. Laura Whitehorn, "America's Most Unwanted," *Poz,* August 2000, Internet, http:/www.thebody.com/poz/inside/08_00/unwanted.html.

5. Centers for Disease Control and Prevention, Division of HIV/AIDS Prevention, "Basic Statistics," Internet, http://www.cdc.gov/hiv/stats. htm.

6. Rachel L. Swarns, "For South Africa's Poorest AIDS Victims, a Place to Die," *New York Times,* December 28, 2002, A1, A8.

7. JoAnn Wypijewski, "The Secret Sharer: Sex, Race, and Denial in an American Small Town," *Harper's,* July 1998, 46.

8. Stanley Cohen, *Folk Devils and Moral Panics: The Creation of the Mods and Rockers* (London: MacGibbon & Kee, 1972).

9. Ibid., 9.

10. See David Underdown, *Revel, Riot, and Rebellion: Popular Politics and Culture in England, 1603–1660* (Oxford: Oxford University Press, 1985); Christina Larner, *Enemies of God: The Witch-Hunt in Scotland* (London: Chatto & Windus, 1981).

11. Quoted in Allan M. Brandt, *No Magic Bullet: A Social History of Venereal Disease in the United States since 1880* (Oxford: Oxford University Press, 1987), 33–34.

12. Reginald Wright Kauffman, *The House of Bondage* (Upper Saddle River, N.J.: Gregg, 1910).

13. Mark Thomas Connelly, *The Response to Prostitution in the Progressive Era* (Chapel Hill: University of North Carolina Press, 1980), 114–16.

14. Ibid., 130–31.

15. Max Weber, *The Protestant Ethic and the Spirit of Capitalism* (Chicago: Fitzroy Dearborn, 2001).

16. Erich Goode asserts: "Stuart Hall and his colleagues yearned for a vehicle to deconstruct the crisis of capitalism, but moral panics did not constitute that vehicle. Moral panics cut across the political spectrum; they erupt in all societies, capitalist, socialist, and pre-industrial alike; they come in all shapes and sizes; some are engineered by elites, some by middle-level interest groups, and still others bubble up almost spontaneously from the grassroots." Erich Goode, "No Need to Panic? A Bumper Crop of Books on Moral Panics," *Sociological Forum* 25 (2000): 545. In this assertion, he articulates an ahistorical approach to moral panics, in effect suggesting that they are universal elements of the human social condition. Given that I am primarily concerned here with the specifics of a particular moral panic, this is not the place to engage a detailed critique of Goode's position. I would contend, however, that the structural components of postindustrial capitalism (media technologies as well as patterns of ownership and control) have shaped the processes by which moral panics unfold and the effects that they have. That moral panics may, in some form, exist in all societies does not mean that their character is not shaped by the structural aspects of a given social system. Just as capitalism marks the apogee of a particular form of economic organization (the market system), so might we expect the moral panics generated within such a system to be both severe and ubiquitous, as they seem to be. For a good summary of approaches to moral panic theory, see Arnold Hunt, "Moral Panic and the Moral Language of the Media," *British Journal of Sociology* 48 (1997): 629–49.

17. Stuart Hall, Chas Critcher, Tony Jefferson, John Clarke, and Brian Roberts, *Policing the Crisis: Mugging, the State, and Law and Order* (New York: Holmes & Meier, 1978).

18. Ibid., 183.

19. Ibid., 278.

20. Mark Fishman, "Crime Waves as Ideology," *Social Problems* 25 (1978): 531–643.

21. Sophia E. Voumvakis and Richard V. Ericson, *News Accounts of Attacks on Women: A Comparison of Three Toronto Newspapers* (Toronto: Center for Criminology, 1984).

22. Ray Surrette, *Media, Crime, and Criminal Justice: Images and Realities* (Belmont, Calif.: Wadsworth, 1998), 78.

23. Barry Glassner argues that Americans are, in general, frightened by the "wrong" things in our society, such as Internet addiction and road rage, while

the most important social problems, such as the maldistribution of wealth, go largely unnoticed or ignored. Barry Glassner, *The Culture of Fear: Why Americans Are Afraid of the Wrong Things* (New York: Basic Books, 1999). Although I would take issue with specific aspects of Glassner's analysis (in terms of what threats are "imaginary" or "real"), the evidence that I have gathered in the Williams case supports Glassner's general thesis.

24. W. Gordon West has suggested that the media in Canada have generated a moral panic around school shootings. W. Gordon West, "Escalating Problem or Moral Panic? A Critical Perspective," *Orbit* 24 (March 1993): 6–7.

25. David J. Krajicek, *Scooped! Media Miss Real Story on Crime While Chasing Sex, Sleaze, and Celebrities* (New York: Columbia University Press, 1998), 7.

26. Quoted in Susan Sontag, "AIDS and Its Metaphors," *New York Review of Books,* October 27, 1988, 90.

27. William F. Buckley, "Identify All the Carriers," *New York Times,* March 18, 1988, A27.

28. Probably the most notorious of these was the LaRouche Initiative in California, which would have required HIV testing of all twenty-seven million Californians, registration of all HIV-infected persons, and the quarantine of anyone who came into contact with the virus. AIDS activists were forced to raise three million dollars to fight and eventually defeated the proposal. Mark S. Senak, "The Lesbian and Gay Community," in *AIDS and the Law: A Guide for the Public,* ed. Harlon L. Dalton (New Haven, Conn.: Yale University Press, 1978).

29. Simon Watney, *Policing Desire: Pornography, AIDS, and the Media* (Minneapolis: University of Minnesota Press, 1989), 9.

30. Cindy Patton, *Inventing AIDS* (New York: Routledge, 1990).

31. Sontag, "AIDS and Its Metaphors," 90.

32. Richard Chirimuuta and Rosalind Chirimuuta, *AIDS, Africa, and Racism* (London: Free Association, 1989), 9.

33. Ibid., 71.

34. Current mainstream scientific speculation locates the origins of the most prevalent form of HIV in chimpanzees rather than in monkeys. In 2000, Edward Hooper published *The River: A Journey to the Source of HIV and AIDS* (New York: Back Bay, 2000), in which he argues that HIV "jumped species" when researchers used chimpanzee kidneys in the production of an oral polio vaccine that was then distributed in a research project to subjects in central Africa in the mid-1950s. Hooper's thesis has been mostly debunked at this point. See Jon Cohen, "Vaccine Theory of AIDS Origins Disputed at Royal Society," *Science* 289 (September 2000): 1850. Yet the "cut monkey" theory, which contends that HIV was transferred when humans killed and ate chimpanzees and monkeys, cannot account for the fact that four separate forms of the virus seem to have appeared from different sources independently all at approximately the same time. See "AIDS Wars," *Economist,* September 15, 2000, 87.

35. Herman Gray, *Watching Race: Television and the Struggle for "Blackness"* (Minneapolis: University of Minnesota Press, 1995), 75.

36. Ibid,. 76.

37. Ibid., 78.

38. Ibid., 81.

39. Kristal Brenk Zook, "All Hype, No Action," *New Crisis* 109 (March–April 2002): 21–24.

40. In 1986, the U.S. Congress passed the Anti–Drug Abuse Act, the so-called crack statute, which rates crack cocaine at a ratio of one hundred to one in relation to the powdered form of cocaine in terms of criminal charges and sentencing. The disparate impact on jail terms for African Americans versus non–African Americans has been well documented. Jason A. Gilmer provides an excellent analysis in "*U.S. v Clary*: Equal Protection and the Crack Statute," *American University Law Review* 45 (1995): 497–565.

41. See Toni Morrison and Claudia Brodsky Lacour, eds., *Birth of a Nation'hood: Gaze, Script, and Spectacle in the O. J. Simpson Case* (New York: Pantheon, 1997).

42. See Carolyn Thompson, "HIV-Positive Man Knew He Infected Teens, Say New York Authorities," *Chicago Tribune*, October 28, 1997, 2; "Upstate New York AIDS Scare May Spread," CNN Interactive, Internet, http://www.cnn.com/us/9710/28/hiv.students.folo/index.html.

43. Quoted in Shirley E. Perlman and Chau Lam, "Town Exposed: Secrets, Sadness Surface in the Wake of Nushawn Willams," *New York Newsday*, November 2, 1997, A5. In my interview with Dr. Berke, he complained that he was misquoted by the local Jamestown newspaper, the *Post-Journal*, regarding his accounts of the numbers involved, and that his statements were exaggerated. But CNN correspondent John Holliman, who spoke to Berke directly, reported that Berke said "that the number of people who may be affected because of direct sexual contact, or indirect or secondary sexual contact could be as many as 100 in this county alone." Donna Kelley and John Holliman, "New York Man in Jail for Spreading HIV and Selling Drugs," *CNN Morning News*, October 28, 1997, Internet, accessed through LexisNexis (http://web.lexis-nexis.com).

44. Quoted in "HIV-Infected Man's Partners Could Reach into Dozens," *Chicago Tribune*, October 29, 1997, 13.

45. Tara George and Patrice O'Shaughnessy, "Dead End in the Rust Belt," *New York Daily News*, November 2, 1997, 40.

46. Dr. Berke's full statement, quoted numerous times in various media, was, "This guy is some kind of score-keeper. He seems to take delight in keeping records. He has been fairly reliable in what he has given up to us." Blaine Harden, "AIDS Carrier Kept Score, Officials Say; Inmate Lists More than 50 Sex Partners for Health Investigators," *Washington Post*, October 29, 1997, A3. A person reading or hearing this could not be blamed if she or he interpreted it to mean that Williams kept some kind of a written diary. That was my impression when I first heard it. CNN correspondent Martin Savidge apparently thought the same thing when he asked Sheriff Joseph Gerace whether Williams's record keeping might not be "good fortune." Gerace responded, "He didn't keep written records that we know of, but a mental record of the individuals that he allegedly had sex with." Martin Savidge, "Sexual Predator Exposes New York Community to AIDS," *CNN Early Edition*, October 29, 1997, Internet, accessed through LexisNexis (http://web.lexis-nexis.com).

47. Quoted in "Upstate New York AIDS Scare May Spread," CNN Interactive, Internet, http://www.cnn.com/us/9710/28/hiv.students.folo/index.html.

48. "News in Brief," *Guardian*, October 28, 1997, 14.

49. Shannon Brownlees et al., "AIDS Comes to Small Town America," *U.S. News & World Report*, November 10, 1997, 52.

50. Shirley E. Perlman, "Man's HIV-Infection List Grows," *Seatttle Times*, October 29, 1997, A4 (emphasis added).

51. "Dozens Get HIV Tests," *Sacramento Bee*, October 31, 1997, A19 (emphasis added).

52. Kathleen Parker, "Condom-mania Is Folly," *Denver Post*, November 2, 1997, I2. Parker's hyperbole (or perhaps ignorance) did not stop at her prediction of hundreds of AIDS patients from Williams's activities. She appeared to view AIDS as equivalent to the black plague: "As one AIDS-infected person infects another, who infects another, and so on, the magic moment can take on nightmarish proportions *in a matter of days*" (emphasis added).

53. Quoted in Karen Matthews, "Publicity May Bring Forward More Partners," *Dayton Daily News*, October 29, 1997, A13.

54. Agnes Palazzetti, "Suspect Kept Score: Williams' Records Helped Track Infected Women," *Buffalo News*, October 29, 1997, A1.

55. Bob Houston, "Four New HIV Cases Reported," *Jamestown Post-Journal*, December 9, 1997, 1.

56. This number is my best estimate based on information drawn from newspaper and interview accounts. "Two Infants with HIV Are Linked to Williams," *Jamestown Post-Journal*, January 29, 1998, 1; Robert Berke, interview by author, July 2, 1999; Neil Rzepkowski, interview by author, January 3, 2003.

57. Henry L. Davis, "Two Births May Bring Williams' HIV Toll to 16," *Buffalo News*, January 29, 1998, B4.

58. Donn Esmonde, "Cycle of Hopelessness Will Endure Long after Williams' Legacy Fades," *Buffalo News*, November 13, 1997, B1; Tom Precious, "Test Results Ease AIDS Fears in Chautauqua," *Buffalo News*, November 12, 1997, A1.

59. Ginia Bellafante, "A Huge AIDS Cluster Reveals a Troubling Mix of Youth, Drugs, and Sex," *Time*, November 10, 1997, 58.

60. Ted Koppel, statement made on *ABC News Nightline*, October 31, 1997, Internet, accessed through LexisNexis (http://web.lexis-nexis.com).

61. Esmonde, "Cycle of Hopelessness," B1.

62. "AIDS Tests Produce Optimism," *Washington Post*, November 14, 1997, A23.

63. William F. Buckley, "Chautauqua Talk," *National Review*, November 24, 1997, 66.

64. Quoted on *ABC News Nightline*, October 31, 1997, Internet, accessed through LexisNexis (http://web.lexis-nexis.com).

65. Blaine Harden, "HIV Outbreak in N.Y. Town Tied to 1 Man; Drug Convict Suspected of Giving AIDS Virus to 11 Young Women," *Washington Post*, October 28, 1997, A1; Tara George, "Panic over HIV Spree," *New York Daily News*, October 28, 1997, 7; Delthia Ricks, "Vagabond a Latter-Day Patient Zero," *New York Newsday*, October 29, 1997, A70; James Subjack, quoted in Lou Michel, "Neighbors

See HIV Figure as 'Troubled Kid,'" *Buffalo News*, October 29, 1997, A1; Esmonde, "Cycle of Hopelessness," B1; "Silence Does Equal Death," *New York Daily News*, October 29, 1997, 40; Donn Esmonde, "Existing Laws Aren't Enough for a Walking Epidemic," *Buffalo News*, October 29, 1997, B1.

66. Rick Hampson, "AIDS Scare Rips through Upstate N.Y.: Teenagers Outbreak Blamed on One Man, Puts Communities in Shock," *USA Today*, October 29, 1997, D1.

67. Esmonde, "Existing Laws," B1.

68. In response to correspondent Bill Hemmer's question concerning whether Williams might be charged with "attempted murder" if one of his victims died, Van Susteren responded, "It [would] not trump to *attempted* murder, but trump to murder. If you commit some conduct that results in murder, and you do it with, perhaps premeditation and you do it deliberately, well, you could face charges of first degree murder." Bill Hemmera and Greta Van Susteren, "Williams Suspected of Infecting Nine Women with HIV," *CNN Morning News*, October 30, 1997, Internet, accessed through LexisNexis (http://web.lexis-nexis.com).

69. Geraldo Rivera, "Williams Infecting Unsuspected Victims with the HIV Virus in New York." *Rivera Live*, October 29, 1997, Internet, accessed through LexisNexis (http://web.lexis-nexis.com).

70. Quoted on *ABC News Nightline*, October 31, 1997, Internet, accessed through LexisNexis (http://web.lexis-nexis.com).

71. Rivera, "Williams Infecting Unsuspected Victims."

72. Ibid. The sentiment that Williams should receive a death sentence was expressed often. In a *Buffalo News* article published on the occasion of Williams's sentencing, a person described as a Jamestown "senior citizen" was quoted as saying, "I don't like the guy. He should plainly die. Nobody should get away with that." And a "former neighbor" said, "Personally, I think he ought to be shot." Lou Michel and Charity Vogel, "Who Is to Blame? Nushawn's Sex Partners Differ over Fault," *Buffalo News*, February 28, 1999, A1. Numerous others reportedly expressed similar views. See Lou Michel, "Nushawn Pleads Guilty: Deal Expected to Result in Four Year Term," *Buffalo News*, February 27, 1999, A1.

73. Quoted in Fred Kaplan, "N.Y. Man Knowingly Spread HIV to Dozens, Officials Say," *Boston Globe*, October 28, 1997, A3.

74. Quoted in George, "Panic over HIV Spree," 7.

75. David Hinckley, "Risky Assumptions: Case of HIV-Spreading Romeo Oughtta Open Parents' Eyes," *New York Daily News*, November 2, 1997, 6.

76. Gabi Horn, "Dread Locked: Nushawn Pleads Guilty," *Poz*, July 1999, Internet, http://www.thebody. com/poz/gazette/7_99/dread.html.

77. For a discussion of the contents of the report that resulted from that psychiatric exam, see chapter 3.

78. George, "Panic over HIV Spree," 7.

79. Williams was not a crack cocaine user. In fact, in my conversations with him he expressed disdain for "crackheads." This, I believe, was partly because of his own experience—he had seen what the drug did to others, including his

mother, who abandoned her family for the drug. Williams did, however, freely admit to "smoking weed."

80. Quoted in Richard Wolf, "AIDS Revelation Has County Reeling: Crisis in Rural Upstate New York Brings to Forefront Disturbing Questions," *USA Today,* October 28, 1997, A2.

81. "Upstate New York AIDS Scare May Spread," CNN Interactive, October 28, 1997, Internet, http://www.cnn.com/us/9710/28/hiv.students.folo/index.html.

82. Martin Savidge and John Holliman, "NY AIDS Scare Spreading Across State," *CNN Early Edition,* October 29, 1997, Internet, accessed through Lexis-Nexis (http://web.lexis-nexis.com).

83. Quoted in Anthony Cardinale, "AIDS Activists Say Education Is Needed More than Revising HIV Confidentiality Laws." *Buffalo News,* October 28, 1997, A6.

84. *World News Tonight with Peter Jennings* (ABC), November 3, 1997, Internet, accessed through LexisNexis (http://web.lexis-nexis.com).

85. Quoted in Hampson, "Aids Scare," D1.

86. I have no doubt that drugs, especially marijuana, were a part of the sexual activities in which Williams and his partners engaged. But the difference between using drugs during social and sexual activities and "trading" drugs for sex is, I would contend, an important one. The former implies that the drug use is part of a social context, an activity of sharing that no doubt takes place on college campuses all across the United States on a regular basis. The latter implies that a drug dealer is taking advantage of a desperate addict who will do anything, even prostitute herself, in order to get access to the drug. Clearly, these two scenarios play out very differently in the press. The latter is much more provocative, especially when the story involves a black man and younger white girls.

87. Quoted in Perlman, "Man's HIV-Infection List Grows," A4.

88. Jacqueline Adams, "Health Officials Go Public with Warnings of Alleged HIV-Infected Drug User in New York," *CBS This Morning,* October 30, 1997, Internet, accessed through LexisNexis (http://web.lexis-nexis.com).

89. Michel and Vogel, "Who Is to Blame?" A1.

90. "Man Admits to Exposing Girl, 15, to AIDS Virus," *Star Tribune* (Minneapolis), February 19, 1999, A16.

91. "Lost *almost* completely" would actually be more accurate. A few voices of reason did occasionally speak over the din of hysteria generated by the case. On *Good Morning America,* Lisa McRee interviewed law professor Lawrence Gostin and Cheryl Healton, president of a public health foundation, about Williams. Healton noted that Williams "provided the names of his sexual contacts. Instead, he is being portrayed as a list maker. And obviously, he did what many, many people do not do in their CDC interview with a public health adviser. He actually provided the names of his partners." Steve Aveson and Lisa McRee, "HIV Confidentiality Law," *Good Morning America* (ABC), October 30, 1997, Internet, accessed through LexisNexis (http://web.lexis-nexis.com). Also, Catherine Hanssens of the Lambda Legal Defense Fund stated on CNN, "One of the real tragedies of the Nushawn Williams case is the focus on an individual, as if identifying this person and villainizing this person is the answer to AIDS prevention." "Nushawn Wil-

liams in Court," *CNN Morning News*, December 4, 1997, Internet, accessed through LexisNexis (http://web.lexis-nexis.com). See also Wypijewski, 35.

92. *World News Tonight with Peter Jennings* (ABC), November 3, 1997.

93. "Upstate New York AIDS Scare."

94. Jacqueline Adams, "Police Try to Trace Footsteps of HIV-Infected Man Who Passed AIDS Virus on to Several Young Women," *CBS This Morning*, October 28, 1997, Internet, accessed through LexisNexis (http://web. lexis-nexis.com).

95. "Man Pleads Guilty in Rape Cases and Exposing Woman to H.I.V.," *New York Times*, February 27, 1999, B6.

96. Chris Bury and Ted Koppel, "Sex Drugs, and HIV," *ABC News Nightline*, October 31, 1997, Internet, accessed through LexisNexis (http://web. lexis-nexis. com). The Joe Gerace who took part in this exchange is the father of Chautauqua county Sheriff Joseph Gerace.

97. John Miller and Peter Jennings, "Williams in Court on Drug Charges," *World News Tonight with Peter Jennings*, November 3, 1997, Internet, accessed through LexisNexis (http://web. lexis-nexis.com).

98. Aveson and McRee, "HIV Confidentiality Law."

99. Kevin Newman, "Chautaqua HIV Predator," *Good Morning America* (ABC), October 28, 1997, Internet, accessed through LexisNexis (http://web.lexis-nexis. com).

100. Quoted in Jerry Zremski, "AIDS Outbreak in Small Town Was Easy to Spot Experts Say," *Buffalo News*, October 31, 1997, A1.

101. Adam Nossiter, "Man Knowingly Exposed Women to AIDS Virus; Health Officials Looking for More Partners," *New York Times*, April 19, 1998, 7; Jeff Flock and Lou Waters, "New York AIDS Spree Brings Back Memories for St. Louis Area," *CNN Early Prime*, November 6, 1997, Internet, accessed through LexisNexis (http://web. lexis-nexis.com).

102. Kaplan, "N.Y. Man," A3.

103. Joe Kafka, "South Dakota Town Deals with HIV Outbreak; Chicago Basketball Player Jailed," Associated Press, May 3, 2002, Internet, accessed through LexisNexis (http://web. lexis-nexis.com).

104. Katie Couric and Matt Lauer, "South Dakota Student Charged with Exposing People to HIV Virus," *Today* (NBC), May 2, 2002.

105. Joe Kafka, "Hundreds Will Be Tested for AIDS in South Dakota after HIV-positive Athlete Is Arrested," Associated Press, April 26, 2002, Internet, accessed through LexisNexis (http://web. lexis-nexis.com).

106. Quoted in ibid.

107. Quoted in "Judge Sets Thursday Preliminary Hearing for Briteramos," Associated Press, April 29, 2002, Internet, accessed through LexisNexis (http://web. lexis-nexis.com); and in Cara Hetland, "South Dakota College Student Charged for Knowingly Transmitting the Virus That Causes AIDS," *All Things Considered*, National Public Radio, May 3, 2002.

108. Hetland, "South Dakota College Student."

109. John W. Fountain, "After Arrest, Campus Queues for H.I.V. Tests," *New York*

Times, April 30, 2002, A16; "Sporty Lover-Boy Leaves HIV Trail," *Sunday Mail* (Qld), April 28, 2002, 42.

110. Joe Kafka, "Man Sentenced for Violating Parole," Associated Press, October 1, 2002, Internet, accessed through LexisNexis (http://web.lexis-nexis.com).

111. Joe Kafka, "Judge Says Briteramos Guilty of Escape," Associated Press, September 17, 2002, Internet, accessed through LexisNexis (http://web.lexis-nexis.com).

112. Kafka, "Man Sentenced for Violating Parole."

113. Parker, "Condom-mania Is Folly," I2; Maggie Gallagher, "AIDS Comes to Mayville, Raising Disquieting Issues," *Sacramento Bee,* November 10, 1997, B5.

114. Quoted in Michel and Vogel, "Who Is to Blame?" A1.

115. Quoted in ibid.

116. Quoted in Jennifer Frey, "Nushawn's Girls," *Washington Post,* June 1, 1999, C1.

117. Andrea Caruso, interview by author, January 7, 2003.

118. Rzepkowski, interview.

119. See, for example, John Stuart Mill, *On Liberty* (New York: W. W. Norton, 1975).

120. Alan Pergament, "The Talk of the Nation," *Buffalo News,* October 19, 1997, 1D.

121. A good example is the *CBS Morning News* report that stated: "You can probably imagine the kind of fear that people must be feeling in the small town of Mayville in Western New York State. As we have reported this morning, at least 11 of Mayville's young women and teen-age girls may have become infected with the virus that causes AIDS." "Dr. Robert Berke, Chautauqua County Health Commissioner, Warns the Public about Nushawn Williams, the Man who Has Knowingly Transmitted the AIDS Virus to Several People," *CBS Morning News,* October 28, 1997, Internet, accessed through LexisNexis (http://web.lexis-nexis.com). CNN correspondent John Holliman made the same mistake. See John Holliman and Lou Waters, "The Man Spreading AIDS Has Infected More than First Thought," *CNN Today,* October 28, 1997, Internet, accessed through LexisNexis (http://web.lexis-nexis.com).

122. Tara George and Michele McPhee, "Epidemic of Fear Follows Trail of Sex," *New York Daily News,* October 9, 1997, 6; Randall Pinkston, "Residents of Chautauqua County, New York, Gather for AIDS Information Meeting," *CBS This Morning,* October 30, 1997, Internet, accessed through LexisNexis (http://web.lexis-nexis.com).

123. Hampson, "AIDS Scare," D1; Jeff Gammage, "Brutal Lesson for Town and Its Kids: HIV Can Happen Anywhere, and to Anyone Who Ignores It," *Des Moines Register,* November 2, 1997, 1.

124. Hampson, "AIDS Scare," D1.

125. Richard Cohen, "Preventable Tragedies in Chautauqua," *Washington Post,* October 30, 1997, A23.

126. Celeste Williams, "Story of Sick Stranger Tarnishes Memories of Safe Small Town Life," *Indianapolis Star,* November 10, 1997, B3.

127. George, "Panic over HIV Spree," 8.

128. Quoted in Bellafante, "Huge AIDS Cluster," 58.

129. Perlman and Lam, "Town Exposed," A5.

130. George and O'Shaughnessy, "Dead End in the Rust Belt," 40.

131. Jane Gross, "Trail of Arrests, H.I.V. Fears, and a Woman's Tale of Love," *New York Times,* October 29, 1997, A1.

132. Pam Lamber, "One-Man Plague: A Deadly Drifter Spreads HIV among Small-Town Teens Looking for Love," *People Magazine,* November 17, 1997, 239.

133. Wypijewski, "The Secret Sharer." Of the dozen or more signs that announce entry into Jamestown, the one that was chosen for the article is one that sits in an older, and somewhat worn, industrial area. It is also the sign least likely to be seen by a casual visitor entering the city. Depicting the sign found along the most accessible route (from the north) into Jamestown, near a mostly residential area, would clearly have been out of keeping with the atmosphere of deterioration that the art designer for the article was apparently attempting to create.

134. Ibid., 36.

135. Ibid., 40.

136. Ibid., 54. The tenor of Wypijewski's piece was not missed by people in the local community, as my interviews with some of them revealed.

137. Donn Esmonde, "To Prevent Nushawn Tragedies, We Must Start Early," *Buffalo News,* January 24, 1997, C2.

138. Media criticism of the press's handling of the Williams case was quite muted. Geraldo Rivera and Montel Williams were easy victims, as the hosts of "tabloid television" shows. The *Buffalo News*'s Alan Pergament accused both of "exploitation." Alan Pergament, "Talk Show Treatment of Chautauqua HIV Crisis Is a Question of Caring," *Buffalo News,* November 6, 1997, D5. True, Rivera suggested that inmates (or guards) "do the right thing" to Williams, but such proposals hardly seem shocking given the atmosphere created by most "respectable" newspaper reporters and columnists. In truth, the distinction between "tabloid coverage" and "real" journalism, in terms of either style or substance, is often very difficult to discern. This was clearly true in the Williams case.

139. Quoted in Houston, "Four New HIV Cases," 1.

140. Wypijewski, "The Secret Sharer," 39.

141. Russ Tilaro, interview by author, May 26, 1998.

142. James Subjack, interview by author, July 2, 1999.

143. Ibid.

144. Neil Rzepkowski, interview by author, January 13, 1999.

145. See Craig Wolff, "Doctor's Resignation Is First Tied to New AIDS Guidelines," *New York Times,* July 27, 1991, 1.

146. Neil Rzepkowski, interview by author, January 13, 1999.

147. Matt Milovich, interview by author, October 8, 1998.

148. Sheila McCarthy, interview by author, June 30, 1998.

149. Joan Patrie, interview by author, May 26, 1998.

150. Donna Vanstrom, interview by author, May 26, 1998.

151. Berke, interview.

152. "Official Calls HIV Crisis Bad for New Business," *Jamestown-Post Journal,* July 9, 1998, 1.

153. "Is There No Shame?" *New York Daily News,* November 1, 1997, 16.

154. Agnes Palazzetti, "Chautauqua Names HIV Carrier Accused of Infecting at Least Eleven," *Buffalo News,* October 28, 1997, A1.

155. Quoted in "Drifter Charged in Rape," *New York Newsday,* May 22, 1998, A22.

156. Quoted in Tom Precious, "State's HIV Confidentiality Law May Change," *Buffalo News,* November 1, 1997, A1.

157. Tom Precious, "HIV Proposals Call for Testing, Disclosure," *Buffalo News,* December 18, 1998.

158. Quoted in Michael Zeigler, "NY Lacks a Law Pegged to Knowingly Spreading HIV," *Rochester Democrat and Chronicle,* October 29, 1997, 1.

159. Quoted in ibid.

160. Quoted in ibid.

161. Amy Decker, "Criminalizing the Intentional or Reckless Exposure to HIV: A Wake-Up Call to Kansas," *Kansas Law Review* 46 (1998): 333–64.

162. For a good discussion of this topic, see Harlan L. Dalton, Scott Burris, and the Yale AIDS law Project, eds., *AIDS and the Law: A Guide for the Public* (New Haven, Conn.: Yale University Press, 1987).

163. Precious, "HIV Proposals," A1. The Williams case also invigorated national efforts. Congressman Tom Coburn of Oklahoma, a Republican, proposed national legislation to require HIV reporting.

164. Lynda Richardson, "Albany Likely to Get Names of People with HIV," *New York Times,* January 14, 1998, B1.

165. Ibid.

166. Lynda Richardson, "New Jersey's HIV List: Valuable, and Still Secret," *New York Times,* May 29, 1998, B8.

167. For more complete appraisals of Williams's motives and culpability, see chapters 3 and 5.

2. Small-Town Mythologies and the History of a Place

1. Quoted in Richard Hofstadter, *The American Political Tradition* (New York: Vintage, 1948), 27.

2. Richard K. Matthews, *The Radical Politics of Thomas Jefferson: A Revisionist View* (Lawrence: University Press of Kansas, 1984).

3. Everett Carl Ladd Jr., *Ideology in America: Change and Response in a City, a Suburb, and a Small Town* (Ithaca, N.Y.: Cornell University Press, 1969), 24–25.

4. James Oliver Robertson, *American Myth, American Reality* (New York: Hill & Wang, 1980), 216.

5. Ibid., 226.

6. Robert S. Lynd and Helen Merrell Lynd, *Middletown: A Study in American Culture* (New York: Harcourt, Brace, 1929).

7. Dwight W. Hoover, *Middletown Revisited* (Muncie, Ind.: Ball State University, 1990), 6–7.

8. Lynd and Lynd, *Middletown*, 3–6.

9. Ibid., 9.

10. Ibid., 22.

11. Ibid., 23–24.

12. Ibid., 52–72.

13. Ibid., 87.

14. Hoover, *Middletown Revisited*, 7.

15. Robert S. Lynd and Helen Merrell Lynd, *Middletown in Transition: A Study in Cultural Conflicts* (New York: Harcourt, Brace, 1937).

16. Theodore Caplow, Howard M. Bahr, Bruce A. Chadwick, Reuben Hill, and Margaret Holmes Williamson, *Middletown Families: Fifty Years of Change and Continuity* (Minneapolis: University of Minnesota Press, 1982).

17. Robert N. Bellah, Richard Madsen, William M. Sullivan, Ann Swidler, and Steven M. Tipton, *Habits of the Heart: Individualism and Commitment in American Life* (Berkeley: University of California Press, 1985).

18. Hoover, *Middletown Revisited*, 37–38.

19. J. F. Steiner, *The American Community in Action* (New York: Henry Holt, 1928).

20. James West, *Plainville, U.S.A.* (New York: Columbia University Press, 1945).

21. Arthur J. Vidich and Joseph Bensman, *Small Town in Mass Society: Class, Power and Religion in a Rural Community*, 2d ed. (Princeton, N.J.: Princeton University Press, 1968), 29, 33, 36, 38.

22. Ibid., 320, 318.

23. Ibid., 303, 80.

24. Ibid., xiv.

25. Ibid., xi.

26. Joseph B. Lyford, *The Talk of Vandalia* (Charlotte, N.C.: McNally & Loftin, 1962).

27. David Plowden, *Small Town America* (New York: Harry N. Abrams, 1994).

28. David Morley and Kevin Robbins, *Spaces of Identity: Global Media, Electronic Landscapes and Cultural Boundaries* (New York: Routledge, 1995), 87.

29. Ibid., 133.

30. Helen G. McMahon, *Chautauqua County: A History* (Buffalo, N.Y.: Henry Stewart, 1958), 109.

31. Paul A. Spengler, *Yankee, Swedish, and Italian Acculturation and Economic Mobility in Jamestown, New York from 1860 to 1920* (New York: Arno, 1980), 33.

32. Ibid., 21.

33. McMahon, *Chautauqua County*, 53.

34. Ibid., 33.

35. Ibid., 38.

36. Ibid., 39.

37. Ibid., 41.

38. Planning Commission, City of Jamestown, *Comprehensive Plan: City of Jamestown, New York* (1980).

39. McMahon, *Chautauqua County*, 84–87.

40. Spengler, *Yankee, Swedish, and Italian Acculturation*, 34.

41. Ibid., 43.

42. McMahon, *Chautauqua County*, 273.

43. Ibid., 274.

44. Spengler, *Yankee, Swedish, and Italian Acculturation*, 64.

45. Arthur Wellington Anderson, "Introduction," in Samuel B. Carlson, *The Saga of a City and a New Concept of Government* (Cleveland: E. George Lindstrom, 1935), 1–11.

46. McMahon, *Chautauqua County*, 197–98.

47. Anderson, "Introduction," 3.

48. Ibid., 4.

49. Samuel B. Carlson, *The Saga of a City and a New Concept of Government* (Cleveland: E. George Lindstrom, 1935), 76–84.

50. Helen G. Ebersole, *Electricity and Politics: Jamestown 1891–1931* (Jamestown: Fenton Historical Society, 1973), 3.

51. Carlson, *Saga of a City*, 65.

52. Carlson's opponents sometimes characterized him as a "Socialist," but his ideas about governance and his political rhetoric seem closest to the Progressive tradition. For example, he consistently inveighed against the "boss" system and campaigned for nonpartisan government, the elimination of the county system, the strengthening of the U.S. Congress against the states, and an end to bicameralism (ibid., 12–24). The milk campaign was infused with the rhetoric of cleanliness, science, and public health that was central to Progressive thought. At the same time, like other Progressives, Carlson believed that business is central to economic progress and development, and that competition in business is essential to a prosperous economy.

53. Ebersole, *Electricity and Politics*, 199.

54. Planning Commission, *Comprehensive Plan*, 8.

55. Ebersole, *Electricity and Politics*, 1. Jamestown was susceptible to declines in the manufacturing sector because of the proportion of its population employed in industry. In 1970, for example, 40 percent of Jamestown's workforce was employed in manufacturing, compared with 24 percent in New York State as a whole. Planning Commission, *Comprehensive Plan*, 25. At the same time, however, local historian Dolores Thompson, was able to write this upbeat statement about the city in 1974: "As people enter the city's limits, they are welcomed by a sign that reads 'Jamestown—All American City—People Working Together.' It is not simply a promotional slogan. The words have real meaning in the diverse manufacturing town. In fact, in 1974, based on strong evidence that people from all sectors and levels of the community were indeed working together to improve their city, Jamestown was selected as 'All American City' by the National Municipal League. Creating problem-solving partnerships among the industrial, commercial, educational and government sectors of the mature city have strengthened its economy, enhanced its quality of life, and furthered its progress." Dolores Thompson, *Jamestown and Chautauqua County: An Illustrated History* (Woodland Hills, Calif.: Windsor, 1984), 95.

56. Planning Commission, *Comprehensive Plan*, 6.

57. Ibid., 8. The 1980 Jamestown *Comprehensive Plan* provides a fascinating glimpse of optimism in the face of economic decline. To the plan's authors' credit, they did not minimize the consequences of long-term industrial decline for the city. But the plan shows virtually no recognition on the part of the Planning Commission that basic structural changes in the national and international economies were affecting cities in ways that would make it extremely difficult, if not impossible, for local governments to respond meaningfully. Thus the commission focused on the creation of new buildings and public spaces as indicators that the city was on the upswing. It recommended such measures as expanding the city bus system, building new highways around the city, expanding public parks, and adopting a historic preservation ordinance. Although certainly laudable, the commission's efforts were proven in time to be completely inadequate to deal with the enormity and depth of the economic transformation that was occurring.

58. U.S. Department of Housing and Urban Development (HUD), *Now Is the Time: Places Left Behind in the New Economy: America's Northeast* (Washington, D.C.: U.S. Government Printing Office, 1999), 7, 42, 41. HUD defines "the Northeast" as the following states: Connecticut, Maine, Massachusetts, New Hampshire, New Jersey, New York, Pennsylvania, and Rhode Island.

59. Ibid., 43.

60. U.S. Bureau of the Census, "State and County Quick Facts, Chautauqua County, New York," Internet, http:// quickfacts.census.gov /qfd/states /36/36013.html.

61. Jerry Zremski, "Work Force Fails to Cash in on High-Tech Economy," *Buffalo News*, April 4, 1998, A6.

62. Sam Teresi, interview by author, July 2, 1998.

63. Zremski, "Work Force Fails," A6.

64. HUD, *Now Is the Time*, 13.

65. Quoted in Zremski, "Work Force Fails," A6.

66. Teresi, interview.

67. Quoted in Zremski, "Work Force Fails," A6.

68. Teresi, interview.

69. U.S. Bureau of the Census, "Median Household Income by County: 1969, 1979, 1989," Internet, http://www.census.gov/hhes/income/histinc/county/county4.html.

70. U.S. Bureau of the Census, "State and County Quick Facts."

71. HUD, *Now Is the Time*, 44.

72. David Whitman et al., "The White Underclass," *U.S. News & World Report*, October 17, 1994, 40–42.

73. Richard J. Herrnstein and Charles Murray, *The Bell Curve: Intelligence and Class Structure in American Life* (New York: Simon & Schuster, 1996).

74. Whitman et al., "The White Underclass," 40. The *Jamestown Post-Journal* was understandably critical of the magazine's study. See Paul Kalomiris, "City Ranks 15th on List for Poverty: Development Cited as a Must by Kimball," *Jamestown Post-Journal*, October 14, 1994, 1.

75. HUD, *Now Is the Time*, 44.

76. Ibid., 45.

77. Ibid., 43.

78. Robert B. Reich, *The Work of Nations: Preparing Ourselves for 21st Century Capitalism* (New York: Vintage, 1992).

79. Teresi, interview.

80. Ibid.

81. Ibid.

82. Jerry Zremski, "Bad for Business: Taxes, Regulations, Strangle Firms," *Buffalo News,* March 30, 1998, A1, A4.

83. Teresi, interview.

84. Ibid.

85. Ibid.

86. Craig Gordon, "NAFTA's Toll Minimal (Unless You Got Laid Off)," *New York Newsday,* November 26, 1997, A53.

87. Zremski, "Work Force Fails," A6.

88. Douglas Turner, "Real Numbers on NAFTA Are Worse than They Seem," *Buffalo News,* April 7, 1997, B2.

89. Jerry Zremski, "As Jobs Trickle across Border, Free Trade Takes Toll on Area," *Buffalo News,* April 3, 1998, A1, A6.

90. Ibid., A6.

91. David Robinson, "Not Mexico, but Canada Becomes Area's NAFTA Goblin," *Buffalo News,* February 7, 1999, B7.

92. Zremski, "As Jobs Trickle," A6.

93. David Elias, *Dow 40,000: Strategies for Profiting from the Greatest Bull Market in History* (New York: McGraw-Hill, 2000).

94. Quoted in Elizabeth Moore, "Upstate Economy at Issue in Senate Race," *New York Newsday,* October 4, 2000, A17.

95. Ibid.

96. Quoted in Adam Nagourney, "Mrs. Clinton and Lazio Disagree on Upstate Economy," *New York Times,* September 22, 2000, B4.

97. Michael Grunwald, "Clinton Sees Upstate New York as Key; Frequent Visits Have Made Region the Crucial Battleground in Senate Race," *Washington Post,* November 1, 2000, A17.

98. Quoted in ibid.

99. Ibid.

100. Marie Cocco, "Shoe Leather Won Race for Hillary," *New York Newsday,* November 8, 2000, A43.

101. Moore, "Upstate Economy," A17.

102. Cocco, "Shoe Leather," A43.

103. Douglas Turner, "Clinton Bills Focus on Upstate," *Buffalo News,* March 2, 2001, A1.

104. Jerry Zremski, "Selling the Upstate Plan," *Buffalo News,* March 11, 2001, A1.

105. Craig Reinarman and Harry G. Levine, "The Crack Attack: Politics and the Media in the Crack Scare," in *Crack in America: Demon Drugs and Social Justice,* ed. Craig Reinarman and Harry G. Levine (Berkeley: University of California Press, 1997), 20.

106. Ibid., 21.

107. Ibid.

108.The demonization of crack reached its high point with the constitution of the "crack baby." As Drew Humphries explains, "Crack mothers," a term coined by the media, referred primarily to women who used cocaine or crack during pregnancy. Socially constructed as black and urban, this group of women became a threatening symbol of everything that was wrong with America. Its cities, its poverty, and its welfare dependency were laid at the feet of crack mothers, who were also blamed for undermining the family and driving up the rates of infant mortality and morbidity." Drew Humphries, *Crack Mothers: Pregnancy, Drugs, and the Media* (Columbus: Ohio State University Press, 1999). Crack mothers were the epitome of irresponsibility and social decline. Unwilling or unable to forgo the drug, even for the health of their fetuses, they were targeted for moral attack and often imprisonment, as district attorneys across the country saw political opportunities in demonizing them.

The use of crack by pregnant women was interpreted as being responsible for a variety of medical problems: increased infant mortality and various kinds of problems in the babies who lived, such as congenital birth defects (organ malformation, central nervous system and heart defects), neurobehavioral problems (motor skill impairments, jitteriness, tremors, emotional instability), and developmental impairments, including loss of IQ (ibid., 53–57). As it turned out, however, as the panic subsided, the suspect character of many of the original findings about the toxicity of cocaine exposure to fetuses was revealed. Problems with the early studies included small sample sizes and an inability to separate cocaine use from other socioeconomic and health factors. Unwarranted assumptions about the causes of particular problems also contributed to the uncritical acceptance of initial findings that seemed to reinforce a sense of panic about crack. Later, however, one researcher noted, "Though there seemed to be an association of cocaine use in the third trimester with premature labor, most exposed infants presented in the nursery as remarkably normal and asymptomatic." D. E. Hutchings, "The Puzzle of Cocaine's Effects Following Maternal Use during Pregnancy: Are There Irreconcilable Differences?" *Neurotoxicology and Teratology* 15 (1993): 28, quoted in Humphries, *Crack Mothers*, 63.

109. Quoted in Humphries, *Crack Mothers*, 22.

110. Ibid., 22–23.

111. Ibid., 29.

112. John P. Morgan and Lynn Zimmer contend, based on their analysis of National Institute for Drug Abuse data, that there are "*lower* continuation use rates for cocaine use than for most other drugs." According to NIDA figures, they state, "among high school seniors who have tried cocaine, only 5.2% report having tried unsuccessfully to stop using it—a lower percentage than for most other drugs." The evidence is pretty convincing that most people who use cocaine do not become addicts. According to Morgan and Zimmer, "Most cocaine users take the drug occasionally and recreationally—without experiencing compulsion, without bingeing, and without developing symptoms of drug dependence." Moreover,

although "some people who use cocaine do become 'dependent' on it . . . many also, at some point, stop or reduce their use often without obtaining drug treatment." John P. Morgan and Lynn Zimmer, "The Social Pharmacology of Smokable Cocaine: Not All It's Cracked Up to Be," in *Crack in America: Demon Drugs and Social Justice*, ed. Craig Reinarman and Harry G. Levine (Berkeley: University of California Press, 1997), 146.

113. See the following chapters in Craig Reinarman and Harry G. Levine, eds., *Crack in America: Demon Drugs and Social Justice* (Berkeley: University of California Press, 1997): Yuet W. Cheung and Patricia G. Erickson, "Crack Use in Canada: A Distant American Cousin," 175–93; Peter D. A. Cohen, "Crack in the Netherlands: Effective Social Policy Is Effective Drug Policy," 214–24; Stephen K. Mugford, "Crack in Australia: Why Is There No Problem?" 194–213.

114. Terry Williams, *Crackhouse: Notes from the End of the Line* (New York: Penguin, 1993), 88.

115. Phillipe Bourgeois, "In Search of Horatio Alger: Culture and Ideology in the Crack Economy," in Reinarman and Levine, *Crack in America*, 69.

116. Ibid., 100–102.

117. Ibid., 69.

118. William MacLaughlin, interview by author, May 25, 1999.

119. Ibid. Jamestown is apparently not the only place where this phenomenon is reported to have occurred. Police crackdowns in the larger cities of Massachusetts pushed crime into the smaller communities of that state as well. Police Chief Russell Sienkiewicz of Northhampton, Massachusetts, one of the affected smaller towns in the state, has called this the problem of "crime transference." The experience of Springfield, Massachusetts, represents a good example of this. In 1997, the *Boston Globe* reported that whereas "Springfield police have cracked down on gangs and expanded neighborhood policing," resulting in a 62 percent drop in the murder rate, "all of the communities north of Springfield . . . have experienced a rise in crime. The highway offers easy access for criminals, and the suburban environments provide appetizing targets." In contrast to upstate New York, where crime increases have been related primarily to drugs, in Massachusetts most of the increases have involved property crimes. David Armstrong, "Cities' Crime Moves to Suburbs; More Effective Police Tactics Are Driving Bad Element Out," *Boston Globe*, May 19, 1997, A1.

120. Anonymous respondent, interview by author, May 25, 1999. (The officer asked that I not use his name.)

121. MacLaughlin, interview.

122. Ibid.

123. Ibid.

124. I have gathered the information I relate in this section regarding Williams's perspective (including quotations) in a variety of ways over a three-year period. My sources include letters and other writings that Nushawn has given to me, phone conversations with Nushawn, and many face-to-face conversations that I have had with him in prison.

125. Lisa Kennedy, "The Making of Monsters: The Miseducation of Nushawn Williams," *Poz*, August 2000, 39–43, 63.

126. A typical encounter went like this, according to Nushawn's written memoirs: "I heard a knock at the door, so I opened it and seen that it was a crack head looking for some crack. So I looked in back of him and I saw his jeep. So I asked him if that was his jeep. He said yes. I asked him how much he was looking for. He said $120 worth. So I said, I'll give you five twenty dollar bags and I'll give you another twenty dollar bag to hold your jeep. He asked what time I wanted to come by and pick it up. I said, come by tomorrow morning, same time as now. He said, your name is 'Face' right? I said, if that's what you want to call me. He said alright. I went back in the house and finished getting dressed."

127. Jonathan Law, interview by author, May 25, 1999.

128. MacLaughlin, interview.

129. Teresi, interview.

130. MacLaughlin, interview.

131. Pat Holcombe, "Lewis Case Goes to Grand Jury," *Jamestown Post-Journal*, September 25, 1999, A1, A3.

132. Pat Holcombe, "Arrests, Indictments Send Message," *Jamestown Post-Journal*, December 18, 1999, A1, A3.

133. MacLaughlin, interview.

134. Carolyn Witt, "State, City Police Join Together in Initiative," *Jamestown Post-Journal*, January 19, 2000, A1.

3. Of Myths and Monsters

1. "Monster" was both the text and often, the subtext. Dr. Berke was reported to have labeled Nushawn a "monster" in Cynthia Dockrell, "A Town Down on Its Luck; Uneasy Memories," *Boston Globe*, October 29, 1998, 1. The girls with whom he was involved were called the "AIDS monster's victims" in Maggie Gallagher, "AIDS Comes to Mayville, Raising Disquieting Issues," *Sacramento Bee*, November 10, 1997, B5. One person who knew Nushawn in Jamestown felt compelled to *deny* that he was a monster in the face of the onslaught. Quoted in Reginald Fields and Doug Mandelaro, "HIV Suspect Has Links to Monroe County," *Rochester Democrat and Chronicle*, October 29, 1997, 1. Lisa Kennedy carried the monster theme into her article on Nushawn in *Poz* magazine. Lisa Kennedy, "The Making of Monsters: The Miseducation of Nushawn Williams," *Poz*, August 2000, 39–43, 63. Nushawn recognized himself as a person who had been cast as a monster as well.

2. *The Shorter Oxford Dictionary: On Historical Principles*, ed. William Little, H. W. Fowler, and Jessie Coulson (Oxford: Clarendon, 1973).

3. Jeffrey Jerome Cohen, "Monster Culture (Seven Theses)," in *Monster Theory: Reading Culture*, ed. Jeffrey Jerome Cohen (Minneapolis: University of Minnesota Press, 1996), 4.

4. Ibid., 16.

5. See, for example, Joseph D. Andriano, *Immortal Monster: The Mythological Evolution of the Fantastic Beast in Modern Fiction and Film* (Westport, Conn.:

Greenwood, 1999); Judith Halberstam, *Skin Shows: Gothic Horror and the Technology of Monsters* (Durham, N.C.: Duke University Press, 1995).

6. See, for example, Allison Pingree's discussion of the hold that Siamese twins had on American culture in the nineteenth century in "America's 'United Siamese Brothers': Chang and Eng and Nineteenth-Century Ideologies of Democracy and Domesticity," in *Monster Theory: Reading Culture*, ed. Jeffrey Jerome Cohen (Minneapolis: University of Minnesota Press, 1996).

7. Lawrence D. Kritzman, "Representing the Monster: Cognition, Cripples, and Other Limp Parts in Montaigne's 'Des Boyteux,'"; and Stephen Pender, "'No Monsters at the Resurrection': Inside Some Conjoined Twins," both in *Monster Theory: Reading Culture*, ed. Jeffrey Jerome Cohen (Minneapolis: University of Minnesota Press, 1996).

8. Frank Cawson, *The Monsters in the Mind: The Face of Evil in Myth, Literature, and Contemporary Life* (Sussex: Book Guild, 1995), 20.

9. "The Monsters Next Door: What Made Them Do It?" Cover headline, *Time*, May 3, 1999.

10. Peter Applebome, "What Murder Says about the Society It Exists In," *New York Times*, May 29, 1999, B9.

11. Sanyika Shakur, aka Monster Kody Scott, *Monster: The Autobiography of an L.A. Gang Member* (New York: Penguin, 1994), 11.

12. Ibid., 15.

13. Ibid., 102.

14. Ibid., 103.

15. This material is drawn from excerpts of a one-hour interview that were broadcast on WPIX News over a three-day period, July 29–31, 1999.

16. Quoted in Charity Vogel, "No Remorse: Speaking from Prison, HIV Predator Nushawn Williams Says He Had Unprotected Sex with as Many as 300 Young Women," *Buffalo News*, July 30, 1999, A1.

17. Quoted in Raphael Sugarman and Ralph R. Ortega, "HIV Infected Man Gets 6-Year Term," *New York Daily News*, April 16, 1999, 31.

18. See, for example, Tony Kornheiser, "The Draw Straws Poll," *Washington Post*, October 18, 1999, B1; Liz Smith, "Trumpeting Trump," *New York Newsday*, November 26, 1999, A15.

19. Luisa Chuialkowska, "Sex and Democracy, a Balance of Power," *Ottawa Citizen*, April 15, 1998.

20. John Tierney, "The Big City: What It Takes to Become a Father," *New York Times*, August 2, 1999, B1.

21. Michael Cooper, "Drifter Says He Had Sex with Up to 300," *New York Times*, July 29, 1999, B5.

22. Nushawn Williams, letter to author, January 10, 2000.

23. Nushawn Williams, letter to author, February 10, 2000.

24. Although Newgate Prison in New York City, founded in 1797, is older, Auburn is considered the first penitentiary because of its emphasis on reform and because of the architectural innovations developed there for housing inmates, specifically the cell block system. See John N. Miskell, "Why Auburn: The Relationships

between Auburn and the Prison," 1991, Internet, http://www.correctionhistory.org/ auburn&osborne/miskell/miskell_index.html.

25. Robert Gangi and Vincent Schiraldi, "New York State of Mind? Higher Education vs. Prison Funding in the Empire State, 1988–1998." Center on Juvenile and Criminal Justice, Internet, http://www.cjcj.org/ jpi/nysom.html.

26. Ibid.

27. Ibid.

28. Apparently, the prison officials had a good deal of difficulty enforcing this regime. According to Miskell, "The silent system of Auburn Prison is perhaps one of the best known features of the early prison. The silence was not perfect. In 1845, for example, 173 convicts were whipped for talking or communicating, yet only a fraction of the offenders were actually caught" ("Why Auburn").

29. "Drug-Sentencing Battle in Albany," New York Times, March 19, 2001, A18; Judy Mann, "Getting Wise to Stupid Drugs Laws," Washington Post, May 30, 2001; Sheryl McCarthy, "Effort to Reform Drug Laws Has Only Been Half-Baked," New York Newsday, May 10, 2001, A48.

30. Kennedy, "The Making of Monsters," 39, 40, 43, 63.

31. Louis Schipano, letter to author, February 22, 2001.

32. Nushawn Williams, "The Life and Times of Nushawn Williams," unpublished manuscript, July 15, 2001.

33. Signed form from the New York State Department of Health, "Informed Consent to Perform an HIV Test," August 15, 1996.

34. Robert Berke, affidavit, "Application of Chautauqua County for Court Order Authorizing Release of Confidential HIV Related Information," State of New York, Supreme Court: County of Chautauqua, October 16, 1997.

35. Cember asked in his "bill of particulars," "(5) Was the defendant aware of the alleged HIV status at the time of the alleged crime?" Memo from M. Nathan Cember, Cember and Cember, P.C., to Maria Rivero, assistant district attorney, County of the Bronx, 2, September 1, 1998. The assistant district attorney's response was, "See attached Exhibit Three, NYS Department of Health letter to Chautauqua County Health Commissioner containing defendant's HIV test results and defendant's informed consent for HIV testing." Memo from Maria Rivero, Office of the District Attorney, Bronx County, to William A. Cember, Cember and Cember, P.C. 3, September 22, 1998.

36. Alexander S. Bardey, psychiatric evaluation of Nushawn Williams, Bellevue Hospital Center, February 19, 1998, 3.

37. See Bob Herbert, "In America: A Black Epidemic," New York Times, June 4, 2001, 17. The reasons for many African Americans' distrust of the medical establishment are not hard to understand. The infamous Tuskegee syphilis experiments are one of the best-known examples of how white public health officials have shamelessly exploited black patients who trusted them. See Susan Reverby, ed., Tuskegee's Truths: Rethinking the Tuskegee Syphilis Study (Chapel Hill: University of North Carolina Press, 2000).

38. Erica Goode, "With Fears Fading, More Gays Spurn Old Preventive Message," New York Times, August 19, 2002, 1.

39. Quoted in Jeremiah Griffey, "First Parole Hearing Set for Nushawn Williams," *Jamestown Post-Journal*, July 31, 2001, 1.

40. State of New York Executive Department, Division of Parole, decision, Shyteek Johnson, August 14, 2001, 12.

41. Ibid.

42. Tom Precious, "Aids Predator Is Denied Bid for Parole," *Buffalo News*, August 3, 2001, C4.

4. State Power, Law, and the Sequestration of Disease

1. Gussow provides numerous case studies of ancient and modern social practices organized to control leprosy. He argues that in spite of moves toward "secularizing" the disease that began in the late nineteenth century, leprosy still holds a symbolic "taint" in the minds of both American and European laypersons and medical professionals alike. This is now partly the result of its association with people of the Third World. Zachary Gussow, *Leprosy, Racism, and Public Health: Social Policy and Chronic Disease Control* (Boulder, Colo.: Westview, 1989).

2. Peter Lewis Allen, *The Wages of Sin: Sex and Disease, Past and Present* (Chicago: University of Chicago Press, 2000), 39–40. Allen attributes much of leprosy's power to the horrific nature of the symptoms, which, if untreated, include horrible disfigurement, a distinctive vocal rasp, loss of hair, tubercular lesions, and the emission of a powerful, unpleasant odor (25–26).

3. During the reigns of Henry II of England and Philip V of France, however, lepers were routinely strapped to posts and set on fire. During the reign of Edward I of France, lepers were buried alive. Saul Nathaniel Brody, *The Disease of the Soul: Leprosy in Medieval Literature* (Ithaca, N.Y.: Cornell University Press, 1974), 69.

4. Ibid., 66, 67, 69.

5. Allen, *Wages of Sin*, 29–30. Sexual activity (even between a husband and wife) was subject to especially rigorous controls, and participation in such activity could lead to severe punishments, including imprisonment or expulsion from a hospital. Ibid., 33–34.

6. Ibid., 81.

7. Brody, *Disease of the Soul*, 93.

8. Ibid., 93–95. Along these same lines, Peter Richards informs us that "wherever a leper lived he was not strictly under house arrest. Rules of many institutions confirm that those admitted to hospital in the early middle ages were not completely confined to the hospital precincts. A curious ambivalence of separation and participation pervades the regulations and warns against conclusions which may seem self-evident today, but which may not have been logical to those concerned. At St. Julian's near St. Albans, for example, leper brothers were forbidden to loiter on the path outside the hospital or to converse with others there. Yet one at least of their number was permitted to visit the mill and brewery, another supervised the farm work, for which outside laborers were hired, and all were entitled to seek leave from the master to visit St. Albans and to spend the night away from the hospital." Richards attributes this ambivalence partly to the uncertainties surrounding the rationale for confinement. Until the seventeenth century, lepers were

separated primarily on religious grounds. In the early medieval period there was little recognition of leprosy's infectious potential. Peter Richards, *The Medieval Leper and His Northern Heirs* (Totowa, N.J.: Rowman & Littlefield, 1977), 51–52.

9. Jean Imbert, *Le Hopitaux en France* (Paris: Presses Universitaires de France, 1958), 178, quoted in Allen, *Wages of Sin*, 28.

10. Brody, *Disease of the Soul*, 96–97.

11. Carlo M. Cipolla, *Miasmas and Disease: Public Health and the Environment in the Pre-industrial Age* (New Haven, Conn.: Yale University Press, 1992), 3.

12. Allen, *Wages of Sin*, 61.

13. Brody, *Disease of the Soul*, 167.

14. Ibid., 165.

15. Allen, *Wages of Sin*, 61.

16. Brody, *Disease of the Soul*, 168.

17. Johannes Nohl, *The Black Death: A Chronicle of the Plague*, trans. C. H. Clarke (New York: Harper & Brothers, 1924), 161–63.

18. Ibid., 171.

19. Ibid.

20. Ibid.

21. Ibid., 171–72.

22. Ibid., 175. Some evidence does exist that some gravediggers smeared houses with infection to drive out the inhabitants; the gravediggers would then take possession of the houses. Ibid., 174.

23. Robert P. Hudson, *Disease and Its Control: The Shaping of Modern Thought* (Westport, Conn.: Greenwood, 1983), 44–45.

24. Ibid., 45.

25. Ibid., 184.

26. Ibid., 184–85.

27. Both Friedell and Maycock are quoted in Anna Montgomery Campbell, *The Black Death and Men of Learning* (New York: Columbia University Press, 1931), 4, 5.

28. Hudson, *Disease and Its Control*, 40–41.

29. Campbell, *The Black Death*, 5.

30. Hudson, *Disease and Its Control*, 40.

31. Ibid., 112.

32. Ibid., 113. For an excellent case study of the operations of the Florentine health boards, see Cipolla, *Miasmas and Disease*.

33. William H. McNeil, *Plagues and Peoples* (New York: Doubleday, 1977), 150–51.

34. Ibid., 121.

35. John Duffy, *Epidemics in Colonial America* (Baton Rouge: Louisiana State University Press, 1953), 24.

36. Ibid., 103; Geoffrey Marks and William K. Beatty, *The Story of Medicine in America* (New York: Charles Scribner's Sons, 1973), 235–36.

37. Duffy, *Epidemics in Colonial America*, 102.

38. Quoted in ibid.

39. Wendy Parmet, "AIDS and Quarantine: The Revival of an Archaic Doctrine," *Hofstra Law Review* 14 (1985): 57–58.

40. James H. Cassedy, *Medicine in America: A Short History* (Baltimore: Johns Hopkins University Press, 1991), 13. Duffy notes that Boston was probably the only American city in the early nineteenth century to have an effective quarantine system. *Epidemics in Colonial America*, 59–60.

41. Cassedy, *Medicine in America*, 59.

42. Quoted in Charles Mullett, *The Bubonic Plague and England: An Essay in the History of Preventive Medicine* (Lexington: University of Kentucky Press, 1956), 336–37.

43. Ibid., 338.

44. Ibid., 367.

45. Hudson, *Disease and Its Control*, 145.

46. Although this was something of a victory for anticontagionism, there were actually few radical anticontagionists within the medical profession. The contagiousness of measles, smallpox, and most sexually transmitted diseases was widely recognized. The debate tended to hinge on plague, yellow fever, and cholera. Ibid., 146.

47. McNeil, *Plagues and Peoples*, 235.

48. Rush's anticontagionist impulses were at least partly inspired by his dislike of quarantine rules. According to Rush, quarantine "demoralized our citizens . . . extinguished friendship, annihilated religion, and violated the sacraments of nature, by resisting even the loud and vehement cries of filial and parental blood." Quoted in Dan E. Beauchamp, *The Health of the Republic: Epidemics, Medicine, and Moralism as Challenges to Democracy* (Philadelphia: Temple University Press, 1988), 206. For an analysis of Rush's scientific views regarding disease, see James C. Riley, *The Eighteenth Century Campaign to Avoid Disease* (New York: St. Martin's, 1987), 140–50.

49. Marks and Beatty, *Story of Medicine*, 236.

50. On "germism," see Cecil Hellman, *The Body of Frankenstein's Monster: Essays in Myth and Medicine* (New York: W. W. Norton, 1991).

51. Charles E. Rosenberg, *Explaining Epidemics and Other Studies in the History of Medicine* (Cambridge: Cambridge University Press, 1992), 269.

52. Hudson, *Disease and Its Control*, 170.

53. George Rosen, *From Medical Police to Social Medicine: Essays on the History of Health Care* (New York: Neale Watson Academic, 1974).

54. Quoted in ibid., 62.

55. Ibid., 62–63.

56. Ibid., 65.

57. Ibid., 67.

58. Ibid., 67–68.

59. Ibid., 69–70.

60. Ibid., 67–68.

61. Havelock Ellis, *The Nationalization of Health* (London: T. Fisher Unwin, 1892), 17, 18, 21.

62. Ibid., 28.

63. Rosen, *From Medical Police*, 78.

64. Ibid., 85.

65. Quoted in Paul Starr, *The Social Transformation of American Medicine* (New York: Basic Books, 1982), 180.

66. On nineteenth-century debates regarding what constitutes "race," see Daniel Kevles, *In the Name of Eugenics: Genetics and the Uses of Human Heredity* (New York: Alfred A. Knopf, 1985), 128–47.

67. Sander Gilman, *Picturing Health and Illness: Images of Identity and Difference* (Baltimore: Johns Hopkins University Press, 1995), 64–65. For a somewhat different interpretation of the meaning of tuberculosis in the late nineteenth and early twentieth centuries, see Susan Sontag, *Illness as Metaphor and AIDS and Its Metaphors* (New York: Doubleday, 1989).

68. Gilman, *Picturing Health and Illness*, 66.

69. Ibid.

70. Allan M. Brandt, *No Magic Bullet: A Social History of Venereal Disease in the United States since 1880* (Oxford: Oxford University Press, 1987), 92–94.

71. Kevles, *In the Name of Eugenics*, 74.

72. Ibid., 106. The U.S. Supreme Court upheld one of these laws in the case of *Buck v. Bell*, 274 U.S. 200 (1927), in which Justice Oliver Wendell Holmes dismissed the constitutional rights of the plaintiff with his infamous quip, "Three generations of imbeciles is enough."

73. Beauchamp, *Health of the Republic*, 205–6 (emphasis added). For a fine analysis of how bias against the poor figured into campaigns against polio in the first half of the twentieth century, see Naomi Rogers, *Dirt and Disease: Polio before FDR* (New Brunswick, N.J.: Rutgers University Press, 1990).

74. *Marshall v. Kansas City, Mo.*, 355 S.W. 2d 877, 883 (1915).

75. *Mugler v. Kansas*, 23 U.S. 623 (1887).

76. *Lochner v. New York*, 198 U.S. 45 (1905).

77. *Gibbons v. Ogden*, 22 U.S. 1 (1824).

78. *Haverty v. Bass*, 66 Me. 71 (1876).

79. Ibid., 74.

80. Ibid.

81. *Dowling v. Harden*, 18 Ala. App. 63, 64 (1921).

82. *Crayton v. Larabee*, 220 N.Y. 493, 503, 504 (1917).

83. *Barmore v. Robertson*, 302 Ill. 422, 425 (1922).

84. Ibid., 430, 432, 433.

85. Judith Walzer Leavitt, *Typhoid Mary* (Boston: Beacon, 1997), 7.

86. Ibid., 97, 101.

87. *Louisiana v. Texas*, 176 U.S. 1, 3–6 (1900). Because of its climate, its size, and the amount of commercial activity between the city and the Caribbean, New Orleans was often subject to disease outbreaks. Until the New Orleans Sanitary Association was organized in the late 1880s, the city was also known for the laxity of its quarantine regulations. John H. Ellis, *Yellow Fever and Public Health in the New South* (Lexington: University Press of Kentucky, 1992), 83–104.

88. *Louisiana v. Texas*, 12.

89. Ibid., 22.

90. Duffy, *Epidemics in Colonial America*, 103.

91. *Minneapolis, St. P. & S.S.M. Railroad Co. v. Milner*, 57 F. 276 (1893).

92. *Compagnie Francaise de Navigation a Vapeur v. Louisiana State Board of Health*, 186 U.S. 380, 385 (1902).

93. Ibid., 392.

94. Ibid., 399, 401.

95. *Plessy v. Ferguson*, 163 U.S. 537 (1896); *Jew Ho v. Williamson*, 103 F. 10 (1900); *Wong Wai v. Williamson et al.*, 103 F. 1 (1900).

96. *Jew Ho v. Williamson*, 11.

97. Ibid., 12.

98. Ibid., 13.

99. Ibid.

100. Ibid., 13–14.

101. Ibid., 24, 29.

102. Ibid., 34, 35.

103. *Wong Wai v. Williamson*, 1, 11, 15.

104. Leavitt, *Typhoid Mary*, 93.

105. A good case in point is the narrative of "incorporation," which assumes that Marshall was correct to exclude Bill of Rights protections to citizens of states and localities in *Barron v. Baltimore* (32 U.S. 243, 1833), that this was partly corrected, and that the ambiguity of the amendment allowed cautious but wise Supreme Courts eventually to bring various individual rights under the rubric of the U.S. Constitution. For a representation of this view, see Henry Abraham and Barbara Perry, *Freedom and the Court: Civil Rights and Liberties in the United States* (Oxford: Oxford University Press, 1977).

106. For a good defense and extension of Warren Court jurisprudence, see John Hart Ely, *Democracy and Distrust: A Theory of Judicial Review* (Cambridge: Harvard University Press, 1980).

107. *Brown v. the Board of Education of Topeka Kansas*, 348 U.S. 886 (1954); *Roe v. Wade*, 410 U.S. 959 (1973).

108. Kollin K. Min, "The White Plague Returns: Law and the New Tuberculosis," *Washington Law Review* 69 (1994): 1133.

109. Ibid., 1133–34.

110. *School Board of Nassau County v. Arline*, 480 U.S. 273 (1987).

111. Min, "The White Plague Returns," 1134.

112. For good legal analyses of quarantine laws in relation to HIV and AIDs, see John Gleason, "Quarantine: An Unreasonable Solution to the AIDS Dilemma," *Washington Law Review* 55 (1986): 217–35; Parmet, "AIDS and Quarantine."

113. The exception here is prisons. Courts have upheld the state's interest in segregating HIV prisoners from the rest of the prison population. Gleason, "Quarantine," 224.

114. See Lisa Kennedy, "The Making of Monsters: The Miseducation of Nushawn Williams," *Poz*, August 2000, 39–43, 63.

115. J. R. Claiborne, "Ithaca Man Indicted for Passing HIV," *Ithaca Journal,* May 10, 2000, A2; "Man Sentenced for Having Sex with Ithaca Runaway," *Ithaca Journal,* June 2, 2000, A4.

116. Laura Whitehorn, "America's Most Unwanted," *Poz,* August 2000, Internet, http://www.thebody.com/poz/inside/08_00/unwanted.html.

117. Anthony Lewis, "Breaking the Silence," *New York Times,* July 29, 2000, A13. This figure of half a million represents a tenfold increase since 1980. For comparison's sake, it is worth noting that the entire European Union, which has a population one hundred million greater than the United States, has only one hundred thousand people in all of its prisons.

118. An estimated 13 percent of regular drug users in the United States are black, whereas 62.7 percent of drug offenders sentenced to prison are black. Ibid.

119. Stuart Hall, Chas Critcher, Tony Jefferson, John Clarke, and Brian Roberts, *Policing the Crisis: Mugging, the State, and Law and Order* (New York: Holmes & Meier, 1978). See also Kenneth Jenkins, *Moral Panics* (New York: Routledge, 1978).

120. David Morley and Kevin Robins, *Spaces of Identity: Global Media, Electronic Landscapes, and Cultural Boundaries* (New York: Routledge, 1995).

121. Robert B. Reich, *The Work of Nations: Preparing Ourselves for 21st Century Capitalism* (New York: Vintage, 1992); William Greider, *One World, Ready or Not: The Manic Logic of Global Capitalism* (New York: Simon & Schuster, 1997).

5. HIV Culpability and the Politics of Crime

1. Eve Goldberg and Linda Evans, *The Prison-Industrial Complex and the Global Economy* (Oakland, Calif.: Regent, 1998).

2. The Arkansas law reads, "Exposing another to human immunodeficiency virus is a Class A felony." ACA sec. 5-14-123 (2001). California provides for a three-year "sentence enhancement" for those who commit sex crimes with the knowledge that they are HIV-positive. Calif. Pen. Code sec. 12022.85 (2001). Colorado provides for "sentence enchancement" of up to life imprisonment for those convicted of commiting sex crimes with the knowledge that they are HIV-positive. Colo. R.S. sec. 16-13-804 (2000). In Florida, criminal transmission of HIV is a third-degree felony punishable by both prison confinement and "criminal quarantine community control." Fla. Stat. sec. 921.187 (2000). Georgia provides a maximum ten-year prison sentence for anyone who "knowingly engages in sexual intercourse or performs or submits to any sexual act involving the sex organs of another person and the mouth or anus of another person and the HIV infected person does not disclose to the other person the fact of that infected person's being an HIV infected person prior to that intercourse or sexual act." OCGA sec. 16-5-60 (2000). The Idaho law reads, "Any person who exposes another in any manner with the intent to infect or, knowing that he or she is or has been afflicted with acquired immunodeficiency syndrome (AIDS), AIDS related complex (ARC), or other manifestations of human immunodeficiency virus (HIV) infection, transfers or attempts to transfer any of his or her body fluid, body tissue or organs to another person is guilty of a felony and shall be punished by imprisonment in the state prison for a period not to exceed fifteen (15) years, by fine not in

excess of five thousand ($5000), or by both such imprisonment and fine." Idaho Code sec. 39-608 (2000). The Illinois law states: "A person commits criminal transmission of HIV when he or she, knowing that he or she is infected with HIV: (1) engages in intimate contact with another; (2) transfers, donates, or provides his or her blood, tissue, semen, organs, or other potentially infectious body fluids for transfusion, transplantation, insemination, or other administration to another; or (3) dispenses, delivers, exchanges, sells, or in any other way transfers to another any nonsterile intravenous or intramuscular drug paraphernalia." 720 Ill. Comp. Stat. Ann. sec. 5/12-16.2 (2001).

Kansas's statute is general in the sense that it concerns "exposing another to a life threatening communicable disease," but it seems most directly concerned with HIV in that it specifies acts that include sexual intercourse and the sharing of hypodermic needles. Violation of the statute is a felony. Kans. S.A. sec. 21-3435 (2000). Under the Kentucky Penal Code, a person convicted of prostitution with knowledge of a "sexually transmitted disease" can be charged with a class A misdemeanor, but if that STD is HIV, the person can be charged with a class D felony. Ky. R.S. sec. 529.090 (2001). In Maryland, for a person who knows he or she is infected with HIV, "contact between the penis and vulva or the penis and the anus," or "contact between the mouth and the penis, the mouth and the vulva, or the mouth and the anus," is a criminal offense if the person does not inform the partner of that status. In Michigan, "a person who knows that he or she has or has been diagnosed as having acquired immunodeficiency syndrome or acquired immunodeficiency syndrome related complex, or who knows that he or she is HIV infected and who engages in sexual penetration with another person without having first informed the other person that he or she has acquired immunodeficiency syndrome or acquired immunodeficiency syndrome related complex or is HIV infected, is guilty of a felony." Mich. Comp. Laws sec. 333.5210. According to Missouri law, "It shall be unlawful for any individual knowingly infected with HIV to (1) Be or attempt to be a blood, blood products, organ, sperm or tissue donor except as deemed necessary for medical research; or (2) Act in a reckless manner by exposing another person to HIV without the knowledge and consent of that person to be exposed to HIV, through contact with blood, semen, or vaginal fluid in the course of oral, anal or vaginal sexual intercourse, or by sharing of needles." Violation constitutes a class D felony, unless violation occurs with a person under the age of seventeen, in which case it is a class C felony. Rev. Stat. Mo. sec. 191.677 (2000).

Nevada law focuses primarily on prostitution, stating that a person "engaging in prostitution or solicitation in prostitution . . . after testing positive in a test approved by the state board of health for exposure to the human immunodeficiency virus and receiving notice of that fact is guilty of a category B felony and shall be punished by imprisonment in the state prison for a minimum term of not less than 2 years and a maximum term of not more than 10 years, or by a fine of not more than $10,000, or by both fine and imprisonment." Nev. Rev. Stat. Ann. sec. 201.358 (2001). According to New Jersey law, "A person is guilty of a crime of the third degree who, knowing that he or she is infected with human immune deficiency virus (HIV) or any other related virus identified as a probably causative agent of acquired immune deficiency syndrome (AIDS), commits an act of sexual penetration without the informed consent of the other person." N.J. Stat. sec. 2C:34-5 (2001). Ohio, like Nevada, covers instances of transmission involving prostitution: "Whoever [has knowledge of HIV infection and solicits for prostitution] is guilty of engaging in solicitation after a positive HIV test. If the offender commits the violation prior to July 1, 1996, engaging in solicitation after a positive HIV test is a felony of the second degree. If the offender commits the violation on or after July 1, 1996, engaging in solicitation after a positive HIV test is a felony of the third degree." Ohio R.C. Ann. sec. 2907.24 (2001).

In Oklahoma, the law states, "It shall be unlawful for any person knowing that he or she has Acquired Immune Deficiency Synrome (AIDS) or is a carrier of human immunodeficiency virus (HIV) and with intent to infect another, to engage in conduct reasonably likely to result in the transfer of the person's own blood, bodily fluids containing visible blood, semen, or vaginal secretions into the bloodstream of another, or through the skin or other membranes of another person." 21 Okla. Stat. sec. 1192.1 (2000). In Pennsylvania, a person guilty of prostitution has committed a "felony of the third degree if the person who committed the offense knew that he or she was human immunodeficiency virus (HIV) positive or manifesting acquired immune deficiency syndrome." 21 18 Pa. C.S. sec. 5902 (2001). In South Carolina, a person "who knows that he is infected with Human Immunodeficiency Virus" who "knowingly engage[s] in sexual intercourse, vaginal, anal, or oral, with another person without first informing that person of his HIV status" can be fined up to five thousand dollars and may receive a ten-year jail sentence. S.C. Code Ann. sec. 44-29-145 (2000).

Under the South Dakota code, "intentional exposure to HIV" is a class 3 felony, and "actual transmission is not required." S.D. Codified Laws sec. 22-18-31, 22-18-34 (2001). According to the Tennessee code, "A person commits the offense of criminal exposure of another to HIV when, knowing that such person is infected with HIV, such person knowingly ... engages in intimate contact with another." The statute specifies that if the infectee knew of the infected's condition and gave advance consent, that would offer an "affirmative defense to prosecution." Convictions are treated as class C felonies. Tenn. Code Ann. sec. 39-13-109 (2001). Under Utah's statute, a person arrested for prostitution is tested for HIV, and if the results are positive, the individual is given written notice and counseling. A person so counseled who is subsequently arrested for and found quilty of solicitation is "guilty of a felony in the third degree." Utah Code Ann. sec. 76-10-1312 (2001). The Virginia code is gender specific and narrow in requiring evidence of intent, but broad in terms of infections encompassed, stating, "Any person who, knowing he is infected with HIV, syphilis, or heptitis B, has sexual intercourse, cunnilingus, fellatio, analingus or anal intercourse with the intent to transmit the infection to another person shall be guilty of a class 6 felony." Va. Code Ann. sec. 18.2-67.:1 (2001). See "State Laws on Criminal Exposure," *AIDS Policy and Law*, July 24, 1998.

3. The Illinois statute has been controversial since it was first passed in 1989. See "Combatting AIDS's Acoustic Shadow," *Loyola University of Chicago Law Journal*

21 (1990–91): 497–515; Michael L. Closen and Jeffrey S. Deutschman, "A Proposal to Repeal the Illinois Transmission Statute," *Illinois Bar Journal* 78 (1990): 592–600.

4. "HIV/AIDS and the States: A Look at Laws Passed in 1997," *AIDS Policy and Law*, December 26, 1997, 6–10.

5. "Iowa Makes Nonconsensual HIV Exposure through Sex a Felony," *AIDS Policy and Law*, April 17, 1998, 15. Criminal HIV statutes have twice been introduced for consideration by the New York State Legislature. Although New York has altered anonymous testing rules to ease the identification of potential HIV transmitters, it has not taken the invitation to jump on the criminalization bandwagon.

6. "Three States Ready to Approve Bills on Criminal Exposure," *AIDS Policy and Law*, December 1, 1999, 4.

7. "North Dakota Law Allows Confinement on HIV Suspicion," *AIDS Policy and Law*, May 2, 1997, 1, 10–11.

8. "Washington Toughens Sanctions against Intentional Exposure," *AIDS Policy and Law*, June 13, 1997, 4.

9. Laura Whitehorn, "America's Most Unwanted," *Poz*, August 2000, Internet, http:/www. thebody.com/poz/inside/08_00/unwanted.html.

10. James Subjack, interview by author, July 2, 1999. All of Subjack's comments quoted in this chapter are from this interview.

11. *Black's Law Dictionary: Definitions of the Terms and Phrases of American and English Jurisprudence, Ancient and Modern* (St. Paul, Minn.: West, 1979), 108.

12. River Huston, "A Woman under the Influence," *Poz*, April 1999, Internet, http://www.poz. com/archive/april1999/columns/river.html.

13. The medical establishment, which is, with all of its flaws, highly regarded by middle-class white Americans, has participated, along with other institutional authorities, in the historical oppression and exploitation of African Americans. Medical authorities have often supported the notion that black people are genetically inferior to whites. In the infamous Tuskegee experiments, the Public Health Service showed utter disregard for the health of African American patients who had put their trust in PHS physicians. See James H. Jones, *Bad Blood: The Tuskegee Syphilis Experiment* (New York: Free Press, 1993).

14. Andrea Caruso, interview by author, January 7, 2003.

15. Comparisons of virus DNA are especially tricky because of the capacity of viruses to mutate. *State v. Schmidt* remains the only HIV criminal transmission case in which phylogenetic analysis was admitted into evidence and was central to obtaining a conviction. *State v. Schmidt*, 699 So. 2d 448 (1997).

16. Susan Brink, "Improved AIDS Treatments Bring Life and Hope—at a Cost," *U.S. News & World Report*, January 29, 2001, 44–45.

17. HIV/AIDS mortality rates dropped by more than 70 percent from 1996 to 1998, and dropped by another 4 percent in 1999. Certain groups are disproportionately affected, however; for example, AIDS continues to be a leading cause of death for black men ages 25–44. "Epidemiology: Mortality Declines in U.S. for Several Leading Causes of Death in 1999," *Medical Letter on the CDC & FDA*, July 15–21, 2001, 10.

18. J. R. Claiborne, "Ithaca Man Indicted for Passing HIV," *Ithaca Journal*, May 10, 2000, A2.

19. "Oregon: HIV Transmission (Policy) New York Case Recalls 'AIDS as Weapon' Convictions," *AIDS Weekly Plus*, December 15, 1997, 31.

20. *Oregon v. Hinkhouse*, 139 Ore. App. 446 (1995).

21. Ibid., 450–51.

22. Ibid., 453.

23. Ibid. See also "H.I.V.-Infected Man Admits Endangering Sexual Partners," *New York Times*, March 29, 1992, sec. 1, p. 7.

24. "Oregon: HIV Transmission (Policy)."

25. *State v. Stark*, 832 P. 2d 109, 113 (1992).

26. Ibid., 112.

27. Ibid., 117.

28. *Guevara v. Superior Court*, 62 Cal. App. 4th 864, 868 (1998).

29. Mike McKeen, "Sex with HIV+ May Be Assault, Sixth District Says," *Recorder*, December 23, 1997, 3.

30. *Smallwood v. State*, 343 Md. 97, 100 (1995).

31. The Maryland Code had a provision that provided for criminal sanctions against any person who knowingly transferred or attempted to transfer HIV to another person. The maximum penalty allowed, however, was three years, as opposed to the thirty years Smallwood received for the attempted murder convictions.

32. *Smallwood v. State*, 101.

33. Ibid., 102, 106.

34. "CO App. Ct. Lifts HIV+ Man's Attempted Murder Conviction," *AIDS Litigation Reporter*, November 9, 1998, 8.

35. "Judge Rejects Motion in HIV Case," Associated Press, August 8, 2002, Internet, accessed through LexisNexis (http://web.lexis-nexis.com).

36. *State of Louisiana v. Salvadore Andrew Gamberella*, 633 So. 2d 595, 604 (1993).

37. Ibid. The statute was eventually amended to include "any means of contact," including "spitting, biting, stabbing with an AIDS contaminated object, or throwing blood or other bodily substances." La. Acts, No. 411, 1 (1993).

38. *State v. Gamberella*, 605.

39. Ibid., 601.

40. Ibid., 602.

41. Kim Bell, "Old HIV Law Makes Consenting Adults into Criminals," *St. Louis Post-Dispatch*, May 17, 1998, B3.

42. "Missouri's HIV Exposure Law Upheld as Constitutional," *AIDS Policy and Law*, July 24, 1998, 11–12.

43. Bell, "Old HIV Law," B3.

44. Kim Bell, "Law Aims to Curb AIDS Crimes: People Who Infect Others Face Easier Path to Prison," *St. Louis Post-Dispatch*, July 2, 1997, A1.

45. "Missouri's HIV Exposure Law."

46. *State v. Russell* and *State v. Lunsford*, 158 Ill. 2d 23 (1994).

47. "Maryland Appeals Court Says Trial Courts Can Consider Defendant's HIV Status," *AIDS Litigation Reporter*, June 8, 1998, 4.

48. *Tennessee v. Pipkin*, C.C.A. No. 01C01-9605-CR-00210, Tenn. Crim. App. 1 (1997).

49. *Najera v. State of Texas*, 95 S.W. 2d 698 (1997). See "Courts Explore Implications of Laws on Exposure to HIV," *AIDS Policy and Law*, July 24, 1998, suppl., 3–4.

50. Dave Harmon and Rebecca Thatcher, "Najera Must Pay $8 Million in Divorce," *Austin American-Statesman*, March 12, 1996, B1.

51. Dave Harmon, "Najera Convicted in Sexaul Assault Trial," *Austin American-Statesman*, February 16, 1996, B1.

52. "Criminal Issues: State of Washington v. Ferguson," *AIDS Litigation Report*, January 29, 2001, 7.

53. *Washington v. Ferguson*, 142 Wn. 2d 631 (2001).

54. *State v. Schmidt*, 449, 450.

55. Ibid., 450, 451.

56. Ibid., 448.

57. Gina Holland, "U.S. High Court Denies Lafayette Doctor's Appeal," *Advocate* (Baton Rouge), March 5, 2002, 1B.

58. Kevin Flynn, "Nurse's Aide Tied to Plot to Kill Husband," *New York Times*, August 25, 2001, B3.

59. *State v. Caine*, 652 So. 2d 611 (1995).

60. Perhaps the strangest "injection case" involved the so-called needle bandit. Warren "Red" White was charged with robbing a West Virginia bank for $8,548 on January 29, 1996. White demanded money and threatened to stab a teller with a syringe loaded with HIV-tainted blood. White was convicted of the bank robbery, although evidence of HIV in the syringe was not introduced during the trial. In this case, the presence or absence of HIV was of secondary relevance to the disposition of the case. In fact, it was not raised as an issue during the trial by the defense counsel, who argued that the prosecutors had the wrong man. Chris Stirewalt, "Jury Convicts 'Needle Bandit': Charleston Man Found Guilty in Bank Robbery," *Charleston Daily Mail*, March 9, 2001, A7.

61. *Weeks v. Scott*, 55 F. 3d 1059, 1061 (1995).

62. Ibid., 1065, 1064, 1063.

63. "Ohio Supreme Court Affirms Felonious Assault Conviction in Spitting Case," *AIDS Litigation Reporter*, May 25, 1998, 3; *State v. Bird*, 692 N.E. 2d 1013 (1998).

64. Quoted in "Ohio Supreme Court Affirms," 3.

65. *Scroggins v. State*, 198 Ga. App. 29, 32, 34, 36 (1990).

66. "Expert Failed to Justify Testing of Man Who Bit Officer," *AIDS Policy and Law*, October 30, 1998, 15.

67. "Transmission: Eighty Swedish Women Tested for HIV While Suspect Is at Large," *AIDS Weekly Plus*, November 9, 1998, 1.

68. "American Jailed in Finland for HIV Manslaughter," *AIDS Weekly Plus*, July 21, 1997, 14.

69. "Gay Man Must Pay $25,000 for Putting Lover at Risk for HIV," *AIDS Policy and Law*, September, 18, 1998, 1–7.

70. Mike McKee, "HIV-Positive Man Held Liable for Love," *Recorder*, August 25, 1998, 5.

Conclusion

1. "Elmira: Nation's First Reformatory," in *History of New York State Prisons*, Internet, http://www. geocities.com/motorcity/downs/3548/history.html.

2. *New York v. Shyteek Johnson*, Criminal Court of the City of New York, County of the Bronx, September 22, 1997.

3. Quoted in *Shyteek Johnson v. Byrne, Johnson, and Vacco*, Affirmation in Support of Petitioner's Application for a Writ of Mandamus, William Cember, February 25, 1998.

4. *People v. Selikoff*, 35 N.Y. 2d 227 (1974).

5. *New York v. Johnson*, proceedings, February 20, 1998. 6.

6. Ibid., 9; *People v. McConnell*, 49 N.Y. 2d 340 (1980).

7. Letter, Daniel Dubno to Nushawn Williams, October 30, 1997.

8. Letter, Mary Garofalo to Shyteck *[sic]* Johnson, October 27, 1997.

9. Letter, Bradley Davis to Shyteek Johnson, October 27, 1997.

10. Letter, Michael Day to Shyteek Johnson, October 27, 1997; letter, Gina Huerta to Shyteek Johnson, October 30, 1997.

11. David A. Trachtenberg, Forensic Psychiatric Services Article 730 CPS Psychiatric Report, Bellevue Hospital Center, February 19, 1998; Alexander S. Bardey, Forensic Psychiatric Services Article 730 CPS Psychiatric Report, Bellevue Hospital Center, February 19, 1998.

12. Trachtenberg, Psychiatric Report, 1; Bardey, Psychiatric Report, 1.

13. Trachtenberg, Psychiatric Report, 4, 5.

14. Bardey, Psychiatric Report, 3, 4.

Index

ABC, 19, 27, 28, 180
AIDS, xii, xix, 160; and Africa, 2, 11;
    confused with HIV, 152; and crimi-
    nal law, xx, 2; as crisis of represen-
    tation, 10–11; as divine judgment,
    10; epidemic, xxi, 2, 103, 170; as
    "gay plague," 32–33; morality rates,
    202n17; and quarantine, xix, 133;
    and race, 11; and Nushawn Wil-
    liams, 13, 14, 97, 105
Albany, New York, 51, 62, 81, 105, 164
Alesi, Senator Jim, 32
Alger, Horatio, 62
Allen, Peter Lewis, 194n1
American Dream, 62
"Andrew B," 147
Arnold, Amber, 23
Auburn, New York, 80–88, 88
Auburn State Correctional Facility,
    81, 82–87, 92–93, 96, 97–99, 107,
    163–64, 192–93n24
"Auburn system," 83, 193n28

"Bags," 94–95
Ball, Lucille, 25
Bardey, Alexander, 103
Barmore v. Robertson, 126–27
Barron v. Baltimore, 198n105
Beatlemania, 7
Beauchamp, Daniel, 123
Beelzebub, 72
Bellah, Robert N., 40
Bellevue Hospital, 167
Bennett, William, 60

Bensman, Joseph, 39–41
Berke, Dr. Robert, xiii, 2, 23, 33–34,
    83, 87, 100, 101; evaluation of
    media, 30; HIV contacts estimated
    by, 13–14, 177n43, 177n46; on
    Nushawn Williams, 16, 19, 102–3,
    191n1
Bird, Jimmy Lee, 159
"Bobo," 95–96
Bourgeois, Phillipe, 61–62
Brady, Ian, 74
Briteramos, Nikko, 20–21; as "mon-
    ster," 21; penalty imposed on, 21
Brockway, Zebulon Reed, 164
Brown v. Board of Education, 132
Buchanan, Patrick, 10, 133
Buckley, William F., 15–16, 133
Buck v. Bell, 197n72
Buffalo, New York, 50, 51, 53, 57, 59, 62
Buffalo News, xii, 18, 25–26, 63, 107
Burroughs, William, 60
Bury, Chris, 19
Bush, George H., 60, 132
Byrne, Justice John T., 165, 166

capitalism, 5–6, 69
Carlson, Mayor Samuel B., 46–47,
    186n53
Caroll, Bill, 146
Caruso, Andrea, 23
Cawson, Frank, 74
CBS, 28, 59, 166
Cember, William, 102, 165–66, 193n35
Chadakoin River, 45, 47

134, 167–68; and criminalization of HIV, 136, 137, 138–45; as generating media panic, 8, 13–15; and HIV confidentiality laws, 33; in Jamestown, 64–67; "reality" of, 9, 34–35; Subjack's analysis of, 138–44

Winslow, Edward Amory, 121

Winter, Fred, 14

Wong Wai v. Williamson, 131

WPIX, 77–79, 84

Wypijewksi, JoAnn, 2–3, 25, 27, 28, 69, 172n3, 183n133

Zimmer, Lynn, 189–90n112

Thomas Shevory is professor of politics at Ithaca College, where he teaches environmental and U.S. politics. He is the author of *John Marshall's Law: Interpretation, Ideology, and Interest* and *Body/Politics: Studies in Reproduction, Production, and (Re)construction,* and he has published articles in the fields of law, public policy, and popular culture. He grew up in Jamestown, New York, and has lived most of his life in upstate New York.